The Harassed Worker

Carroll M. Brodsky
University of California-San
Francisco

Lexington Books
D.C. Heath and Company
Lexington, Massachusetts
Toronto

Library of Congress Cataloging in Publication Data

Brodsky, Carroll M
    The harassed worker.

    Includes index.
    1. Industrial psychiatry. 2. Persecution–Psychological aspects.
I. Title.
RC967.5.B76   158'.26   76-43115
ISBN 0-669-01041-3

Second printing, July 1979.

Published simultaneously in Canada

Printed in the United States of America

International Standard Book Number: 0-669-01041-3

Library of Congress Catalog Card Number: 76-43115

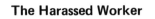

The Harassed Worker

Contents

Preface

The tradition recounted in several thousand years of literature does not lessen the shocking impact of modern ecounters with the cruelty represented by harassment. Like countless dramatists and novelists, I have always wondered at the brutality human beings can show to each other for no apparent reason. Yet, knowing the reasons can make the cruelty seem even more pathetic and tragic, especially when other, more humane, ways to achieve the same ends are readily available.

I have reviewed well over a thousand cases of workers who claimed that they had been injured and had not recovered from their injuries. Some were maimed, some were crippled, all claimed to be in pain. Some complained that their employers had violated safety rules or had neglected to take the kind of precautions that might have spared the workers from injuries. But I also saw another type of patient, one who usually was not physically injured; his disability was not a result of a violation of safety regulations. Instead, these workers complained that they had been treated cruelly, either physically or mentally. Further, they believed that this cruel treatment, whether intentional or unintentional, had resulted in either physical symptoms or mental injury and had made them less capable of coping with work and with life in general. After I had expressed an interest in such cases, and started seeing more and more of them, it seemed to me that they represented the most preventable of all injuries. Although it might be impossible to make a workplace accident-proof, because of the dangers inherent in machines and moving parts, slippery surfaces and noxious vapors, it should certainly be possible to make a workplace cruelty-proof, harassment-proof, and possibly work pressure-proof. I decided to undertake the study of a substantial number of such patients in order to determine the parameters of harassment and work pressure with the hope that these could be prevented and that those persons who had already been victimized could be helped.

This book is the result of that study. Through it, I came to the conclusion that harassment is a basic mechanism in human interaction. The workplace is like the family place, the school place, the military place—a site where all the reactions and patterns that humanity has known are still being reinacted. I am no longer sure that the injuries I studied are the most preventable of injuries, but I do believe that much can be done to build into the social structure of the workplace the elements needed to encourage productive rather than destructive interaction. The changes that are needed can be brought about through the individual and the cooperative efforts of all those who are involved in the work system, including not only employers and employees but also those who deal with the breakdowns in the system that are represented by workers' compensation claims.

The workers' compensation system appears to be an adversary òne. Sometimes it is. But I have been impressed by its nonadversary aspects and by the positive feeling that exists on the part of the applicants' attorneys, the defense attorneys, and the claims adjusters, as they meet in conference to reduce the applicants' conflicts and to rehabilitate them to the greatest possible extent. By and large, I have found that all the participants in the process truly wish to help the applicant. I have a great deal of confidence in both their desire and their ability to initiate, support, and implement programs that might make the workplace a safer and healthier place.

This book is written for those concerned with work problems—lawyers, claims adjusters, legislators, union officials, vocational and rehabilitation counselors, family physicians, employers, personnel officers, supervisors, and workers themselves. It is my hope that this consideration of the harassed worker will help them in their efforts to prevent and to remedy the often tragic effects of the various forms of harassment on physical and mental health.

Acknowledgments

I should like to acknowledge the contributions of Kay Knox, who worked with me as a research assistant and for whom each of these patients came to be a highly personalized, individual human being. Her questions and suggestions were invaluable. Her search of the literature provided materials that added to the breadth of my understanding.

I should like to thank Sara Clarenbach. This young lawyer studied the legal aspects of the problem and brought clarity to much of the data by applying the legal mind to anthropological and psychiatric thinking.

I should like to thank Mimi Riordan for her editorial help, her very gentle criticism, and her determination to bring to a close a manuscript that could have gone on forever.

I should like to thank Mary Ann Esser for providing overall editorial supervision marked by breadth of critical judgment and scrupulous attention to detail, and for guiding the manuscript through the complex final stages of preparation for publication.

I am grateful to the Department of Psychiatry and the Langley Porter Neuropsychiatric Institute for supporting this research through grants from the General Research Support Grant and from other sources, and to Dr. Leon Epstein who facilitated these grants.

I should like to thank all the applicants who claimed they were injured, whose psychological pain and suffering stimulated the writing of this volume, and the claims adjusters and the lawyers who worked with these applicants in an effort to help resolve their cases and restore them to health and to their full work capacity. I am grateful to all of them for the privilege of having been invited to work with them.

Introduction

This book describes the process of harassment and how that process is manifested in working situations, how it affects the worker and his coworkers, family, and community. The book is based on certain claims filed with the California Workers' Compensation Appeals Board and Nevada Industrial Commission, claims of workers who stated that they were ill and unable to work because of ill-treatment by employers, coworkers, or consumers, or because of excessive demands for work output. In some cases the claimants alleged permanent, continuing, or total disability.

These are cases that went through the claims system and probably are only the tip of an iceberg in relation to the actual incidence of harassment at work and its contribution to the general malaise. The effects of harassment on mental health, physical health, and worker productivity are pervasive and crippling. Harassment contributes to workers' proclivity toward accidents and toward willful and inadvertent damage of machinery and products. Harassment can increase the incidence of psychophysiological disorder such as hypertension and gastrointestinal and musculoskeletal disorders. Whether recognized and admitted or not, its human and economic loss is felt not only by the workers and their families but by industry, by insurance carriers, and by the public.

The sample of workers claiming disability based on work-related injuries came to the author through referral from insurance carriers, from applicants' attorneys, and from both parties jointly, when they agreed to accept the author's diagnosis. Others were referred by the Workers' Compensation Appeals Board to the author in his role as Independent Medical Examiner. Many were referred when the author's interest in problems of harassment and work pressure became known. They came from a wide range of work levels and included blue collar and white collar workers, executives and academicians, from the public and private sectors of employment.

It is unlikely, of course, that these workers constitute a representative sample of all harassed workers. First of all, we do not know the full extent of the problem of harassment. Second, we cannot calculate the number of claims for disability stemming from harassment or work pressure [22]. As a check on the representativeness of the sample, however, we discussed the varieties of harassment in our sample with attorneys and claims adjusters who have had much contact with such cases. They agreed that these cases of harassment, work pressure, and even eventual suicide are indeed representative of the types they had seen frequently in their practices.

We interviewed each patient, following an outline that included inquiry into most aspects of consciousness, awareness of changes in feelings and in physical and mental functioning, changes in relationships in the home and at work and with friends in nonwork organizations. In addition, we interviewed the patient's relatives, usually the spouse, and in some cases parents and offspring. Most of the records were extensive. We compared the history given to us by the patient with what had been given to other physicians.

The average length of time between the date of claim and the date of examination was twenty-one months for those claiming harassment and eleven months for those claiming work pressure. Because of this delay, initial accident reports and earlier physicians' reports were invaluable in providing information about the patient, giving earlier views of the relationship between work and disability. For example, one claimant, Matt, in ten years of treatment for physical symptoms and depression, never related his symptoms to his work until a physician mentioned the possibility to him. This was noted in the medical record by the physician who made the statement.

Medical records, previous litigation records, and documents subpoenaed in association with them were useful [124], for they occasionally revealed factors of which the claimant might or might not have been aware. For example, in one case such records showed that the patient had complained of the same mental symptoms a year before the attack he cited as the cause of his problems. At that earlier time, he had complained that he could not continue with a job-training program because he was too nervous to go anywhere without a weapon. A year later, he was attacked while working as a security guard. He then complained that he dared not go anywhere without a weapon and attributed his "traumatic neurosis" to the attack.

Although the interviews followed an outline, they generally were nondirective and focused on two requests: "Tell me all about your illness," and "Tell me all about yourself." Patients were not interrupted except when they left a large gap or when they reported something of possible importance so tersely that the interviewer had to ask them to elaborate.

The examiner tested the limits of quantitative statements. A typical sequence was "Are you married?" "Yes." "Was this your first marriage?" "No, I was married before." "Was that the first time?" "No," or "Yes," etc. Similarly, after the patient told about the medication he took, the examiner would inquire about dosage, the total number per day, maximum amount ever taken during a day or month, etc.

The last portion of the interview was a formal mental status examination that included tests of intellectual function and memory and some simple performance tests, such as drawing a clock, that often indicated the need for more extensive psychological testing. Further tests often were necessary to determine the full extent of impairment and whether it resulted from organic central-nervous-system dysfunction, whether it could be localized, and whether it could be dated from childhood or was of more recent onset. After this, the examiner asked direct questions from the schedule in order to complete the patient's history and further clarify details noted in the records.

Perhaps the best sources of comparative and sometimes corroborative data were the reports of other psychiatrists. Although the workers' compensation system represents the first broad application of a "no fault" system of compensation for loss or injury in California, it still contains large adversarial elements, in contrast to systems existing in Nevada and in Ontario, Canada [123]. In most of our cases, both the fact of injury and its cause were disputed by the insurance company or by the employer. As a result, each side was represented by its own attorney, and each side sought out a psychiatrist who would examine the claimant and render an opinion. In records of cases that had been in litigation for years, there often were reports from many psychiatrists, some of whom had seen the patient several times.

Many of these psychiatrists were experienced in evaluating patients for medical-legal purposes, and their reports not only were detailed but also were models of good evaluation technique. Most often, the stories the patients told one psychiatrist were almost exactly the one told to other psychiatrists and to this author. While the psychiatrists' opinions differed widely, their facts did not. When wide differences in the facts related by the patient to different psychiatrists appeared, we were alerted to the possibility that there might be unconscious memory or personality problems or problems of conscious malingering. Indeed, these were present in all instances where there was a great disparity of fact among several reports.

A sample for comparison was provided by a group of workers seen in the author's own psychotherapy practice, patients from the Work Clinic at the University of California Hospital in San Francisco, and numerous employees of the University of California Medical Center in San Francisco who had been referred because they experienced emotional problems on the job. These were often in what we designated a "preaccident state." That is, although they had not filed a claim, they shared many characteristics with workers who are accident-prone and especially likely to claim disability resulting from an industrial accident, harassment, or work pressure. Such characteristics include complaints that work is too hard and conditions unsafe; the belief that the job pressures are too great; claims of individual harassment by supervisors and of racial discrimination; the presence of tension symptoms such as headaches, dizziness, fatigue, and weakness; and, in general, a belief that the job offers a limited scope for the worker's talents.

The conclusions presented are based on the following body of data: the patient's spoken words; the longitudinal medical records, including previous industrial accident claims; the records of the employers; interviews with family members; and observations made at hearings in which coworkers, supervisors, former employers, physicians, and private investigators testified. The data are both hard and soft—hard in that records provide dates of events, medications, and the like, soft in that much of the data are based on the reports of involved persons, who may be consciously or unconsciously biased.

The approach to the data is typological. As we reviewed our cases and as new ones were referred, it became apparent that the patients could be grouped according to similarities in the personalities of the workers, the types of job, the special environments at the job, or extra-job factors—such as a desire to move, to change occupation, or to retire. Within the text, case histories are presented as examples of these types.

1

Harassment in the Working Environment

Attitudes toward Work

There is a growing awareness among social scientists and governmental agencies of the contribution that work experience makes to the worker's sense of satisfaction with life in general and to the way he relates to those around him—his spouse, children, and peers [31,71,153,164]. In the social and physical environments in which a worker spends most waking hours are localized elements that can cause, on the one hand, misery, pain, and illness [58,70,149] and, on the other hand, pleasure and satisfaction [58,70,86,112,148].

Work is pleasurable when a job provides an abundance of rewards and a minimum of discomfort. Rewards, which include money, status, respect and acceptance by coworkers and high regard from superiors and subordinates, contribute to a sense of satisfaction [9,62,66,113,119,125,157]. Certain fringe benefits—work-social groups such as bowling teams, the after-work drink with coworkers, are desirable to some people but are regarded as drawbacks by others [77,118]. Similarly, special job features such as the freedom to travel or to set one's own schedule are bonuses for some workers but disadvantages for others [35,105]. The latter may hate to leave their families and be away from home overnight, or they may need to "know" when their day's work is done, or they may prefer a situation in which their work is measured by time spent rather than by volume sold, pages typed, or products manufactured. Even changes in work rules that are fought for and enjoyed by some workers make other workers angry and uncomfortable [98]. Relaxed rules that permit, for example, greater flexibility in clothing, in hair styles, and in hiring practices that involve the presence of more women and minorities trigger strong reaction in some who are disquieted by change.

Nevertheless, although there are many such instances where "one person's meat is another person's poison," job satisfaction is not entirely subjective [47]. All workers appreciate the core features of status, money, respect, and security [1,8]. Workers who find in their jobs most of those features may well appear to be "work neurotics" to their family and friends [165], especially if they prefer work to any other activity. Work is the place where they are happiest. Work as it fulfills survival needs represents a mastery over the environment, which does indeed provide a sense of well-being [112].

In the absence of these rewards, work can become dull [105]. If viewed solely as a means to the end of survival, work can be just another form of burdensome tax that one would avoid if possible. For some workers, a job is neither pleasurable nor dull, it is hell. A job once tolerable can become unbearable if it demands more work or skill than it did formerly, if one's coworkers turn on or abandon one, if one is passed over for promotion, or if customers, students, inmates [50], or patients [51] attack one verbally or physically. A new supervisor or new coworkers or a new breed of consumer—the passenger on the bus or the inmate in the prison—can turn a good job into a hellish one.

Harassment Defined and Described

The term "harassment" is both generic and specific. It encompasses a continuum of various forms of behavior, ranging from humor to teasing to specific harassment, i.e., scapegoating and verbal and physical abuse.

Harassment behavior involves repeated and persistent attempts by one person to torment, wear down, frustrate, or get a reaction from another. It is treatment that persistently provokes, pressures, frightens, intimidates, or otherwise discomforts another person. This overt behavior may go on for a week or many years, not stopping until the harassee strongly demands its termination. If the demand is too feeble, the harassment likely will continue, for the harasser recognizes the weakness of his victim. Rarely is harassment a way of raising consciousness, as teasing is; rather, it is a way of pressuring or of keeping a person in a corner. Although its ultimate purpose, either real or rationalized, may be to discipline, to increase productivity, or to condition reflexes (as in the military services), the primary effect of harassment is always unpleasant, and it is usually resented by the harassed.

Repeated harassment behavior is not necessarily from the same person, however. For instance, a bus driver may feel harassed by many different passengers in the course of a day's work, as the prison guard may be harassed by a number of his charges. Continued harassment behavior is felt by the target to place him in a cornered position. He is teased, badgered, and insulted and feels he has little recourse to retaliation in kind. The target may be of a lower status and may not feel he has the power to return an insult to someone of higher status. A highway patrolman realizes that it is inappropriate for him to shout back at an angered ticket recipient. The bus driver accomplishes little by returning insult for insult, as this only interferes with the efficiency of his job. Clearly, harassment often is part of a job. The problem begins when harassment is excessive or when the harassee's tolerance for such treatment is low, and he experiences it as negative intimidation.

Harassment implies a lack of humor, involves negative affect, and tends to be interpreted as an attack on a person, for the harassing behavior preys directly upon the felt inadequacies of the personality.

"Subjective harassment" refers to the awareness of harassment by the target and "objective harassment" to a harassment situation in which actual external evidence of harassment is found, for example, in statements from coworkers, employers, subordinates, or independent observers. Neither kind of harassment is an independent, pure type. The concepts are relative concepts whose perception depends on the individual. If one is objectively being harassed, one usually has the subjective sense of being harassed. Many persons, however, probably are subjected to the same kind of treatment and yet do not think of themselves as being harassed. They might say, "This is just a game—this is the way it always is around here, a lot of horseplay and practical jokes," "that boss of mine is always after someone."

Subjective harassment is important not only as a perception of very real pain that the target is suffering but also as an expression of his other feelings. One aspect of a process that takes place outside of awareness is that the mind defers action until the proper occasion arises. For instance, as we see repeatedly in these harassed subjects, a person may consciously realize that all is not going well in a particular relationship yet is hesitant to take the next decisive step directly, because the channel for doing so is unclear. A man who is unhappy with his job and wants to change occupations may not be able to go to his wife and friends and say, "I've had it, I'm going to quit my job." His "exit" may be to become injured. Often the injury is physical, but in some cases the occasion for leaving work is a psychological event. The "victim" might be completely unaware that he is using someone's teasing or goading as the occasion for quitting a job he already wants to quit.

In contrast, some people use such an occasion consciously as a way of dealing with a problem. Their behavior makes the statement, "I have been injured by this harassing event and as a result I am disabled now." This is the person who is trying to accept and prepare for a change of some kind. The tension is mounting; suddenly, a traumatic event occurs, and he becomes disabled. The disability is, "I can't work," not, "I can't move my leg." This person's disability resolves his social conflict in regard to his relationship with other people [135]. There is "a commingling of internal and external perception. This may be designated a putative injury; that is, the psychological effects perceived by the injured as 'real' are as valid for him as if he had received an injury validated by an external observer" [20, p.961].

Numerous authors have isolated qualities that consistently accompany subjective perception of hurt or harassment. The humorless person, the person who cannot see what is funny in a joke, is most likely to feel harassed [96]. There is a "state of readiness" to view another person as threatening, with "autistic hostility" developing from excessive egocentricity and self-absorption, and this characterizes the person who constantly expects to be attacked [120]. Those who cannot express hostility are also those who cannot differentiate hostile from nonhostile humor, but perceive all humor as hostile [30]. "Noninsightful" persons who are also hostile, miscalculate hostility in others, thereby perceiving more hostility than there actually is [116] . Patients in a vulnerable and ambivalent position often regard humor as hostility [87] .

Harassment as Competition for Privilege

Competition is ubiquitous in all social, ethnic, and racial groups. There is a constant process of testing, of matching of self against others in order to establish one's place in the hierarchy, and there is a use of acceptance and exclusion as devices for enhancing one's own position and status. Ultimately, this process is designed to serve the person practicing it by providing him with privilege. Competition and the establishment of rules for admission and rejection in the working environment deal with the privilege to do easier work, less work, the same amount of work but with higher pay, the privilege to live in a larger, warmer, more protected, more comfortable house, to have better food, to pay others for one's care rather than to have to provide it for oneself, and other such privileges generally held in high regard. As important as the material comfort itself is the respect that is given to the possessor of these privileges. The importance of the positive feeling that comes when others know that we "have it made" should not be underrated.

As significant as the comfort and respect that come from privilege is the security a person has that he will always have first choice in the good things of the world and that it is unlikely he will ever be relegated to the place of the poor and underprivileged. Everyone wants to be a "have." "Haves" fear becoming "have nots." Much has been written about consequent discrimination on the basis of ethnicity, social class, race, sex, or religion. Formal, overt, institutionalized discrimination is frowned on, but there are covert, unverbalized, and frequently unrecognized mechanisms for achieving the same goal.

Harassment is a mechanism for achieving exclusion and protection of privilege in situations where there are no formal mechanisms available. When one person harasses another in order to achieve visible gains—a job, a better seat, a more comfortable spot—we think of it as competition, aggressiveness, or assertiveness. We are more likely to identify harassment when it seems purposeless and seems to fulfill no function for the harasser. An external observer may wonder why one person is engaging in this exercise with another. It may appear that the aggressor is practicing, is flexing his muscles. Harassment indeed has this function of permitting the aggressor to test himself and improve his skills, in order to reassure himself that when the occasion arises, he can do well against an opponent. Whether it occurs among nations or among individuals at the highest or lowest socioeconomic and political levels, harassment seems to be a social instinct. In the same way that a small dog of a species with instinctive bird-hunting abilities, or an animal trained to hunt rodents, goes through the entire ritual even though there are no birds or no rodents around, human beings fall easily into harassment behavior even when there seems to be no rational objective.

The Institutionalization of Harassment

Harassment has been institutionalized as a way in which persons in certain roles should relate to each other. As such, it is not an aberration of human behavior but a formula for interacting. 'Spare the rod and spoil the child' is a statement of this belief that harassment and punishment are legitimate and often necessary means for compelling compliance with the rules and regulations of society.

It is as difficult to trace the evolution of harassment as a work institution as to trace other social developments. Ethnographic reports about primitive societies indicate that teasing is a form of social interaction in almost all of them. It has been noted in both the Firelanders of the southernmost tip of South America [61] and the Pygmies of the Belgian Congo. There is no evidence of true work harassment until society evolved into a more complex structure that conferred on a few of its members special privilege with the ownership of land and animals. This transition brought with it stratifications of position and status, power and privilege. Gradually, an even more complicated structure evolved, exemplified by feudal societies and, in the extreme, by slavery, the ultimate work-harassment institution. The worker had few rights; the employer or master could do pretty much as he wished, consistent with the prevailing public sense of decency. The slave had no legal rights, no recourse in the courts. The feudal serf, though somewhat better off, still was subject to exploitation by his master. Only gradually did the notion of human rights, children's rights, women's rights develop. Governments freed slaves, workers organized into unions in order to match the power of their employers and fight for better wages, indemnification for disability resulting from work-incurred injuries, improved working conditions, and the right to their jobs.

Certain bastions of privilege to harass, in geographic areas of this country in which segregation and behavior patterns going back to the days of slavery were maintained, fell as a result of the civil rights movements. The treatment of enlisted men in the military became more humane during World War II when large numbers of middle- and upper-class men were inducted into the military service. After this war, some effort was made to codify the rights of enlisted men and to include them in military management and judicial structure. The women's movement, the ethnic movements, and the student movements of the late 1950s and 1960s rebelled against the existing structure of privilege, and they won. Educational institutions changed, hiring practices changed, housing practices changed. These groups insisted that the social structure is not a norm, that harassment is not "natural." They based their fight on a belief that harassment as a privilege is historical and is perpetuated by those who derive privilege from it.

We see the subjects of our study as persons who have used the workers' compensation laws to combat, to prevent, and to be indemnified for harassment in one area. It is not the function of this report to present a social analysis of the forces that are working to perpetuate and those that are working to eliminate harassment, but we should like to present an overview of those factors.

Harassment has always existed, and that fact alone signifies the important function it serves in society, as an integral part of our culture that people view as a natural way of interacting. Most of those who are not victims at a given moment see nothing wrong in harassment. It is one of the control mechanisms of society.

Whole training programs are based on the notion of harassment. Since World War II, the newspapers have dealt recurrently with the problem of harassment in the United States Marine Corps, where harassment is institutionalized in the relationship of the drill instructor and the trainee. In spite of disclosures of drownings and beatings and the most sadistic kinds of interplay forced on the trainees and participated in by the drill instructors, very little seems to have been done to stop this horror. We must assume that the military authorities, especially the leadership of the Marines, could control this behavior and reduce most of the brutality and harassment. We must ask why they have not done so. One explanation is that the privilege of harassing, the right to be sadistic, is a fringe benefit of the job. While the perquisites of some jobs are automobiles, airplanes, helicopters, or servants, the perquisites of others are the privilege of striking, discomforting, aggravating, and harassing one's subordinates. In the Marine Corps, there are few other rewards or privileges for the drill instructor. Anyone who has observed Marines in basic training is impressed with the fact that the drill instructor works as hard or harder than his trainees. He has to answer for their performance. He has to run with them, climb with them, and be up early in the morning and go to bed late at night because he shepherds them. He is the subject of harassment from above. What really compensates him for doing this job? The salary is low and is fixed by Congress. He can be rewarded and given status only by being permitted some articles of uniform that others do not wear and by being given the privilege of harassing those beneath him. Most human beings, for reasons too profound to consider here, do see the right to harass as a privilege and will accept an opportunity presented to them.

If harassment in an institution or in an organization is to be considered a principle, then it must be accepted as right at all levels. It would not be right for the lieutenant to treat the sergeant in certain kinds of rank-appropriate ways unless the sergeant could treat the corporal in the same rank-appropriate ways. Harassment pervades certain establishments, especially military and paramilitary establishments, that are almost structured on it as a principle of achieving conformity, obedience, uniformity, and loyalty. Whether the organization is industrial, academic, or military, harassment is defended and protected as a necessary privilege, to be exercised to maintain control and to justify the harassment those at each level receive from above. There is a basic belief, unsubstantiated but unrefuted, that fear is necessary—or at least is the easiest way—to control persons, so that harassment becomes a method of preventing nonconformity or disobedience.

Harassment signifies status. If the pecking order indicates that those above shall have the right to annoy or displace those below, and if there is no pecking order and no harassment, then one must find other symbols of status. The privilege to harass is an inexpensive way of conferring status, requiring no capital investment or outlay. Alternatives to harassment as ways of conferring status are more complex, more highly evolved, and are not readily applicable to most situations. Because of this, harassment has become part of most management systems. Changes in harassment patterns represent changes in status and privilege that threaten to disturb operational systems that have relied on it. Those who select executives look for a certain kind of "toughness" in their candidates. They and their subordinates consider those who are unwilling or unable to participate in pecking or in harassing as weak. If their refusal to participate stems from principle, then they are seen as traitors to their class, and the result is exclusion from the society of those holding status.

Culture Change and Harassment

Certain kinds of people have special problems that may lead to harassment. Some persons who come to this country from other cultures and do not achieve the goals they anticipated find it hard to attribute their failure to personal flaws and deficiencies. The more perceptive, more intelligent, less defensive may understand that there is an element of luck and chance in success, but many of the problems of persons who come from other societies or cultures stem from their notion that success will be easy to achieve in this new environment. The belief that they will certainly become rich or famous or achieve great success and become executives overrides their awareness of their language insufficiency and lack of education.

Some are able to acknowledge that "it isn't exactly the way I thought it was going to be." But many have to find external causes for their failure. In the group we studied were many who left other cultures because they felt they were unappreciated and they looked to a new culture for the appreciation it seemed to promise, as well as for the tangibles it offered. They had the ambition and the drive to break out of their own society, but when they discovered they did not do better than before, they were faced with a terrible crisis. "Am I to blame or is society?" The more natural tendency is to blame someone else. We have no statistics as to how many blame themselves and become depressed, although we may assume some do. We do know from our study that many blame others.

Some of these workers believe they have been harassed. The accusation of harassment is not entirely invalid, but there is an understandable process by which harassment occurs in such circumstances. Rather grandiose and expectant of quick rewards, without the patience and the deliberate approach that might make it possible to learn the rules of work and the communications games of the system, these workers tend to attack the system head on. Such a person is immediately seen by those around him as aggressive, driving, possibly unrealistic. In some work situations, if he is very able, he might indeed succeed within a very short time. But if he does not have the ability or skills that he thinks he has, he becomes ludicrous. His coworkers see him as pretentious, a braggart, sometimes as a fool, and they do what is done to such a person—they tease him. Such persons react violently to teasing, aware as they are of their own failures and their insecure position, not just in work but with their families and with the people in the society they left behind. Since part of their breaking out had to do with impressing people back home with how well they could do in the United States, if it turns out that they do not do well here either, then they have a serious problem of maintaining self-esteem.

Many persist and somehow join the system. Others withdraw at this point and we never see them again. The remainder, who are represented by our claimants, are determined that they are going to break the system. They are not going to put up with ridicule, teasing, and harassment, which they have labeled as injustice. They complain and they fight back.

By the time of the second or third phase of this kind of harassment situation, the person is indeed being discriminated against and harassed. At this point, he may become more aggressive and seek remedies wherever he can find them, by going to superiors, by going to racial caucuses, by direct confrontation with his coworkers and superiors. At times this may result in actual physical combat, fights that usually amount only to quick exchanges or pushes. At some point, at the end of the push, whether he is the winner or loser, the claimant may find that he is crippled forever.

The functions of that damage are clear. He has revenge against the employer and the system and he no longer has to participate in the system, or in any system, for that matter. He has some measure of financial support; he has an acceptable explanation for not working, for his family and his friends. In fact, within his group his incapacity might be equivalent of a purple heart medal. He was attacked by the majority aggressor, an explanation that satisfies him and his family and may be equally important as an explanation for the people back home. He has been injured in the war, so to speak, and this accounts for his lack of success.

There are, of course, differences in family support systems among different societies. In Latin American societies, which are more oriented to the extended family, the male who cannot support his family does not lose status to the same extent as a disabled male in the United States. The extended family provides the necessary support without considering it a sacrifice.

In our sample we found an enormous range of personalities within all ethnic groups. The members of any one ethnic group are not necessarily similar, and predictions cannot be made about how they are going to behave. No type of behavior seen in one ethnic group has not also been seen in every other ethnic group. The frequency might vary but the incidence is universal. Thus, grossly hysterical kinds of behavior, grossly paranoid kinds of behavior, severely depressed kinds of behavior have been seen in each of the subgroups we have studied.

Everyday Conflict in the Work Situation

The very structure of jobs seems to be an important variable affecting the course and character of harassment. In almost all jobs there are common areas of potential conflict. One of the most ever-present areas of conflict is territoriality. There are personal and cultural definitions of spatial arrangements between individuals, as, interpersonal space (the space between individuals) and personal space (the area surrounding a person) [63,146]. If people come too close to each other or overlap spatially, each experiences invasion by the other, and they become uncomfortable without knowing why. Within the work setting, sharing tools, equipment, and space can cause conflict when the parties have different ideas of who has priority in these territories.

In our subjects, harassment occurred in stable and defined jobs. Workers generally spent a good deal of time together, were forced to interact within a confined situation, and necessarily had to share territory. They were not independently mobile (as a salesman is) but were occupationally wedded—a situation providing many opportunities for harassment. One of our subjects was situated in the main line of office traffic, where people were constantly interrupting her by brushing past her desk or walking around her, and this spatial invasion contributed to her feeling of harassment.

Another area of potential conflict in all work situations is the differing motivations of the supervisors and the supervised [97], which often result in communication problems. A basic cause of failure in superior-subordinate relations is a breakdown in conflicting values [107]. The supervisor's concern is economic—to finish the job in the shortest time possible while keeping costs down. His watchword is efficiency. The worker, on the other hand, wants to achieve good performance, but he also wishes to be seen as an individual [85]. He does not want to be pushed beyond his self-determined capacity and resents being pressured by his superior. The superior may be additionally burdened by having a supervisor above him, producing the problems of the "middle man" whose motivations are complex, because he must please subordinates, peers, and supervisors [132,160]. Among our harassment population were many examples of the "middle man" conflict. One man served as an acting director of social services during a time of decreased government spending and increased case loads for social workers. He was so overwhelmed by demands from above and complaints from below that he became unable to function on the job.

Work hierarchies lend themselves to harassing behavior toward both those who are extremely high in the hierarchy and those who are extremely low. Passive persons (generally subordinates) tend to exaggerate communication with active persons and tend to be hypersensitive to both positive and negative comments, while active persons (generally superiors) tend to underestimate the power of their interactions and therefore might do more harm than intended [160].

Another job quality conducive to harassment is conflict regarding worker output. Defined standards of productivity facilitate harassment or selective use of work pressure because there is a ready yardstick against which to measure people's behavior. A worker may be slow or sloppy and become a target for harassment by supervisors. Or a worker may be too conscientious or productive and become a target for harassment by peers [60].

Class differences in work produce differing forms of harassment. For example, harassment at the executive level tends to be subtle and exclusionary. It moves its victims to another area out of the councils of influence or out of the channels of progress. At the middle level, harassment excludes victims from the accepted social exchanges. Quite frequently this harassment takes the form of gentle kidding or of displacement. Lower-level jobs, such as laboring positions, seem to encourage harassment in the form of practical jokes and horseplay, where the harassee is physically involved.

2 The Harassment Process

Precipitants of Harassment

Change that the victim cannot integrate is the most common factor triggering harassment. Whether a change in locale, personal life, occupational life, or health status, its unexpectedness and seeming immediacy shock the victim into feeling vulnerable.

Most people realize that negative change can occur; economic recessions, plant shutdowns, demotions, the advent of new supervisors come as no surprise. The reaction may be anger, depression, and anxiety, together with laments that the system never recognizes the individual. The average person, however, does not see himself as a persecuted victim but as one of many sufferers. Many harassment claimants, however, think negative change is directed solely at them. Once established in a position, they believe no one should be able to force them to change their ways. Although they know that their employers have the right to make a change, they nevertheless resent it because they consider it directed at them personally. None of us likes change imposed upon us, although we often seek to make changes ourselves. We like to imagine that we can control our lives, so that if we are unhappy with what we are doing we can select other programs for ourselves, find other jobs, meet other people. When we select change, we generally select it from among a set of known alternatives. Change imposed when we are satisfied is threatening, because it always carries with it the risk that what follows will be bad.

Other factors that precipitate harassment include the perception of differences between the group and the victim in culture, race, appearance, dress, behavior, or sexual preference. Some claimants resent not only change in itself, but the result of change, which may, for example, deprive them of the love of a tolerant, parental supervisor when that superior is transferred or retires.

Albert singled himself out for harassment by his behavior when he did not find the love and approval, the "home on the job," that he felt he needed. The arrival of a new boss constituted a change in father image for Albert. This and his inability to cope with other changed relationships at work caused Albert to feel harassed.

Thirty-eight-years old, Albert was the youngest of eleven children of an emigré couple from middle Europe. He had acquired his father's great respect for authority. In that household one obeyed "the boss" because that was the only way families, countries, and business organizations could run. Conversely, when one was "the boss" himself, one expected to be obeyed. After high school and several odd jobs, urged by his in-laws, Albert joined the police department, a job offering higher status, employment security, and retirement benefits.

From the moment Albert entered the police department, he loved it. He enjoyed being a policeman; he enjoyed his colleagues; and most significantly, he loved and admired his chief. "He was a great man; he was a great chief." Albert and the chief enjoyed a father-son relationship, and Albert was secure in his position. He could do no wrong. Unfortunately, five years later, when this chief retired, life changed abruptly for Albert. The new chief was a "white glove man," who constantly checked up on everybody and everything. "Keep the body moving" became the watchword of the department. The new chief knew about Albert's relationship with his predecessor and thought Albert was very manipulative. He decided to stop Albert's manipulations and became especially hard on him, criticizing him, humiliating him in front of others, and threatening him with loss of his job. The new chief accused Albert of living with a woman to whom he was not married, and even demanded to see his marriage license. At one time, 95 percent of the police department signed a petition opposing this chief, but even after this censure he did not alter his behavior. Albert continued to be known throughout the department as the chief's "number 1 target." This reciprocal interaction, with Albert resenting being checked on and the chief in turn pressing him even more heavily, continued for four years.

Albert's life was hell. He began to dread going to work in the morning. He was unable to sleep. Because of anxiety and tension, he felt he could no longer relate to anyone. His marriage broke up and his wife and stepson left him. His parents died. He went to a physician who prescribed Valium but questioned whether Albert could safely continue his duties while taking the drug. As he took more medication, Albert felt he could not think and at times functioned in a daze. Finally, his physician sent him to a psychiatrist, and the psychiatrist urged him to stop working.

Albert left the police department and for a short period of time continued his second job as a maintenance man for an industrial organization. Within four months, he had to stop working there, too, because his anxiety had become so intense. Slowly, he had phased himself out of the work world, unable to express his rage and sadness effectively.

After he stopped working altogether, Albert seemed unable to organize himself. He said that he spent most of his time "going crazy." He watched television. He tried to read, but could not. Even fishing no longer held his interest. All he wanted to do was to get away from the area in which he lived. He hoped to go to some place where life was quieter, more peaceful. He tried moving away, but after two months returned home disillusioned.

In the same way, Albert had sought perfection in the working world. He wanted a job that assured security in the present and in the future, where he had camaraderie and he could obey and respect his superiors. We can only speculate on why the first police chief was so fond of Albert and why he was in turn so fond of the first chief. We must assume that the first chief selected as his favorites the people he liked, and Albert was chosen. There is nothing more pleasing than being selected as one who is wanted. They cared for each other's ego needs, the chief needing the adulation of his men and enjoying Albert's special adulation. Like the baby of a family, Albert felt secure in the chief's love.

A relatively dependent personality, Albert could not integrate the change from being the favorite son to being the object of a rigid, disciplined relationship. With his old chief, he had come to expect love and approval from a superior, and without this Albert's whole system of expectations had been shattered. He could no longer predict what the future would hold; he was crushed and outraged by the turn of events.

Albert's disability claim was more than a request for his "due." He wanted justification, verification, and validation of the rightness of his position, that is, that he had indeed been damaged by this treatment. As a result of his great dependency needs and his unrealized search for the benovolent and all-protective boss, Albert had become a displaced person. He had no status with his old friends on the force and, unemployed and drifting, had no status with his family either.

The same harassment-producing change in environment can occur when one is promoted or changes jobs and must function at a higher emotional level than previously demanded.

Louise was forty-five years old, had seven children (one of whom lived with her at home) and six grandchildren. She lived with her seventy-two-year-old mother, as she had all her life. Louise had recently left her job as a receptionist because of what she called a "nervous breakdown." About a year before, in order to obtain a promotion, she had taken a position in a large city four hundred miles away. When she arrived to begin her new job, she felt terrible pressure because she had much more responsibility than ever before. For the first four and a half months on the new job, she did not once meet with her new supervisor; after that, their encounters were continuous. Instead of supplying support, her supervisor harassed her, demanded more of her, and became increasingly critical. Because the pressure was more than she could bear, Louise went to see a psychiatrist for the first time in her life, and she found the treatment helpful. But her supervisor "changed her tactics" and insisted on a bi-weekly conference. During these sessions, she was criticized unceasingly. Louise reported, "I was always wrong in whatever I did. Between my two supervisors, I had to watch one so that I didn't get stabbed in the stomach and the other so that I didn't get stabbed in the back." Louise felt additional conflict because her new employers refused to pay her moving expenses, which she believed they had agreed to do when she accepted the job.

Louise decided to leave her position, but because she did not want to break up her son's schooling, she was forced to wait until the end of the school year to make the change. She would have preferred to return to her home town, but there were no jobs open, so she located a similar position in another town. When she transferred to this third city, which was closer to her original home, she met exactly the same problems. She felt that the new supervisors there were even worse. She soon began to have headaches and vomiting, her physical condition degenerated, and her spirits lagged. A short time later, she was "fired," when it was discovered that she had "leukemia" and previous physical illness, even though she had been hired with a congenital deformity. Louise felt that she was at her wit's end and tried to commit suicide by hitting a concrete abutment of an underpass, but she only damaged the bumper of her car.

She and her son moved back with her mother. Louise felt that she was much too nervous to go back to any kind of work and spent her days at home, cooking and sewing and visiting her children.

Louise was diagnosed by a psychiatrist as a rigid and self-demanding woman whose high expectations of her own performance were easily disrupted when others criticized her. Her decision to leave her relatively safe haven at home with her mother, to move to a large city where she knew no one, merely in order to gain a promotion, indicated her need to win approval and to achieve. Almost from the beginning she had difficulty, both in that city and in the next one. Many of these difficulties were self-created because she had exceeded her level of emotional competence. As a result of her own tensions and apprehensions, combined with those of her supervisors, she found it impossible to continue working and cannot bring herself to work again.

Mechanisms of Integration and Rejection

Socialization and enculturation are mechanisms of integration and rejection. Socialization usually focuses on what happens to the individual, how the individual learns to work with his society, to acquire the techniques of living in his society, values, and roles that are assigned him and permitted to him. Enculturation is the process of absorbing, for the most part unconsciously, the values and rules of the culture and the group in which one lives. Although all persons go through enculturation and socialization, the processes are not the same for everyone. Even in the same family, the individual members are exposed to different experiences. The "trainers" in the family, the parents or surrogate parents or those associated with them such as members of the extended family who live in the nuclear household, change in the course of time, and the enculturation and socialization processes change with them. Other processes also affect enculturation and socialization, processes having to do with the selection of individuals for special training and the acceptance or rejection of certain individuals.

Acceptance and rejection do not occur arbitrarily, although at times it might seem that they do. There are criteria to determine who can and cannot be accepted, and there are tests to decide whether someone measures up to the standards of the group and is worthy of being a member, and whether he represents a good investment for the group to train more extensively than it does other members of the unit.

Upon occasion, these tests are formal. For example, the person who performs well in school may be given opportunities for further training, the well coordinated child may be given tennis lessons or golf lessons, or the child with a "good ear" and sense of rhythm may be given music lessons.

Sometimes, the decision making is less rational. The handsome child may be given more advantages and training and preparation for acceptance and leadership than a more talented sibling who is less well endowed with beauty. The tall child may be given more than the short child, the light-colored child more than the dark-skinned child. One of our cases was that of a young black man who said he had been rejected even within his own family. His mother's second husband was lighter than her first husband, and the patient was the darkest of the children of both marriages. He believed he was rejected by his parents for this reason and given far less than the other children.

Acceptance and rejection begin early in life, the testing process probably beginning at birth. Tests of acceptance and rejection are met throughout life, and the mechanisms of acceptance and rejection are important in determining how well individuals are integrated into our society. This is particularly true in our mobile society, where the rules for acceptance and rejection that were laid down in the early childhood associations no longer hold. Even in the most stable societies there is change, but there is a level of constancy that we do not find in a mobile society from which many members have left and into which many new members have come. It becomes important in such mobile societies to study the mechanisms of acceptance and rejection in order to influence those mechanisms to reduce the potential for destructive rejection. A concomitant reduction of the hostility and antagonism that develops between groups should result.

Harassment and work pressure are devices for testing individuals and indicating to them they have failed the test and are being rejected. Although the primary reason for increasing the workload on individuals is to increase productivity, there is also a testing effect. When one increases the workload on an individual, one is saying, "Let's see if you measure up. Can you perform at this new level? If you can work at a higher level of productivity, we will insist that you do. If you cannot or choose not to, we do not want you in our company." Work pressure can constitute a selective test, and many workers resent it as special testing applied to them because they do not meet other qualifications, such as those of race, ethnicity, or education. Only if they can do more work than others will they be accepted. Blacks and women have coined the term "superblack" and "superwoman" to indicate that the requirements for their acceptance into an organization or into a group will be much higher than they are for other individuals. They resent this demand and may react to it, either overtly or covertly, in the form of psychological discomfort and physical symptoms.

Harassment is a form of testing that often is used to determine whether an individual will take it. Does he agree that the group he is about to enter has value? If so, he must pay a membership fee, and since there are not many ways social partnerships can be bought into, different testing procedures or different prices are established. The familiar initiation rite of the fraternity is one, and there is an initiation rite for some persons coming into a work organization. It is not always possible to determine exactly why some members are selected by this process, when others come in easily, as if they were recognized as being peers from the very beginning. For the others, there is an elaborate testing procedure, with teasing, practical joking, being made fun of, and assignment to the more obnoxious or the less desirable tasks in the organization.

The process of identifying and selecting a person for rejection can be either conscious or unconscious. The process begins at the moment an individual is considered for admission to an organization. A recruiter for a baseball team will reject most of the players he sees on a college team, his eye falling on just one or two. He does not even know he is rejecting the others. They have not even presented themselves for consideration in his mind, the first requirement for acceptance. The same happens in any work environment or work organization. A screening process takes place at the moment hirer and applicant meet. If the job to be filled is that of a college president, the scrutiny will be rigorous on both sides. If the job opening is at a lower level, especially if there is considerable turnover, the scrutiny may be minimal. The applicant says he is interested in and eager for the job; he appears to be physically capable. A simple questionnaire reveals no reason to disqualify him. If it turns out he is not a good worker, he can be fired before the end of the day.

The next level of appraisal takes place in the actual work environment. The worker will be appraised by his superiors and by his coworkers, and by his subordinates if he is in a supervisory position. His superiors will judge him according to his productivity and his ability to work with others, and perhaps by how much of a threat he seems likely to be to them. His coworkers will judge him in other terms. Is he going to relieve them of some of the load? Is he going to break up established patterns of relationships? Is he going to make them feel uncomfortable by behaving as if he were superior? Out of all of these considerations comes an initial impression, and this is tested in one of two ways. It can be tested by inviting the new worker to come closer and by learning more about him and how he works, how he relates if he is offered a positive relationship. Or, he can be attacked, gently and carefully at first, because he might turn out to be the kind of person who strikes back, whom one does not want to alienate. At the end of the testing process, the worker is rated "keep," or "tentative," or "reject." If the decision is keep, there is no problem. If the conclusion is that he should be tested further or that one should be watchful in his presence, then the testing process might continue, but in a modified, usually subdued form.

If the decision is to reject, the pressure is increased, either by isolating the person and ignoring him, itself a form of harassment, or by aggressive teasing, practical joking, sabotaging, or insulting, making it clear to the new worker that he is not one of the crowd. Most workers in this situation resign or are fired. They are too disturbing to the work organization to be permitted to stay. At times such workers do not permit themselves to be rejected. They know and invoke their rights. The organization then has to decide whether to redouble its efforts to get rid of the worker or to permit him to stay.

When the entire organization, coworkers and superiors, agree that a worker should be rejected, there is a high probability that he will be. In some cases, however, because of the worker's tenacity and because of protection against discharge offered by a union or an organization or a civil service commission, the employers might decide it is not worth the effort to try to remove him. Or, an individual may be offensive to his fellow workers but a good producer. The employer might even be pleased that this particular worker is discomforting the other workers, and may even pit him against them. The harassment process then speeds up, as the workers try to reject the foreign body from their presence.

At times when jobs are plentiful, many workers will see little point in remaining in an unpleasant situation and will leave. Sometimes they do not leave, but in time the organization comes to accept them, at some fixed level of continued harassment. Individuals can become fixated at some stage in their lives, so that their development from that point on is aberrant, and the same thing can happen in work relationships. There may be no reason why harassment should continue, but it does, with an adjustment process taking place around it. The harasser does not harass too hard nor do his harassment tactics increase. The target does not react violently and at times even seems to accept the harassment as a pleasant form of interaction. Black workers and Chicano workers often accept teasing as part of their lot in life. They are supposed to permit white workers to make a little bit of fun of them, either to show that they appreciate being admitted into the group or to indicate they recognize their lower status and subordinate social place. A balance may be established that sometimes goes on for many years, perhaps until the worker and his harassers are separated as a result of natural causes or, sometimes the target's tolerance changes, because other things in his life change or because social conditions change, and he suddenly strikes back.

Humor and Teasing at Work

Humor in the work situation serves to generalize specific discomforts. People who work together share common jokes about their superiors or about people who work in another section [18]. They develop ways of regarding what they dislike within their own working environment as part of a system that is impersonally benign, or at least is not malignant. An example is the joking and friendly banter on a production line. Talking, laughter, and fun make more pleasurable what would otherwise be drudgery, sitting at a station continuously, performing the same manual task for eight hours. Shared humor lightens the workers' load because it creates a group relationship. In this manner humor at work operates under a "Parkinson's Law of relationships" [126]: it fills the relationship vacuum and thus forestalls autism and aggression.

While we have no hard evidence that humor either increases or decreases productivity, we could without question use positive humor as a rough index of a happy working situation. Using this index, one might conclude that a work environment that evidences a good bit of humor will show less conflict, less overall unhappiness, and fewer emotional problems than a situation with less humor. Humor is conducive to group cooperation, whereas harassment is destructive. Harassment is humor gone sour, perhaps because the participants have lost their objectivity and react in subjective ways.

Some persons are not able to appreciate humor. They seem unable to tolerate the abstractness in humor, turning it instead into something specific and personal. The failure to understand a joke signifies an underlying conflict [96]. Such a person is not able to use humor adaptively because of his too punitive superego and an inability to relax defenses and permit momentary regression. A true appreciation of humor requires a playful and disengaged psychological stance characterized by minimal defensiveness [142]. If humor is not appreciated, but is interpreted as insult, it leads to aggression, arousal and threat, which lead to defensiveness. Psychotherapists have been advised to use humor sparingly with their patients; it is too easy for patients to interpret humor in idiosyncratic and derogatory ways and to become defensive and vulnerable [87].

Many of the subjects in our harassment population were of humorless disposition. Often hyperconscientious, they took their lives and jobs seriously. Perhaps this seriousness provoked humorous remarks from others, but those remarks were never perceived by the subject as pure humor.

Humor, then, is one method of defining interpersonal relationships. Just as the relative status between superiors and subordinates differs from the relative status of coworkers, the kinds of humor between the two groups can differ. A superior's sour attitude can suppress humor in a work situation where workers would develop humorous outlets if left to themselves. Often, an employer will consider humor to be an antiwork distraction and will discourage it. A supervisor who comes upon a group of workers laughing, and says, "Why don't you people cool it and settle down to work," assumes that laughter is incompatible with productivity; he fails to realize the positive function of the humor. In such cases, humor might go underground or might remain at an inhibited low level because the worker is afraid of trouble if he engages in humor of some kind.

Coworkers who resent humor can constrain their peers as well, although in contrast to superiors, these persons do not have the authority to ban it. A woman who worked as a secretary in a district attorney's office was such a humorless person. For many years after her high school graduation she had worked for a solo practitioner who had trained her to be a legal secretary. When he finally died, she went to work for another lawyer, and then another, and another, because she could not find the "right" job. Finally, she took a job with the district attorney. When she arrived, the office was a "four-girl operation." Within a month she was the "senior girl," because the others left or went on part-time status. Then another "girl" was hired who was "kind of hippie," while the subject herself was extraordinarily straight. The new girl had many "hip" friends who often visited her at work. A short while later, a third girl was hired, who gradually became a close friend of the "hippie." They engaged in a good bit of horseplay around the office. The subject was furious that she could do nothing "against" these two because she was "only" one of the "girls" in the office, and she began developing headaches. She felt that she was forced to carry too much of the workload because the others were "fooling around." Although she told both the district attorney and the two other secretaries how difficult it was to work under these circumstances with so much horseplay, conditions did not improve. Finally she had to leave work and filed a compensation claim alleging injury caused by the behavior of her coworkers.

Humor can, of course, become aggressive. The mildest form of aggressive humor is what we would call teasing or kidding. If humor is a kind of generalization, teasing is the obverse, a shift from the general to the specific. Teasing says something about "you." An act of teasing or a practical joke turns a probability system onto an individual. One would expect, for example, that the chances of grease spilling all over someone's tools are possibly one in a hundred, but the practical joker converts this into a one-in-one chance. Just as humor, which generalizes, tends to make one happier and more comfortable with oneself, teasing, which degeneralizes or specifies, makes one more uncomfortable, more uneasy, more uncertain.

Humor connotes a shared empathy between equals, whereas teasing generally occurs between persons of unequal status. The aggressive teaser assumes the role of adult while reducing the teasee to the status of child. While humor often is characterized by a sudden change or twist in a shared sequential story, the analogue in teasing is its very ambiguity: the teaser implies that he knows more about his target than the target himself does, but the target is uncertain about the other's knowledge (i.e., as when told, "You're just a big baby," or "I saw your wife with another man").

Teasing can be placed on a scale from "light teasing" (kidding, joshing, tantalizing, jeering, and "getting a rise out of someone") to "heavy teasing" (tormenting, bullying, pestering) [147]. The light end of teasing includes play between friends, while the heavy end encompasses the teaser's demand for attention from the teasee and his forceful assertion of superiority.

Teasing, like punching, pushing, or slapping on the back, has a clear potential for hurting. If one slaps another on the back, he might break the other's back or damage his skin or knock him over. Ordinarily, one knows another's approximate resistance and would not slap him hard enough to risk any danger. The slap is meant to startle more than to damage. The same holds true for most teasing or kidding: the "slap" or "push" is not intended to hurt, just to startle.

There is a certain ritual involved in kidding that depends in part upon the relative status of the participants. The lower-status person—the child, the student, the employee—can go only so far in teasing the higher-status figure—the parent, the teacher, the employer. The two have a kind of "teasing budget" or "teasing account." They cannot overdraw the account by teasing each other too much or too harshly. The art of teasing resides in the ability to gauge the force necessary to startle but not to hurt. One must gauge the stamina and the vulnerability of the target. If the teaser is clumsy, his "slap" will knock the victim down; on the other hand, even when the teaser is clumsy, if the target is tough or is quick on his feet, he will not be knocked over. Many of our harassment incidents occurred because an artless teaser met a weak victim.

The components of teasing are interactive participation in eliciting behavior; uncertainty; pretense; unpleasant potentialities; and, the pleasure premium of the unpleasant potentialities not being fulfilled [147]. Countless authors have studied the functions of teasing, viewing it as an important mechanism by which people develop personally and test themselves and others socially. Teasing can be considered part of growth and development, a necessary and positive step in the maturation of a healthy ego [130]. Teasing experiences constitute developmental transitions that a child must withstand before being accepted by various groups, from playmates to schoolmates to clubmates. A child's reactions to teasing determine his evaluation as a good or bad sport, reflecting his ability to "dish it out" or to "take it." Taunting, heckling, name-calling, mimicry, and practical jokes are weapons of ridicule and disapproval that enforce conformity to group standards [5,76].

Many children who fail to master their early teasing experiences have little success as adults with the light, graceful banter that facilitates social intercourse [148]. They often are embarrassed because they cannot differentiate among the coquettish, the flirtatious, and the seductive. An adult who has not outgrown early teasing is the "born tease." His dominant mode of establishing or maintaining social relationships is teasing, which reflects social and emotional immaturity.

Teasing can be an experiment to evaluate a new acquaintance, a way of asking, "What are you like? How do we compare with each other?" Teasing stands somewhere between aggression and love [21]. It is sometimes modulated by adaptive and creative ego processes, and at other times by complex defensive processes. There is significance in the literal meaning of teasing, "to shred finely, to disentangle, to tear to pieces." Teasing or "tearing apart" is a safe way of getting close to loving another human being, for one can be an ambivalent tease. Because teasing has an aggressive element, if one teases and is rejected, he has not "lost." His target has merely told him, "I don't want you to be aggressive toward me, and I will not accept your aggression." This hurts him far less than to be told, "I don't want your love." Thus, teasing can be a cover for love.

Both parties must understand the words in the cultural language of teasing. If the target does not understand, then he may recognize the aggressive component of teasing, but miss the opportunity for love. Some teasing, however, is purely aggressive: the target is clumsy, he does not speak the language, he cannot stop in time. In the vast majority of cases, however, and certainly those in this sample, teasing constitutes a mixed cultural message. Most people at work are able to accept teasing as social testing, an initiation rite. Those who view teasing as combat or as a judgment of individual human worth may react aggressively, and vitiate this cultural formula for relationship testing.

Anthropologists who have studied teasing in other cultures can help us understand teasing in our own society. Teasing has been described as molding character among the Balinese [11]. From the age or five or six months, the unsatisfied suckling was increasingly subjected to abrupt withdrawals from the breast during nursing. The child's reactions were met consistently by the mother's unresponsiveness. The child was subjected to other forms of teasing, such as genital stimulation. Once aroused, the child was ignored; his tormentors threatened to forsake him or to harm his genitals. These early learning experiences contributed to the typical adult Balinese temperament: emotional unresponsiveness or "awayness" in interpersonal relationships.

The Sioux Indians similarly tested an infant by premature withdrawal while breast feeding [42]. The infant's temper tantrum was encouraged because the Sioux believed it promoted the socially desirable qualities of aggression, fierceness, and violent muscular activities, which the Sioux needed to survive in his own culture.

Among the Arapesh, the teased child was encouraged to display suffering and rage, provided that he did not physically harm the teaser [110]. The teaser, who became aghast at the misery he had produced, felt compelled to make amends and to curb his teasing impulses. In this culture, physical aggression was intolerable, and the slightest rejection among adults might produce prolonged displays of rage or weeping.

Japanese practices began to inculcate cultural behavior early in childhood through teasing and threats of rejection or separation [13]. Yet, later on, if children teased others they suffered shame, ridicule, and humiliation, which was a serious and frowned-upon loss of face.

"Joking relationships" exist throughout the world [128]. The relationship varies with the culture but basically is a mix of friendliness and antagonism, a "permitted disrespect." What is described in primitive societies is very much what we have observed about teasing at work, although less ritualized in the latter context.

What is meant by the term 'joking relationship' is a relation between two persons in which one is by custom permitted and in some instances required, to tease or make fun of the other, who in turn is required to take no offense. It is important to distinguish two main varieties. In one the relationship is symmetrical; each of the two persons teases or makes fun of the other. In the other variety the relationship is asymmetrical. A jokes at the expense of B and B accepts the teasing good humoredly without retaliating; or A teases B as much as he pleases and B in return teases A only a little. There are many varieties in the form of this relationship in different societies. In some instances the joking and teasing is only verbal, in others it includes horseplay; in some the joking includes elements of obscenity, in others not [128, p. 90].

Joking relationships often develop in industry during stressful situations [18]. Higher-status figures frequently tease lower-status workers in an attempt to disarm the subordinate of antagonism, which, in the supervisor's view, would maintain the status-quo working relationship. Those who joke readily and participate in this teasing are more popular than those who do not. Those who cannot or do not joke often are isolated, as so often happened with the claimants in our study.

The effect of teasing may be destructive or therapeutic. Destructive teasing undermines the teasee's stability. At the same time, the teaser releases his own feelings of aggression and inadequacy. Often a tortured person, the destructive teaser seeks to demonstrate his power over the teasee in order to counteract his own feelings of impotence. He projects his own deficiencies onto the victim [131]. Some teasers are not only aggressive but also sadistic, that is, they enjoy causing suffering in others.

It is an aspect of social development that teasing can be therapeutic [67]. By laughing with others and by being laughed at, the child develops a consciousness of himself vis-a-vis others. From disapproving laughter, he learns about social authority, coercion, and exclusion. Laughter also focuses his attention on social ethics, standards, and taboos.

Teasing is essential in adult socialization as well, where it educates. It establishes role and status, affirms common values and norms. It channels behavior by showing disapproval of deficient or aberrant conduct.

Teasing can be said to be purely positive when it affirms a relationship, such as the acceptance of ritual teasing between friends. It strengthens their interaction by ventilating minor aggressions rather than jeopardizing the friendship. Positive teasers, in contrast to destructive teasers, are usually of equal ego strength. In that sense, both parties are teasers, and there is no exploited teasee. The following group of cases focuses on a range of reactions to various types of teasing.

A sixty-two-year-old plumber with an eighth-grade education, Jim was the victim of simple teasing that so outraged him, he developed a physical reaction. The unusual manner in which Jim was injured is not insignificant in understanding what followed. While Jim was using the portable outhouse at a construction site, one of his coworkers who drove a scoop truck decided to "have a little fun" and raised the corner of the outhouse with the front of his truck. This caused uproarious laughter and diverted the foreman and coworkers for some time during the afternoon. Jim was not hurt. His only immediate symptom was surprise and confusion. He went home that evening, experienced no symptoms, and was able to watch television. His wife had an appointment with a physician that evening and asked if he thought he should come along. He responded that he was not uncomfortable at the moment and probably would not know until the next morning whether he had been injured. Having thought about his injury all night long, he decided the next morning that he was indeed hurt. He went to the hospital, and was extremely angry when after some weeks he was discharged. He felt that the severity of his symptoms was not appreciated. After that, his symptoms diminished slowly, and he expected them to continue to do so at about the same rate. He attributed all his difficulties to damage to his spine and associated nerves. He explained that nerves recover from injury at the rate of a millimeter a month, and in this way he calculated his own progress.

Jim had a history of numerous surgical procedures during the last thirty years. His social history was chaotic. He had been married four times; among his wives were alcoholics and lesbians. His present wife is ill a good part of the time, and he has had running battles with physicians regarding her care. Exhibitionistic and superficially aggressive, Jim in the past used medical symptoms to gain attention and to achieve what was in his eyes some prominence. His rate of recovery after the outhouse tip seems to have depended upon his decision to improve at his own pace. In this manner, he showed everyone that being bumped in the outhouse was more than a joke.

Whereas in Jim's case a single incident constituted the teasing, David was the victim of chronic teasing. Throughout his life he had been teased because he had a cleft palate. During his ten years as a social worker, his superiors had teased him cruelly about his physical deformity, until his supervisor finally pressured him into having surgery to correct it. The surgery was not effective. Then, David injured his knee, tripping over a drawer at work. Despite corrective surgery, the pain continued, and his leg has never improved. As a result, he was placed on limited duty. He is constantly harassed by fellow staff members and by superiors who "are bugging the hell out of me," he says, and he thinks they want to get rid of him. Both superiors and coworkers have openly accused him of malingering, and he says the program administrator has been heard to say he hoped David would leave because he did not want anyone working there who had David's attitudes. Constant conflicts with supervisors and colleagues have depressed David and made him so nervous he thinks he is going to "flip out" because he is so "uptight." David has never been able to escape the stigma of having been identified by his superior as a proper target for teasing because of a congenital physical handicap and subsequent physical impairment. Because his coworkers and superiors can no longer tolerate their own guilt and hostility, they seek to do away with the "irritant." Meanwhile, David goes to a job that provides little more than misery for him.

Forms of Harassment

Harassment itself is untempered, systematic teasing, the selection of a target for aggressive, hostile, assaultive treatment. Differences between humor and teasing and outright harassment often are only differences in degree. Harassment in some instances represents the continuation of an unworkable relationship that was not resolved through joking or teasing. Harassment can be coated with a thin veneer of humor, or it can go to the extreme of overt bullying.

The harassment process takes many forms, and we have isolated four of these, which are represented in the cases: scapegoating, name-calling, physical abuse, and the selective exercise of work pressure, or the "hurry-up" tactic.

Scapegoating

A well-known and ubiquitous phenomenon, scapegoating [29, 80] represents a displacement, the selection of one person to absorb the aggression of an individual or an entire group. It is a comfortable escape valve for blame [83] and in many ways is used to "drain the reservoir" by seeking other channels and targets [111] when aggression toward the source of frustration is prevented. The participants are saying, in effect, "Let's fix all of our attention on this one area so we don't have to attend to problems in the other areas."

When frustration generates aggressive tendencies, particularly in rigid or highly prejudiced individuals, displaced aggression is externalized onto a disliked person [16]. This person is disliked because he is different or strange or unlikely to resort to retaliatory aggression. The more the target is disliked, the greater the tendency to make him the focus of aggression.

Disliked persons are rejected or scapegoated [44]. For the individual, these experiences are dysfunctional; for the group, scapegoating serves an integrative function. Scapegoating is a unifying mechanism in groups with low levels of functional and interpersonal integration and therefore suggests further deterioration of group integration.

The psychiatrist often sees scapegoating in the home in the context of the "identified patient." A family comes for treatment and the husband or the wife or the child will be the announced "sick" patient, when actually the problem is in the entire family. It is so much simpler for the family to say, "Let's focus all of our blame on that one person," because in that way the others can avoid acknowledging responsibility.

This focusing of aggression onto one person will be felt by him as harassment. When he is turned upon, the scapegoat frequently does not know what hit him. Caught unprotected, he may react with defensive anger. Or, as psychiatrists notice frequently, the scapegoat may come to believe that he deserves what hit him; he begins to hate himself just as his tormentors hate him because he believes that he is indeed the cause of the problem. Self-hatred in many persons is a reflection of such mental processes of absorbing and internalizing self-derogation. Racial minorities and women have long suffered from this. Many women even today deny that a woman should ever be president, because, "How could a woman ever run the government?" Children who see themselves as the cause of all the family problems quite often come to hate themselves. A paranoid person who becomes a scapegoat is especially susceptible to self-hatred, for he is likely to exaggerate the scapegoating far beyond his tormentors' intent. It is possible, of course, for a scapegoat to react philosophically, as did one of our subjects. He recognized that his being made the goat was a social phenomenon, and said, "Someone has to be the scapegoat, and I was the guy who was chosen this time. Next time it will be someone else."

Name-Calling

Known to all of us since the childhood taunt, "Ha, ha, scaredy cat" is this version of teasing: name-calling. "The Dozens" among some blacks is a form of name-calling that has almost become a game by its ritual. It is an adaptive social form growing out of black frustration. In this repartee, one insults another's family, "especially female relatives and particularly the mother, . . . (it is) not simply personal insult to the individual" [55, p. 105] .

A more malicious form of name-calling is "joaning," which is designed to "tease another person with the intention of starting a fight" [37, p. 212] .

For our patients who were called names at work, this was a most destructive form of harassment. The name-caller characteristically exploited a salient physical feature or immutable characteristic in his victim, frequently relating to sex or sex preference. Appelations of "Spic," "Black Mexican," or "Fairy" hurt deeply and more often than not were preludes to a fist fight.

Physical Abuse

Physical abuse in our culture expresses a breakdown of ritual patterns for settling disputes. People have a "physical dialogue" when there is no longer a balance in the joking relationship or in the "teasing account." When either the harasser or the harassee makes a false estimate of the other's tolerance, the cumulative effect of the mounting tension creates an explosion. For some reason, the harasser escalates his aggressive behavior and this "breaks" the victim, who might be increasingly sensitive for reasons totally unrelated to the harasser—for example, because of domestic problems.

We first see physical abuse in childhood: parents spanking children, siblings beating one another up, playmates and classmates fighting. In our experience, the reaction to such physical attack is a constant awareness of the psychological scar the attack caused. An example is noted in the case of the young man from a boarding school who had been teased and beaten up by his fellow students. To the psychiatrist, he described not only his misery, but also his concern that he spent so much time ruminating about how he would like to kill or maim one of his tormentors. He talked about various methods of revenge, ranging from getting up in the middle of the night and stabbing them to waiting until they went into town, standing in a dark alley and striking them with a heavy object. All his fantasies fulfilled the desire to cause pain when the victim would not expect it, not out of fear, but because he wanted his victim to be as defenseless as he himself felt. This young man could continue to go to school despite the beatings he got. But in our work sample, physical abuse was a catastrophic event that in most instances ended the working relationship. This was true whether the attack was by a superior, by a coworker, or by a consumer.

Carlos, from South America, for example, was injured when a coworker threw a piece of equipment at him, hitting him in the chest. In addition to this physical abuse, he felt he had been insulted, teased, and pushed physically, and had been the victim of aggressive behavior in other ways. He was so angry that even one-and-a-half years later, his ambition was to get total revenge and put the company out of business.

Ricardo was the target of physical abuse by his supervisor, when he was caught sitting down on the job, waiting for assistance to lift a 100 pound sack. This angered the boss, who scuffled with and pushed Ricardo on his back, fell on him, and then grabbed and shook him. This has resulted in a seven-year absence from work for Ricardo, although there were no true physical injuries.

In another case, when a passenger attacked a bus driver, the driver withdrew from his job to avoid a repetition of the event. A significant factor in his withdrawal was rage because the attack was unilateral. The victim could defend himself, and even could later file for monetary benefits, but he could not retaliate against his assailant. Left with a feeling of massive rage, the driver spent most of his time ruminating about the injustice done him. He was obsessed with the thoughts of what he would like to do to his attacker, to those who supported his attacker, to all the members of the system who did not rally to his support in order to punish the attacker.

Upset and withdrawal increase in such cases. A wife says that her husband sits in a living room chair and "barks" at her when she asks him for something; he is irritable with the children, and if one of them makes noise or asks him something, the father strikes out or explodes at the child. When asked why he behaves this way, the victim often describes what we could call "autistic retaliation" [120], that is, a state of readiness to attack. The erstwhile victim lashes out at whoever happens to interfere with his system of internal justice in which he is meting out revenge against his attacker. The interloper who has interfered with a satisfying autistic process, whether spouse or child, is rejected and in turn attacked for the interference.

A primary reason why physical abuse has been the end of working relationships may be the subconscious recognition that degeneration of those relationships into physical attack is simply an unacceptable "solution." The old days of dueling or stepping outside to fight it out are long gone. The group cannot integrate or accept such methods of conflict resolution as normal. Nor can the group deal with the subsequent lingering hostility generated by a fight, when group members fear that they may be attacked next.

Sexual Harassment

One mode of harassment of workers by superiors is sexual harassment. The most frequent claim of sexual harassment was that of a female who had been harassed by a male. In most such instances in our study, we had no way of reconstructing the actual facts but, based on the available data, it often seemed that the male aggressor did not actually wish to have sexual relations, nor even an extended social contact, with his female target. Indeed, one often suspected that he chose this victim precisely because he knew she would never agree to his suggestions. His intention was merely to tease. The target, however, took him seriously and became upset. Such harassment has been called "little rape" by one author.

Reactions to it depend on how the woman sees herself and on how she sees her relationship to the suggesting male. If she likes the exchange and indicates by verbal and nonverbal gesture that she is pleasantly annoyed but that she is willing for the interaction to continue, then there is no harassment, no "little rape," at least from her viewpoint. If the male is undesirable either because of age ("the dirty old man"), physiognomy, or personality then the target sends out signals that request termination of the interaction. Such requests are respected by most, but some few persist, recognizing the weakness of the victim or the strength of their own superior position in the organization.

A white assembly line supervisor indicated to a recently hired Mexican-American female that easy tasks and freedom from job pressure would follow her willingness to see him after work. She refused. She had a boyfriend of her own, and this supervisor was "fat and old." Her work life became a nightmare.

Both the seduction and the punishment for refusing were daily events. Criticized and moved from task to task, she went to her family physician who suggested that she take sick leave and talk to a psychiatrist.

A second type of sexual harassment claimed by females is exemplified by the reports of two women, both middle-aged and both employed in county government agencies, who identified black males as the aggressor. In the first instance, a black janitor repeatedly suggested to an older, unmarried Caucasian secretary that she was attractive and that she should "loosen up" sexually with him. Initially, he said this privately but he later repeated it in front of their coworkers. She was unsure how to handle him but each time said "Absolutely no!" The more strongly she reacted, the more he suggested sexual contact. Fearing that she might cry or show symptoms of her chronic nervous tension (twitches and tics), she would not talk with her supervisor about the incidents. Finally, she sought psychiatric treatment.

In the second case, a woman in her late fifties had the same experience with her black supervisor. He often made sexually-related suggestions to her in front of coworkers. After a year of embarrassment, the woman spoke to the director of the organization. He seemed to think it was humorous and that he could not do much about it. Shortly thereafter the black supervisor was moved to another unit, and the woman no longer felt harassed.

In both cases, the white women looked down upon black coworkers and neither would ever consciously consider a friendship, much less a sexual relationship, with a black person. Each was very concerned that her coworkers might think she was actually tempted to engage in sex with a black man. For these race-conscious women, the men's open verbal advances represented a "social rape."

Although we saw no cases where males claimed sexual harassment by females, we did encounter several males who claimed sexual harassment by other males. When the aggressor recognized someone else's discomfort about discussing sex or relating sexually, he would pick away at that sensitive area. Males teased males about their sexual potency or sexual interest. In the target's mind, the implication that he had low level sexual potency also suggested that the harasser thought he had homosexual tendencies. One target was primed for any statement indicating that his harasser considered him homosexual. The target invariably thought that as a result of the harasser's insinuations other workers regarded him as "gay" or "queer." He was constantly obsessed by these thoughts; he was unable to sleep because of his anger, helplessness, and embarrassment; he could not discuss it with his wife because he feared admitting to her that others might consider him anything less than a vigorous, active heterosexual.

In another case, when a new male employee rejected his male supervisor's seduction, the supervisor retaliated by giving him highly undesirable assignments. Finally, the new worker had to leave work, his hopes for a permanent and profitable job shattered.

Functions of Harassment

Just as harassment itself is closely related to humor and teasing, the functions of harassment are similar to those we noted in conjunction with humor and teasing. We can discuss harassment and its functions from two perspectives: inside the work system (harassment by coworkers and by superiors) and outside the work system (harassment by the consumer).

Harassment is one way in which coworkers test and determine their status relative to one another [149]. The new worker joining an office or plant is generally an unknown quantity. He usually arrives through an impersonal hiring office, knowing few if any of his coworkers, and has not been screened or chosen by the older members of the group. In some instances, harassment is part of his "initiation rite." Our experience has been that an "initiation ritual" is deeply ingrained in the more stable, established work groups. It is unclear whether harassment is less rigorous in groups such as construction crews, whose membership varies from job to job and whose life span is short.

Some new workers are not harassed at all, depending upon both the individual characteristics of the newcomer and the composition of the group. For any number of reasons, the older workers from the beginning have judged these new recruits to be "desirable." The reasons for such a judgment may range from pleasing personality characteristics to outside friendship with the older group. A new worker who is known by one or more of the old group or has been brought into the working organization through the influence of older members of the group has in effect been "pretested" as in older social systems, such as some union and apprenticeship positions. The newcomer usually is tested only in a token fashion, the teasing or kidding obviously being friendly. We see this most often in the case of the seventeen- or eighteen-year-old who comes into a group of much older men. They tease him pleasantly, as a child is teased at a family gathering. If he can accept and understand this, then he will soon become a bona fide member of the group.

Other newcomers are not tested because they are too "dangerous" [94]. Some are physically too threatening. Others are emotionally too threatening. One hospital worker joined a hospital work group—a group that had a reputation for teasing initiates—but he was not teased because it was apparent to the members of the group that he was paranoid, suspicious, and easily angered. Instead of harassment, there was a walling off, an isolation of this man. Although people were polite to him, and although there was no evidence of a conspiracy to exclude him, he was left to himself. He was never initiated into the group because it was evident that he would not tolerate the initiation process, and it was feared that he might strike out and injure a member of the group.

In general, then, because a new worker arrives on the job today "cold," the existing group uses various forms of harassment as a method of testing and integrating him [18]. In the course of this integration, the established group must see whether the new member is likely to be pleasant or irritable, supportive or threatening. The older employees might use his reactions to harassment as a way of deciding whether to spend time with him after working hours or whether to limit the association to work.

Teasing and harassing tell the new worker that the existing group has sanctions, that it has ways of punishing those who do not conform to the rules of the group. The message is, "We are a worthwhile entity. We have our own status. We need not accept a new worker, and we can reject you and can make life miserable for you" [18,149]. Such demonstration that the organization has "teeth" is important to its existence as a substitute for a written constitution or other sets of rules of acceptable behavior within the work culture.

A good example of the coercive power of the group appears in "play" that takes place in the industrial setting [151]. Among the assembly-line worker's "line games" is one called "piling." A few workers decide to increase the workload of the "rate buster," a "maverick" who produces more than the agreed-upon quota. They do this because they are forced to work faster or are made to look bad as a result of the rate buster's speed. They "pile up" work for him so that no matter how fast he works, he will never catch up. They also isolate him and tease him about his production. This ultimately brings him into line or makes it impossible for him to interact with his coworkers.

Harassment unifies the group of harassers [150] as the "in-group," making them feel stronger and more secure. The victims too are brought together in a struggle against the hostile force [33,109]. Sometimes they can even negotiate with harassers.

Harassment can be compared to other forms of exploitation, in that the victim must be seen as weak or helpless relative to the strength of the aggressor. As long as the victim believes he is alone or subject to physical, psychological, or economic annihilation, he cannot defend himself. If he can identify others as members of the same subset into which he falls, suffering the same wrongs, he can unite with them. Organized, he can face the exploiter with strength. Labor unions, consumer groups, and racial caucauses are examples of formalized defense.

As suggested elsewhere, much of harassment is simply a demonstration of power. The aggressor proves his vigor by acting as he does [80]. The person whom the potential aggressor perceives as "guilty" in some way may elicit aggression as vengeance, deterence, or an object lesson.

In line with these notions, one can view superiors' harassment of employees as a demonstration of dominance. The job foreman or supervisor who works directly with people in his section may feel threatened by groups of workers. Thus, he seeks to establish his dominance in order to show that he is more than a "straw boss." Harassment is a method of delivering an object lesson. A superior harasses a particular worker to make other employees afraid. Coworkers also use harassment as a sanction to force those whom they view as laggards to "pull their own weight," because they fear the increased workload if one member of the production team slacks off. Numerous authors have observed examples of dominance behavior in animals [3,43,49,137].

A superior may harass an underling purely to indicate that he does not care if his subordinate leaves. This says to the subordinate, "You're not all that important—in fact, you are quite dispensable. I'm going to push you around and if you want to go, you can go. I don't have to be very considerate of you." We know that this is not restricted to the work situation. It happens commonly in marriages and in other situations where one person exerts this kind of leverage upon another.

Harassment keeps the subordinate tense or anxious. The notion is that management must "keep people on their toes" because the more anxious workers are, the better they perform. Left to themselves and unprovoked, workers will become sluggish, will not be motivated, will not perform at maximum capacity. If, however, the worker fears punitive measures, he will produce more. Employees who fear reprisals will be less likely to organize [100,105].

Harassment by consumers, or others external to the work group, serves to make the consumer feel that he is not helpless. He can strike out at whoever is in the controlling position. The *Wall Street Journal* commented on the subway conductor who, because he pushes people in and out and moves the subway, is the man who "really" controls the subway [161]. When the consumer strikes back at perceived authority figures, although he knows that those figures are only individuals, he personifies the system in them. Thus, his action is a kind of "teasing" or specification of the general. The subway conductor or the prison guard [50,161], the store clerk or the police officer is the representative of the evil, suppressive, or frustrating system. In venting his anger on the individual agent, the consumer is protesting the system he dislikes. Most attacks by members of the public are acts of impersonal aggression: throwing objects at a passing vehicle, pelting a conductor with fruits or vegetables, assulting a guard. The actor need not find a specific cause for his feeling; he only acts out an overall anger.

The following cases demonstrate primarily the functions of harassment in unifying an in-group against the "deviant" outsider.

Leonard was a 56-year-old school teacher who was harassed out of his profession because he could not adapt to currently accepted behavior and thought. His social history shows the evolution of a strong sense of morality and duty.

Leonard and his brother grew up in the home of a "foster grandmother," when his father abandoned the family and his mother went to work. Leonard cared deeply for this woman. His relationship with her was strong; for example, even though he was offered several college scholarships, he took none of them because it meant he would have to abandon his foster grandmother. (Even after

Leonard married, his foster grandmother continued to live with him and his wife.)

Soon after high school, Leonard bought a small farm so that he, his brother, and foster grandmother could live together, but because it was a losing venture, he was forced to sell the farm and return to work in a large city. By working eighty to ninety hours a week, he eventually saved enough money to buy another small farm. In addition to farming, he also took a part-time job as a bus driver. Several years later he left that job because he rebelled against the graft within the organization. Although some of the "honest people" in the area urged him to run for public office, he declined. When World War II began, Leonard went to work in an explosives plant.

Although he was married, had three children, had a small farm, and was working in an essential industry, he volunteered for the military service. He did so, Leonard said, because he felt a moral obligation to serve his country if he could. During those two years of military service, he suffered numerous injuries and was honorably discharged with 100 percent disability. After the war he became a teacher.

For a number of years, things went reasonably well. Leonard enjoyed teaching and was extremely active in civic and service activities. Then, various problems began to surface at school. Intentionally or unintentionally, some students slammed a door on him. The blow on the head aggravated his deafness, the result of a war injury. Leonard was a stickler for the rules, and as education went through the crises of the sixties, the rules were increasingly bent, and he could not bend with them. He would request and urge and insist that school administrators enforce the rules, and administrators in turn became more uncomfortable with him. The students realized the Leonard was at odds with the administration and would challenge him, knowing the administration would not support him.

In response to Leonard's rigidity, the administration began assigning him an inordinate share of unpleasant duties infamously known as "latrine" jobs. One such task was literally "latrine duty" in that he had to patrol the boys' bathroom to make sure students were not smoking, taking drugs, or drinking. Another such task was monitoring the study hall for unruly students. Needless to say, he took these jobs seriously and attempted to enforce the rules. Ironically, the very teacher who had the most difficulty in dealing with those who would not conform to the rules was purposely assigned to work with them.

The end came when he was assigned to monitor the parking lot exit roads after school. There was one exit road for school buses and one road for student automobiles. The road for buses was smooth, because the authorities had no fear that school buses would leave the parking lot at excessive rates of speed. The road for students had built-in bumps so that students would have to exit slowly. In Leonard, the students knew that they had a "pigeon." Cars whizzed by him. When he reported this to the administration, nothing was done about it.

Students would test their driving skill to see how close they could come to him without knocking him over. So close did they come that once his briefcase was knocked from his hand.

Finally, the same student who knocked the briefcase out of Leonard's hand had decided that in spite of the teacher's presence, he would drive out the bus road. Leonard was determined to stop him. He went out into the middle of the road and waved his hands. The student came slowly up against his legs and kept pushing him forward, moving the teacher out of his way with the bumper. When Leonard was no longer able to back up fast enough, he tried to get out of the way and the student sped by, catching his shirt sleeve with the sideview mirror and flipping Leonard over.

He was hospitalized for five days. Even after he was discharged, he had pains all over his body and swelling and bruises. Despite the incident, he decided to take a long-planned European summer vacation. The trip was miserable because of his pain, and he returned as soon as possible. Home again, he was shocked to discover that the school administration had done nothing about the event and that the district attorney's office had no knowledge of it. The next fall he was again assigned to "latrine duty." He developed a tremor so severe that it was diagnosed as Parkinson's disease. His pain intensified unbearably, his symptoms eventually became too much for him, and he retired.

It would be difficult to find a more poignant case of both overt and subtle harassment. One has the feeling that this man threatened the world around him by his very goodness. He hated corruption, he hated deceit, he believed that everyone should live by the rules, he believed that one should pay his debts to his community. And he lived all his beliefs himself. But the working world in which he lived was a bending world, a society experiencing great changes in its concepts of authority, generalized relationships, behavior, sexual freedom. Leonard wanted to live by a book that each day became more antiquated.

Because of Leonard's rigidity, the society around him had either to accept and tolerate him or to exclude him, and it chose the latter course. It could not exclude him directly, but an unconscious conspiracy evolved to extrude him. He was teased by his fellow faculty members because he was in some ways a caricature. We do not know whether the students grasped this attitude from the faculty or whether they decided of their own accord that Leonard was a good target. The exchanges between him and the students were test cases that would decide whether such behavior on the part of the students could be tolerated. Leonard lost in each case, and it was he, not the students, who suffered. It was he who was given "latrine duty," and the students knew it. Each such test was an invitation to further harassment by the students until the ultimate, life-threatening event occurred.

In this case harassment became a way of dealing with a deviant who was on the side of the angels rather than on the side of the devil. A film called *Serpico* dealt with the same theme. In it, the "honest cop" was interfering with a system that permitted crime. The outraged and honest Serpico, unwilling to bend with the system, was harassed and finally extruded. The cases of Leonard and Serpico illustrate the difficulties the conscientious or hyperconscientious person has in living in normal society. These cases show, too, that because such people serve as a mirror to their superiors and coworkers, they make them uncomfortable. Eventually, many of the Leonards and Serpicos are martyred by those who fear their influence.

Another outsider who never made it in was Howard, a twenty-five-year-old park ranger who yearned for peace and order and the simple life. When he was sent to a post in a small semirural community, he was delighted. The very thought of going to a small town made him even happier than when he had been accepted into the Park Service, which had been a great moment in itself. Howard had always viewed the Service as a distinguished career. His expectation had been that as a ranger, he would be an important figure who would, above all, enforce the law. It was important to him that rules be enforced and that they be enforced as written, uniformly against all persons.

What Howard actually experienced was a great deal different from what he had expected. He found the area isolated, and he was frustrated by the lack of support staff to help him in case of difficulty. He believed that the community in which he lived was against him. According to Howard, the community had a system of law enforcement that permitted local residents to do almost anything in the park and unfairly clamped down on outsiders. If he issued a citation to a local citizen, the person usually got off with only a warning from the court. The same offense committed by an outsider merited a heavy fine from the local judge. Howard felt community hostility in a variety of ways. The windshield of his car was broken by local adolescents who threw rocks through it. His wife was nearly run off the road by one of the local hot rodders who chose the road in front of his house as their favorite drag strip. Once, when he grabbed one by the collar, the boy's parents complained to his superior and Howard was reprimanded for this action. Howard believed the reprimand especially unjust, because it was made retroactive to his performance report for the preceding year. He thought also that his own superiors were against him. He was refused training in special schools, he was refused a change of housing, he was refused special permission to use his ranger car to drive to baseball practice in another town, all of which were privileges commonly accorded to other rangers.

He felt alone and frightened, rejected and harassed by both his superiors and the community he was to serve. The park community made it very clear that it would not tolerate a nonselective law enforcement foreign to its culture.

In response, Howard began to develop back pains, had trouble breathing, and occasionally came close to passing out. He became extremely irritable: he criticized his wife ceaselessly; he punished his children at the slightest excuse. Formerly fairly gregarious, he began to withdraw, and along with this change in behavior, he changed his appearance, growing a beard and mustache and long hair. Suicidal thoughts obsessed him, and he made several suicide threats. Once he considered suicide on the road; on another occasion he placed a gun against his head and thought of pulling the trigger, but did not. Because of his unusual behavior, he was finally hospitalized and shortly thereafter resigned from the park service.

Howard then spent his days at home. He and his wife lived close to his parents who gave him both financial and emotional support. He owned a number of horses and spent his time training them. He enjoyed this work and said that if he had enough money, he would buy a horse ranch. Still a tense man, he felt that as soon as he was not subjected to community harassment, his condition improved.

Each of us tends to idealize and anticipate a situation, perhaps marriage, school, military service, or work. The positive idealists of the world are capable of imagining a situation in which they will fit perfectly and be perfectly happy. They tend to project onto the anticipated job or relationship all the positive features that they will need in order to be happy. But most of us learned in childhood that the amusement park to which we were going was fun and that the baseball game was great, but neither was idyllic. We learned in many different situations that what existed was not always what had been visualized; sometimes it was better and sometimes worse, and we behave in such a way as to make it as good as possible for ourselves.

So, too, with work. At whatever level, the worker soon discovers that the job he anticipated as being the best job of all or in just the place that he wanted to be—in Alaska where one can fish all the time and where a person is free and unencumbered by the restrictions of civilization, or in Hawaii where one can swim and surf all day and do a little bit of work on the side—is not quite what he expected, but he understands and adjusts, and then idealizes the next situation. Howard was one of those persons who cannot adapt to the difference between his ideal and the real. For a Howard to reevaluate his expectations in the light of reality and to adapt to the real, means that he must give up the ideal, whereas for most people adapting to the real still leaves it possible for them to have the ideal. For a Howard, this adaptation to the real means that he has been cheated, and he reacts by becoming angry. By fighting, he makes the situation worse for himself rather than better, and the worse it becomes, the greater the difference between his ideal and the reality. The harder he fights, the more anxious and angry he becomes. Finally, he is expelled or withdraws from the system.

Another person we saw with the same difficulty was Harley, a man who by the age of thirty had already held and lost three law enforcement jobs. In each, he had been harassed. First, as a police officer in a small community, he soon decided that the community was corrupt; because he could not adapt to the corruption, he was fired. He then became a jailer in a county jail, where he soon discovered that he could not tolerate the dope traffic in that jail. After he filed a complaint with the authorities, he found that he was being harassed by his coworkers and by the inmates. He felt he had no protection from the inmates because his coworkers seemed to ignore slights by the inmates. At this point he moved to another community and became a sheriff's deputy. Here he found that the administration was totally inefficient, and once again his efforts to right the inefficiency resulted in harassment. After this he began an effort to influence legislators to change the state law enforcement system so that it would be less corrupt and law enforcement officers would have more protection against law breakers.

There are many Howards and Harleys in this world, and they are not all alike. They may be like those described above, or they may fight a little and then adapt. Or they may be of another type of whom we see many in work situations, who do not claim harassment but leave as soon as they discover that each job in which they find themselves is not their ideal.

Job Upgrading and Harassment

The clients in our harassment sample would expect to have the greatest difficulty in entering into new situations. Going from the unskilled laboring class or the farm labor class to some kind of factory work might seem a relatively easy transition, but for the unskilled or for the farm worker it represents a tremendous complexity. Farm life is migrant, short term; the employee works with his own people, by and large, who speak his language. The farm worker uses a set of skills that he has acquired over many years, and how well these skills are used activates respect patterns among those who do farm labor.

These people are not prepared by experience or language for the transition to another kind of occupation. The users of the majority language generally are familiar with the nuances and idioms of the language and of the nonverbal language so essential in understanding what is going on. Two people interacting with each other have some notion of how much leeway exists in their relationship before any exchange becomes harassment. Relationships are not fixed or linear, but variable. All relationships have within them a range of tolerance, so that a person can be a bit mean to one person, slightly aggressive toward another, a bit passive toward someone else, within a range that each situation allows. When a person is in a situation where he cannot take anything as a "given," where he does not know the language or the range of tolerance or his own position in relation to others, he may seem slightly paranoid when in fact his response is a kind of rapid scanning of the environment and a tendency to read the worst rather than the best meaning into a given situation. Like the hypervigilant, he tends to interpret a subjectively ambiguous situation as the most dangerous of all possible situations.

At the same time, those who already are on the job are going through the same kind of process. They do not really know what he is saying, or the meaning of his gestures or his reactions. They can afford to be a little more relaxed, because they are the majority. They all speak the same language. They know the rules, they know the cues, they know the nonverbal language. They do not know what kind of threat the newcomer represents. The testing phase of the relationship is not just testing to see whether the new worker is friendly or whether he will be accepted; it is also the kind of testing one sometimes sees in flirtation, when a person cannot always be sure of the meaning of the language. Is he hostile, rejecting, friendly, or inviting? This point marks the beginning of racial problems in harassment. In spite of Supreme Court decisions and laws such as the Economic Opportunities Law, discrimination persists in both North and South.

Minority group workers exhibit many different approaches to the work system. They have been told, and rightly so, that they have been discriminated against educationally, culturally, and certainly materially and that they have rights to remedy that discrimination, rights that are listed in affirmative action laws. One worker takes a passive approach, feeling that "I'll take what I can get and I mustn't expect any more. I can hope for more, but I mustn't really expect more. I'm not sure what they're talking about with this antidiscrimination affirmative action, but I don't think it has anything to do with me. I'll keep on working as blacks have always worked and be grateful when I get a job. It does seem that I can get somewhat better jobs than I used to and that I get paid somewhat more. I'm damn glad."

At the opposite end of the spectrum is the person who expects the system to live up to its promise to upgrade him. It is indeed true that if a member of a minority group is very able, his chances for moving ahead are better than they were formerly. In our sample, however, we often saw minority group members who were not the most able and who did not have the kinds of skills that would immediately mark them for promotion. Some had serious work problems. Without the basic skills for learning the job, they could not produce the quantity or quality of work required. Problems often arise in highly competitive work situations where out of any layer of employees, only one or two are going to be promoted. When a person of limited qualifications finds himself in this situation, he may feel that the reason he is criticized or is not promoted is that he is a member of the minority racial group or victimized gender. If working in an ethnically or sexually homogeneous situation, the same person might feel discriminated against for some other reason, for example, on the basis of nepotism. This person probably would have difficulty in any type of setting because his expectations outdistance his skills and abilities.

We must remember, however, that a person claiming discrimination or harassment is not always doing so because he has a problem; often the situation is exactly as he has described it, namely, there is harassment based on racial or ethnic or gender discrimination.

Several of our cases demonstrated that overt discrimination based on race or gender had been flaunted and defended by the worker's superiors or coworkers, resulting in denial of promotion or of placement in a more desirable job, and in overt verbal harassment. One of our subjects protested, and at a grievance hearing attended by upper level management and union officials, his immediate supervisor said to the assembled group, "I don't like blacks; it's my right not to like blacks; I can't help it. I think they're lazy. I don't think they're productive. I think they're less intelligent. That's my right as an American citizen, and I'm not going to hide it." The claimant became very upset. His blood pressure went up, and he developed other physical symptoms. When his case was litigated, it was decided that he was indeed being discriminated against, and a decision was made by his superiors to promote him. We know from follow-up that he has done very well in that position.

In contrast, another worker filed a disability claim, not because he felt overworked or harassed, but because after four years of work in a sales office, "management and supervision did not fulfill its responsibility to me." He had been a construction worker, cook, gas station attendant, health gym "therapist," telephone apprentice lineman, and salesman. Several of the jobs folded; others he quit because "I never got off the ground" or because of "certain innuendoes." He quit clerking at the Post Office, where he had felt "trapped with a black frame of reference," because he was "not moving anywhere, stagnating, standing completely still." Prior to that, he elected to be discharged from the Army after almost two years service, when he found he could not qualify for OCS. Initially believing this new job "a fantastic opportunity" to get more information and experience so he could make a better living, he was once again disappointed, angry, and puzzled that the world and work had not met his expectations.

Management's not fulfilling one's expectations, whether or not this is intentional, is perceived as a type of harassment by a person who has hoped for something special from an employer. He feels singled out because, from his point of view, something is being withheld from him. He is unable and unwilling to imagine that there is a hierarchy of abilities and talents and that he might not be at the top of that scale.

He accounts for his failure by pointing to past and present patterns of harassment and discrimination. He does not see that although the member of the majority group has a higher probability of achieving success because of his origins, he must still be blessed with talent and acquired skills in order to surpass his fellows.

Effects of Harassment

The effect of harassment upon its victims can be devastating. There is a wide variety of reactions to harassment in the form of laughter, depending upon individual intellect and temperament [67]. Being laughed at can result in embarrassment, humiliation, depression, alienation or anger. A secure person can take the laughter, but an insecure one will experience increased doubt, insecurity, and lack of self-confidence. While individual reactions vary, most of us are shaken by being laughed at.

The subjective experience of being overwhelmed by an authority figure has been called "putative" injury. "When a person is confronted repeatedly by a figure, perceived as inimical, supported by what is considered as immense, incontrovertible, overwhelming authority, the individual feels reduced to smallness and helplessness with a proportional magnification of the authority figure" [20, p.961].

An extreme consequence of the devastation harassment can produce is that of a Detroit auto worker who obtained revenge by killing his supervisor and some fellow workers [155]. After an on-site plant visit and observation of the harassing conditions under which the defendant worked, the jury acquitted him of murder on grounds of insanity. Admittedly, this example is extreme, but it demonstrates that the effects of harassment do result in negative behavior that can be of shocking intensity.

In our study, the effects of harassment were never as extreme as in the preceding example. Prior to their disabilities, most of our patients were productive and more than adequate employees who tried their best in the work situation. Well-regarded by colleagues, many had been promoted on previous jobs, in recognition of their hyperconscientious qualities. They needed approval and many worked hard to please; these were not malingerers or "goof-offs." Because of their previous work successes, they had come to think that their efforts would succeed in keeping them in a favorable light, although basically their hyperconscientious work habits covered their own doubts and fears regarding their abilities.

When suddenly struck by social disaster—harassment—the impact is enormous, because the attack is not anticipated, even by those who might seem to an observer to have provoked their harassers. It is in this connection that it is easy to underestimate the impact of harassment. Sickness or accidents might reasonably be expected to occur, but the shock of harassment for our subjects lay in learning that other human beings had decided to "get" them. This crisis might be compared to that of being unexpectedly hit from behind by a car while stopped at a red light. The unexpectedness of such a shock can be disastrous for the injured party, and this is what happens in situations of abrasive teasing or harassment. In spite of constantly escalating tension, the victim never really expects the explosion.

Our harassment victims exhibited various reactions, some with extreme indignation and rage that resulted in a display of inappropriate aggression, others with depression and a greatly diminished self-image. Those who reacted with anger often found themselves provoking further harassment, for the effects of harassment can be reciprocal. People who became angered when harassed tend to react with hostile, defiant, and aggressive behavior. Hostile verbal response increases rather than decreases the probability of further hostile verbal response [38]. This response by anger serves for many people as a reinstatement of potency and feelings of adequacy and self-worth [156]. Many of the harassment victims who were angered initially later developed feelings of depression and loss of self-regard. Whether the initial reaction was one of depression, diminished self-worth, or rage, the result followed some general disability patterns. Some expressed their reaction by developing vague physical symptoms such as chronic fatigue, loss of strength, various aches, weaknesses, and pains. Others reacted with depression and the symptoms that accompany depression—sleeplessness, impotence, lack of self-esteem, and poor motivation. Still others reacted with psychological symptoms such as nervousness, hypersensitivity, hostility, memory loss, and feelings of victimization; they may also have begun to avoid social contacts.

All appeared to use their complaints as a justification for staying away from the work situation. In short, this is a population of persons who express their life problems through somatic complaints and are basically lacking in psychological insight.

Most people realistically expect a certain degree of "harassment"—teasing, razzing, horseplay—in whatever they do, whether school, recreation, or work. They may resent the ill treatment, but most of them know it is coming. Although they may fight it, they are willing to accept the unpleasantness at least insofar as they engage in the particular activity associated with it. What distinguishes our population is that many of them do not *expect* harassment, and none of them *accepts* it. They are part of this sample precisely because they could not tolerate a situation they perceived as upsetting, so upsetting that it disabled them from working.

Both the development of the harassment scenario and the effect of the harassment process are dramatically illustrated by the cases of Juan and Ray. Because of their obsessive-compulsive natures both men projected a "holier than thou" attitude. Angered at this, their peers fought back via harassment, further isolating their targets.

Juan was outraged because the behavior of his coworkers was not entirely consistent with the rules and regulations. He was furious if a coworker used company time for anything but the job that was to be done, took a paper clip for his own purposes, or used company machinery to produce something for other purposes. It is commonly understood that white collar and blue collar crime consists not only of petty thievery but also of misuse of work time for such purposes as football pools, numbers rackets, and personal letter writing. Within most institutions the culture of the institution is flexible enough to permit a given amount of such activity. Some departments allow such infractions as fringe benefits.

Almost always there is one employee in a group who is troubled by the time wasting or material wasting of his colleagues. Usually he mutters about it or sometimes shares with a coworker his feeling that this behavior should not be permitted, or he might tell his spouse about it. Seldom does he report his coworkers to superiors, confronting them with what in most instances they already know, that is, that the situation exists and that it is not consistent with the stated rules.

Such a confrontation throws the working system out of kilter. Suddenly, managers are asked to change their behavior, to enforce rules that may make a job less desirable. With the tension created, the complaining employee becomes the target of his coworkers' anger and becomes a nuisance to management. Instead of being rewarded for his honesty and devotion to the organization, he finds that he has driven his coworkers and his superiors closer together, and he is even further alienated and isolated from them. Many workers resign at this point. Others are so incensed that they vow to fight corruption to the top. Those who think that such a worker can be intimidated underestimate the energy of the person who *has* to be right. Each bit of pressure increases that worker's determination, and each failure to remedy the situation produces anger, paranoia, and renewed determination. Such is the case of Juan.

For twenty-five years Juan had worked at a shop in the local college. During the last ten years he had been in a constant state of unrest at work because of his inability to tolerate what was in his view improper activity on the part of his coworkers and superiors. According to him, they were doing private work, using college time and equipment. He estimated that the college was losing between $17,000 and $20,000 a year in time and materials, and estimated that each man was earning a considerable amount of extra money per day. He believed that such activities should not be tolerated in the college, and he complained to the business manager. Nothing was done. His coworkers learned of his complaint, became very angry with him, and began insulting him. Shortly thereafter, a new business manager was hired, and Juan again complained to him that his coworkers were "chiseling on time." Juan also warned the foreman that he would have to go to a higher authority unless action was taken. Finally, the new business manager did issue a letter, directing workers in the shop not to do work for private pay. Later, under pressure from still higher authority, the business manager reversed his position in a letter stating that employees could do private work after hours, provided that it did not interfere with their college work. Juan's response was, "Nothing doing. This is illegal. No one has the right to use the taxpayer's equipment."

With this, his fellow workers increased their harassment, calling him a "Black Mexican," a "Spic." They threw away his work or destroyed it, so that he was forced to waste much time redoing projects he had previously completed. Because of this, and because he felt ill much of the time, his productivity declined. He was accused of not working rapidly enough and later received two letters of reprimand. He took the letters of reprimand to a grievance committee and obtained an official pardon. Nonetheless, his running disagreements with his coworkers continued.

The upsetting situation took a physical toll. Juan had stomach trouble, his psoriasis became worse, and he developed cataracts. At the peak of his problems at work he had severe colitis, tachycardia, hypertension, and nightmares.

Juan continued to work at the shop, but there was at best an uneasy detente between him and his shopmates, although they ceased to harass him. He had his cataracts removed and received extensive physical and psychiatric care. At work, he still was accused of being "too slow." He was unhappy but he was not eligible for retirement.

A captain in the fire department, Ray was obsessed by the need to know and obey the rules and regulations. Everyone must agree with his interpretation of the rules and conform. These attitudes repeatedly brought him into conflict with others on the force, culminating in his taking an indeterminate leave of absence.

Several years ago, in the course of a routine physical examination, the county physician wanted to do a blood test. Ray did not want his blood drawn. When the assistant fire chief threatened to suspend him for lack of compliance, Ray appealed to the chief, insisting that he would take the blood test only if they could show him a requirement in the rule book. The chief responded that he wanted to know whether or not Ray was fit for duty, and that was why he had to take the test. Understandably, this disagreement became infamous within the fire department.

Routine within the work situation stabilized again, until Ray announced to the department that the vacation policy was wrong. He asserted that fire department policy was in conflict with civil service regulations. He initiated a volley of letters to the appropriate district authorities explaining that the policy was outdated, describing the conflict with civil service rules and regulations. He included suggestions for improvements in a possible new policy. His superior replied by telling him to take it up with the fire fighter's union. Ray did not expect such a hostile reply. Later, when he selected his vacation according to civil service policy rather than fire district policy, he was refused vacation until he decided to conform to the fire department policy. Finally, because these deviations from the rules were so upsetting to him, Ray saw a physician who prescribed Valium, which created another problem for him. Ray knew that regulations prohibited firemen from taking Valium during working hours. He felt that he could not take the medication without written permission, but when he called in and asked for written permission, he was given only verbal authorization to work while taking Valium. On that permission he worked for several weeks while taking the drug, but later felt compelled to seek written authorization. This insistence created yet another stir within the fire department. Eventually Ray left work over this and other related "rule" matters.

Ray's obsessive-compulsive personality reaches into every aspect of his life, determining that he must take every contigency into account before he acts. In order to safeguard himself, he must abide by the rules, and when the rules come into conflict with his needs, he has a tremendously serious problem. He expects others to be as attentive to the rules and regulations as he is and shows relatively little understanding when his interpretation of the rules disagrees with that of others. He cannot be wrong because that threatens his whole cognitive system. This personality feature caused him to push his superiors further and further; as a result he and the fire department have reached an impasse. Ray feels the need to push for a definition of every rule and regulation and reacts with suspicion to anything that might be considered a negative or hostile gesture. At this point he cannot return to the department because he feels that the requisite certainty is lacking. Because he has pushed so long for legalistic clarifications, he is fearful about retaliation.

Failure of Coping Mechanisms

The patients within our population responded to harassment with a variety of coping mechanisms, with seemingly three phases in the reaction.

The first phase is confusion, shock, and an overwhelmed feeling. The psychological confusion is manifested through physical reactions such as diarrhea, headache, dizziness; through somatic responses, including pain, blurry vision, ringing in the ears, palpitations, tremor, twitching, and tics; through identifiable psychological states of confusion, depression, profound anxiety, and a sense of impending disaster. Socially, even the casual observer notices the patient's withdrawal from family and friends. The victims are confused and concerned about themselves. Understandably, it is difficult to interact with others when one is terribly worried about oneself. In addition, many harassment victims think that if they are not "worthy" of being full members of the group at work as indicated by the harassment, neither are they "worthy" of being full members of the group at home. At this stage of the reaction to the harassment, domestic problems usually surface or intensify.

In phase two, we see a sort of random behavior. Like a disaster victim, the patient gives the impression of just wandering about, but one must assume that he is trying to find a solution to his problem. He is so traumatized that he will often try anything in order to get back to "normal." He is like the panicked student studying for an examination, a little from this book and a little from that book. If one asks, "Why don't you just study one book and then you will learn the material?", the response is, "Well, but what if I miss . . ." The patient is overwhelmed and desperately trying to find a solution. At this stage, still feeling buffeted around and not certain whether he will return to work, the victim is interacting with many people concerned with his illness, doctors, insurance workers, lawyers, etc.

In the third phase, our population can be grouped into three clusters, all with somatic symptoms. One group continues the random phase, never seeming to develop a way of dealing with reality even though they have filed claims for compensation. A second cluster of patients becomes depressed. To some degree they have accepted the accusations of "badness" transmitted by the harassment. These patients feel that Nature, God, Fate, or people have treated them badly. They are distressed at having put themselves in such a position, at not having done what they might to get out, at being so unlucky, or at not being one of God's favorites.

Those who become depressed tend to disappear from view. Never really overcoming the shock of being selected for negative treatment, some never return to work, some begin to drink or become habituated to drugs and progressively decline. Those who do return to work tend initially to sink occupationally, seeking lower-status jobs that make fewer demands and that require little involvement with other people. In some of our cases, such workers looked for jobs as security guards, janitors, or night watchmen, hoping that they would be able to walk around, push a broom, check a firebox, and go home after eight hours. Some few do gradually work back up to their preharassment job level, taking a lower-status job and using it as an opportunity for reorganizing their lives. One man, for example, decided that he was not going to get himself into a similar situation again. He went to a school for new training, started a business of his own, and, in effect, used this disaster as an incentive to rebuild his life.

The third group of patients, by far the largest, consists of those who become angry. This group decides to fight. They are outraged, in part by their own terrible helplessness against an external power. In some instances, there has indeed been a gross injustice done. In other cases, one feels that these patients are excessively litigious. With many, the rage continues for weeks or months and then seems to diminish. They either find a legal channel for coping with the anger, or it gradually dissipates and they go on to do other things. For some few, the anger seems never to dissipate but to become a way of life. Anger is converted into somatic symptoms, and the patient becomes involved in the complex system of medical treatment. Often, an unconscious cyclic dependence on drugs follows. Analgesic medication given for pain can be habit forming in those who tend to form habits. Unconsciously, they must keep having symptoms in order to get drugs. They can honestly say they are not feigning symptoms in order to receive medication, because they actually do experience and believe in the symptoms. Other aspects of medical treatment, carrying with them support and recognition, encourage patients to retain their symptoms, and the prospect of monetary "compensation" for lost time and work nurtures the lingering anger. As long as the litigation process is pending, many of those with a compensation neurosis can be expected to retain their symptoms.

Anger not only can be converted into somatic symptoms but also can become institutionalized through litigation, becoming the social means through which the person derives his identity and status. Anger can become a statement of belief rather than a statement of feeling; when one talks to such a patient, one hears him expressing anger that has long since passed and has become part of a role he is playing, a role of which he is generally quite unconscious. He becomes, in a manner of speaking, professionally angry, much in the manner that groups of displaced persons sometimes continue for many many years to fight the nation that displaced them, long after the original expellees are gone, and sometimes into a third generation. The anger becomes a part of identity rather than a feeling, different in kind from the real anger that has somatic components and disables the person. This kind of anger is a kind of hysterical anger, a role available to the person at the time he needs it. He may fight for two, three, or four years to right a relatively minor wrong, confounding the negotiation and litigation processes as he goes.

The angry patient also may change his position within his family. For some patients, there is no recovery from that initial helpless, random position within the family structure. Many experience all the effects of a traumatic neurosis: withdrawal of interest from activity, irritability, and impotence. As with any illness, there follows a change in family structure and dominance patterns. The harassment victim might achieve a more desirable position as a result of his injury. If he enjoys more care and more attention plus diminished responsibility after the harassment, he may not want to relinquish what he has gained. If, for example, as a result of his initial confusion and unemployment, his spouse has begun to work outside the home and has become the primary provider, he may discover that he really likes it much better at home than at work. He may unconsciously "decide" to stay angry and unemployed. We see this phenomenon in all kinds of injuries, especially in industrial accidents, where the person works out a way of life far more pleasing to him than the one he had before.

At the very minimum then, harassment makes its victims subjectively miserable. It alienates them. It substantially diminishes both their job satisfaction and their productivity. Although they might scramble in order to appear busier, they generally are less efficient because their energies are diverted to planning retaliation against perceived injustices. They develop a sense of being sick and vulnerable, both psychologically and physically. This kind of disaster makes one concerned about all parts of his body. "If I can have this, I might have all kinds of other things—a bad tooth, a bad heart." Numerous physical complaints lead to increased absenteeism, resulting in further losses to both employer and employee, and the cycle continues.

Coworkers who observe this process, whether or not they are a part of the harassing group, begin to feel that the system is not a secure, protective system, but rather a system in which one can be hurt at any time. Coworkers, too, can become less productive, can develop an increased sense of personal vulnerability, and might even develop somatic concerns. The harassment-ridden organization, then, becomes threatening, frightening, unstable. In short, it is dysfunctional.

Systemic Consequences

The benefits to animal societies of dominance/subordination struggles have been described, with the conclusion that these struggles are positive in that they terminate anarchy and establish mechanisms for determining strong leadership [7]. Because strong leadership is established, social friction and disorganization are reduced. But we have no reason to believe that struggles for dominance, discord, combat, or other aggression are either necessary or salutary in human work society. Indeed, we have great reason to believe that they are unnecessary and destructive both of the work environment and of workers [44]. To the extent that humor and gentle teasing serve to make work lighter, happier, and more convivial, these serve useful functions in work society; to the extent that they tend to bring the outside into the work place, they are also helpful. Much of humor, for example, relates to sexual activity, which ordinarily takes place outside of work. A good deal of teasing also refers to performance in leisure-time activities, such as bowling or golf. By increasing the scope of the work field, such allusions make work a more social activity.

But when humor or teasing becomes harassment, tension is added to the system. Cruelty can be both contagious and aimless, and the worker knows that if people can be cruel to each other, some day he himself might become the victim of such cruelty. As a result of harassment, then, an atmosphere is created in which trust is minimal and fear is increased, as is seen in the contrast between paranoid societies and more supportive altruistic societies [14]. At present, we see in many work situations the ingredients for and behavior expected within a paranoid society. Workers do not expect that things will go along in a predictable, supportive, harmonious fashion; instead, they fear that arbitrary behavior by superiors or coworkers will make work painful. While much of the rationale behind harassment is that it improves the work situation, it is our observation that the harassment-filled organization is threatening, frightening, and unstable.

3

Harassment by People

One can say that each work system constitutes a separate culture. Behavior that is approved by one culture would be considered outrageous in another [18], and those who engaged in it would be viewed as harassers. The kind of concrete, physical, almost visceral horseplay that several patients reported on assembly lines in packing houses would not be at all acceptable in a university or in upper-management business circles.

Harassment carried out by people has different features, depending upon the "work culture" within which it occurs [33,56]. At work levels that require less specialization of skill, one appears to get closer to the chronological beginnings of teasing and goading. This includes name-calling, physical contact, and overt accusation. In work situations requiring more specialization, training, and skill, as in business, professions, and academia, harassment surfaces in the form of the attack on professional standing or managerial skill, disparagement of a business deal, or criticisms of writing ability, and is often accompanied by political maneuvering to discredit others. It is perhaps in the context of the work culture that one sees most clearly the use of harassment as an exercise of control.

Several kinds of harassment are illustrated by the cases presented in the following chapters. We have called these harassment by people, by work pressure, and by the system.

Harassment by a person occurs when one person willfully makes another individual uncomfortable. Although the teasing, the goading, or the abuse may be willful, the teaser is not necessarily conscious of the reason for his action [115]. A harasser may, without fully understanding what he is doing, select a target for his teasing because the target irritates or threatens him [17]. Frequently, a teaser joins in the teasing of others simply "to be one of the crowd," even though he does not wish to hurt the target of the teasing [36].

Conscious or unconscious harassment by people ultimately relates to the issue of control [83]. Who has sufficient power to keep someone else in line? The behavior we term "harassment" becomes harassment when it extends beyond a certain culturally determined boundary of what is acceptable. While the line of propriety varies with the circumstances and is frequently hazy, most of the time we can discern what is well beyond that boundary. Of course, the judgment that certain behavior has become harassment depends on a combination of the

47

individual or subjective factors [57] and of the external or objective factors [48, 116]. When this mix of variables goes beyond the bounds of what most people would call normal for a particular subculture, it becomes what we have called harassment.

Harassment certainly occurs first long before people go to work. It begins overtly and primitively in childhood [21]. All of us have lived in situations in school, in the family, on the street, in social groups, on the athletic fields where we have observed harassment or have been the victims or instigators of it. Teasing in children is a part of the development of learning to externalize aggression while learning further social controls [130].

Teasing of younger children by older siblings is often cruel; it is directed at those aspects of his behavior or appearance about which the child is most embarrassed, such as his wet pants or his runny nose. In childhood, extortion and bullying are common, taking the form of either physical threat or actual physical attack [5].

School is, of course, a well known harassment arena. All of us have observed harassment by "superiors," whether older pupils, teachers, or parents, who constantly focus on and openly criticize weaknesses rather than praise strengths. We have seen harassment by "inferiors"—pupils in lower grades who sometimes challenge and tease, even though they risk being beaten up, for they have nothing to lose except the beating and everything to gain by demonstrating their courage. Beginning in the lowest grades, nonconforming manners and dress often become the focus for teasing and mimicking. It is usually the smaller, physically more vulnerable children who are picked on. After once becoming a target, even if these children do begin to conform, they often cannot escape the stigma of being a target of harassment. In high school, harassment changes and becomes more subtle, tending toward social exclusion rather than physical threat. Gossip and subtle remarks join practical jokes, hazing, and mimicry as means of indicating that a person is not acceptable to his classmates. Harassment in the work setting adapts that techniques.

Harassment by Superiors: "It's Easier to Shit Downward than Upward"

A high police official who felt that he was doing a good job was notified one day that he was being transferred to another post. The tradition was that those holding his rank were not transferred unless they requested it. Whenever this rule was not followed, the regulations of this department stipulated that a full explanation would be given to the person being transferred. Such explanations might note special needs at the new post or changing needs of the old post. In this case, however, the official was not asked whether or not he wanted to go, and when he requested an explanation for the transfer, none was given. At that point he consulted a lawyer who suggested that he accept the transfer and raise no fuss about it. A friend also recommended against initiating a grievance procedure, saying, "Remember, George, it's easier to shit downward than upward," that is, one must expect and accept a given amount of injustice or harassment from a- bove and that George would be the loser if he tried to protect himself or to harass back.

George did accept the transfer and went to his new post. Soon afterward, his blood pressure rose from well within normal limits during the month before the transfer to 180/120 in the month following transfer. He was angry, anxious, restless, and irritable. He felt that someone was out to get him. He had known of other officers in the department who became targets or scapegoats, and he understood and accepted this process. But in his own case, he did not know who was responsible or why. As a result, he was tense and apprehensive and was always looking over his shoulder to see who was checking on him. During several periods when he was able to take a vacation, his blood pressure returned to normal. His physician became concerned about the danger of his running such a high blood pressure and insisted that George take several months off work. His blood pres- sure again dropped. After numerous experiments in which he attempted to re- turn to work and each time found that his blood pressure went up, he decided to retire, and with retirement came a drop in blood pressure and a sense of tranquility.

When, after all of this was over, he was asked if he had any idea why he had been singled out, he said he thought that he had been a victim of the same kind of process that frequently affects corporation executives. Once a person reaches a certain status, a number of others will try to "get him," and he happened to be the one this time. He had known of other officials in the department to whom this had happened, for no apparent reason, and he was still outraged that he had been selected.

The sense of helplessness, anger, and frustration that comes when one is attacked from above, when one feels that he has been done an injustice by those more powerful than he, is well known. In George's case the victim was a rela- tively sophisticated person who knew the system in which he worked and under- stood the process. In spite of this, his blood pressure went up. How much worse for the person who is not sophisticated and does not understand the process, who does not know what is happening or why, but assumes some reasonable explanation. Angry and outraged, probably with no lawyer to con- sult, he cannot find terms in which to discuss the disaster with his family. He complains to his doctor of physical symptoms, without relating these to events at work. He becomes depressed or irritable, and his wife will report, "He whips the children for nothing," "He picks on me."

A review of such cases often reveals that what the police official said was true. There seems to be no special reason why a given individual is scapegoated or picked on at any given time. In his case and similar ones, it seems that the superiors had to demonstrate their power to behave in an administratively illegal and improper manner, to warn other members of the organization to be careful. Hanging over each member of the organization was the threat that, if he did not go along with every aspect of his superior's wishes, verbalized or unverbalized, then he might well be the next one eliminated.

A larger, more basic principle seems to be that one never knows what power one actually has until one exercises it, and that others likewise do not know the extent of the power one has until one exercises it. In the same way that nations have from time to time put on displays of power in the hope of cowing other nations, so, too, individuals in working organizations display their power. Those consciously and purposefully perpetrating such injustice often rationalize it with such notions as, "Rank has its privilege," and "We have to keep the troops in line." It is as if some persons in executive positions believe that one of the rewards for having achieved an executive position is the right to pick on others. The relationship of the chief petty officer and his subordinates, of the top sergeant and his subordinates, reveals this pecking-order behavior, although there is no evidence that this kind of atmosphere in fact keeps anyone "in line" or makes for a more effective or more productive organization. Indeed, there is evidence that it produces profound hostility and probably makes the aggressor as tense or almost as tense as it does the target.

Such behavior serves different functions for different persons at different times. Some people enjoy seeing others squirm. They make their subordinates squirm to prove they are subordinate; they will go to great lengths to make their children squirm even though everyone knows that their children are subordinate. One might say they are sadistic because they need constant reassurance of their own authority and power. For others, such behavior is used to show how much power they have. It becomes as much a status symbol as a car or a key to the executive washroom.

Differing approaches to work of superiors and subordinates can also cause bad feelings. Mac's case illustrates a result of the influx of bureaucrats into the idealist's domain. Generally speaking, members of the "old guard" in many social service agencies were motivated by common ideals of humanitarian service. More recently, the politically motivated bureaucrat has joined the ranks, creating conflict for the idealists. The latter group are often outraged that expediency should supercede humanity. Many, such as Mac, simply cannot function in the consequent conflict and develop somatic symptoms.

Since his arrival in the United States seventeen years before, Mac had worked in a state social service agency. Sensitive to oppression, which he fled in his native country, Mac consciously chose social work because he believed in the causes of social justice that are the concern of that profession. He himself had long been active in unpopular causes, including unionism, before coming to the United States.

Work went well for five years, until a new supervisor was appointed. This

Mr. Smith had come from another agency as a senior consultant, and was therefore above Mac in status. Since Smith knew nothing of the practices of Mac's department, it became Mac's job to introduce Smith to departmental procedures. Mac took the supervisor along while investigating a black woman's claim of employment discrimination. During the investigation, Smith made some remarks about the claimant that Mac considered discriminatory. Smith said, "People who live that way are nothing but pigs," which Mac felt to be a highly bigoted statement for someone investigating discrimination practices. Later in the investigation, this woman's employer admitted that he had said to her, "all you blacks ought to go back to Africa where you belong." Although it was evident to Mac that there had been an act of discrimination, Smith argued that there had been none. The case was eventually decided in favor of the claimant, but hard feelings between Mac and his new supervisor lingered.

Mac incurred the wrath of many others in the organization when he and some colleagues lobbied in the legislature for an increased office budget, even though Mac had made the presentation on his own vacation time. Smith's reaction was angry, "No one is screwing around with this budget." Because of this, Mac developed a tremendous backlog of case reports. Smith then ordered that he complete at least one written report per day until the backlog diminished. Because Smith forced him to work so quickly, an inordinate number of appeals resulted from Mac's decisions. With the appeals, his backlog again increased. A "dress-down" for inefficiency followed.

When Mac arrived at work the following Monday, Smith met him at the door, demanding that he continue completing reports until he had submitted a "quota" for the day. Mac began dictating reports, but shortly thereafter was told the secretaries refused to transcribe them because the reports were so muddled. Smith then ordered him to handwrite all his reports. At this point Smith ordered Mac into his office, played all Mac's recordings, and spent the balance of the day criticizing those reports and their author. Mac was overwhelmed. He could not function. He doubled over with stomach pain. He was absolutely astounded at this treatment, because he was accustomed to being treated like a professional and not "like a dog." His physician told him he had developed an ulcer and recommended that Mac leave work.

The initial tension and pressure of Mac's job were worsened by his belief that he was singled out for unjust attack and harassment. He and his immediate supervisor had locked horns in mutual harassment. At the moment of greatest anger and helplessness, Mac, though generally healthy, reacted physically with an incapacitating ulcer.

It is not always the case that the boss is the harasser. Harassed employees sometimes turn on their employers. Natalie was an example of a supervisor who pushed people, and later herself became the victim of harassment. Natalie interpreted reactions to her own controlling behavior as harassment. Because of her need to control others and to dominate the work setting completely, reasonable differences between her and those under her seemed like harassment to her.

Natalie had been uprooted many times, first from her native Russia, then from her second homeland in China. She remembered nothing but hard times in those foreign lands. Finally, when she was fifteen her family emigrated to the United States. The family was poor, and domestic dissension between her parents resulted in separation and finally in divorce. Her father abandoned the family, sending them money only occasionally.

Although the family suffered through lean years, Natalie finished high school with good grades and went to business college. Afterward, she took a job as a bookkeeper. About this time she developed a duodenal ulcer, which recurred several times when she was under stress. For the next fifteen years she worked as a clerk in a store, a valued employee because she could sell merchandise and keep the books, and she was considered reliable and trustworthy. She left the job in order to care for a sick relative and when she could finally return, the job was no longer available.

She then found a job as a bookstore clerk at the local college, and later when an opening occurred in the sports department, she moved into that. She was a hard worker and was promoted several steps. Internal politics, however, made the department chaotic. Bickering, jockeying for position, and uncertainty about role definitions created a void, and Natalie began taking on more and more budget and administrative work. She eventually requested a reclassification so that her job title would reflect her actual work level. She was given this reclassification, although it was of relatively low rank. Shortly thereafter, when her boss resigned in the face of a departmental uproar, everything was "dropped in my lap," and she was made acting department head. Another person was selected for the permanent position, but overwhelmed by personnel and budget difficulties, he too resigned, and again she applied for the position and was refused. She heard via the grapevine that the unit director opposed her appointment, and she believed the opposition was based on personal dislike. After several candidates for the position were interviewed, she finally was given the position as head of the department. She was overjoyed, and she worked day and night. The job became the center of her life. She was instrumental in converting the sports department from a losing operation into a profitable one, but she soon started having problems with subordinates. A battle erupted between her and one subordinate while the unit director was on leave of absence for several months. Later, she was confronted with an attack by several subordinates who sharply criticized her alleged minimal efforts to obtain promotions for them and her not following through on promises to increase their salaries.

Although the unit director attempted to restore peace in the department, Natalie's troubles with her subordinates intensified. Finally, Natalie learned that her department was to be merged with another and she would certainly lose her job as director. Her desperate request to the unit director for written clarification of her probable postmerger status brought no reply. Later, at a meeting with her supervisors, she felt she was "on trial." She felt picked on and pressured to resign. She became increasingly nervous and could not sleep or eat. When she learned that the departmental merger was inevitable, her sense of isolation and defeat was too much. She broke down completely and could not stop crying. Her physician recommended that she stop working for the time being, so she left the department.

Natalie is an example of a person who believes that doing good work is all that matters. No one questioned that she had done an extremely good job. What was in serious question was her "militarist" approach toward her employees. She believed that everything should run perfectly—her way—that her employees should all support her and her superiors reward her. Unforgiveably, she committed the bureaucratic sin of forcing showdowns. She could not recognize that systemically bound institutions that cannot act quickly also cannot tolerate confrontations requiring firm decisions. For Natalie the world had again come to an end. Once again she was uprooted, but unlike the previous dislocations, this one had occurred after she had finally reached the top, where her efforts had been rewarded.

Natalie exemplifies the type of person who flounders and has no clear goal in sight. Her ambitions were generally unconscious, and if she had been accused of being ambitious, she would have denied it. She did well as a clerk in a store, where her functions were relatively well defined and she was never in conflict with the one person above her, namely the owner of the store. When she entered the system in which her problems began, she experienced the sweet taste of success and power. Suddenly she needed more and more of it. She could see herself rising to the top of a hierarchy and anyone who seemed to stand in her way to the top was an obstacle to be removed. For her, making it meant dominating the department completely. She required an almost militaristic efficiency, with no opposition from anyone about her. Suddenly she was faced with a conflict of making it or not making it, whereas formerly she did not have this problem: she just worked. It was as if she had been placed in a competition from which she had always protected herself before.

Her's was a personality that had protected itself over the course of a lifetime by avoiding the kinds of challenges that would make her uncomfortable both in her home life and in her work life. She found herself challenged, the inflexibility of her personality was such that she could not adapt, and she behaved as if she were programmed by forces beyond her control. She was not unwilling to adapt, to adjust, or to compromise, but in fact, she could not.

This case also illustrates the importance of recognizing and dealing with organizational problems such as the one created by Natalie's personality in the context of the organization in which she found herself. (Hers is one of the organizations the author studied directly, and he was therefore able to interview some of those who were involved in the problem. These data are based on some of the reports of others who were involved, both superiors and subordinates.) Natalie and her problems disrupted the organization in which she worked for well over a year. Innumerable work hours were lost as a result of her need to dominate and her inability to adapt, immobilizing the organization for long periods of time. The Natalie situation resulted in suspicion, anxiety, and guilt among various participants; it required an enormous amount of paperwork, with letters, meetings, and hearings. The emotional and economic cost to Natalie herself probably represented a small portion of the true cost to the organization in which she worked, illustrating why it is so important for administrators to be alert to this type of organizational problem, its causes, and its management.

Harassment, of course, need not be active. Successful harassment of superiors by employees is often passive-aggressive. Recognizing that they are protected by the system if they avoid an open confrontation, subordinates can frustrate the boss, as did Claudia, a fifty-five-year-old registered nurse who taught at a nursing school. For some time she had had difficulty with the school's janitorial staff. Her classrooms often were dirty and in disarray, and this lack of order infuriated her. She was forced to clean the rooms and arrange the furniture herself before she could teach. Repeated complaints to the janitorial supervisors brought no relief, except that her complaints seemed to result in even filthier classrooms. The conflict culminated one afternoon prior to her class. As she angrily moved the students' desks, her back snapped. She felt pain in her pelvis; her abdomen became distended, and she had pain in her leg. In spite of treatment, she did not improve and has not worked in the four years since the incident.

Harassment by Peers

In cases where workers have harassed fellow workers, sympathy and cooperation diminish. Coworkers may view a "victim's" request for support against harassment or for relief from the workload as unfair, as cheating, or as malingering. Their rejection only exacerbates the problem.

Dirk claimed that nine months of outright harassment by his coworkers drove him to leave work. While operating a forklift alone in an isolated warehouse, he attempted to shift the load manually and was pinned under 800 pounds of cardboard boxes for half an hour. He truly thought he was dying. He screamed for help, but no one heard him and no one came. Frightened and helpless, he prayed that he would be saved. Finally one of his coworkers came to his assistance. Aside from terrible fright, nervousness, and some bruises, he appeared uninjured. During the succeeding nine months, Dirk did not claim that he was unable to work. Rather, he claimed that he was harassed by fellow employees who made fun of him, especially of his new gait. He was openly accused of malingering and falsely claiming to be disabled. Finally, to "teach him a lesson," Dirk's plantmates hot-wired the wheel of his truck so that when he touched it, he received an electric shock. Dirk said that he then had a nervous breakdown, crying frequently, shaking constantly, aching all over, and describing himself as generally disabled. His wife reported that he made several suicide threats; repeatedly, physicians noted that he had overdosed himself with drugs.

Dirk's one and constant ally in his period of illness was his wife. Indeed, one psychiatrist noted that Dirk's wife might have contributed to his slow recovery. She took up the cudgel against her husband's doctors, whom she regarded as unsympathetic and in one instance less than honest. She was adamant that her husband had been victimized and unjustly deprived of compensation. Interestingly, Dirk and his wife did not communicate about his illness. He kept a diary in which he complained of symptoms and revealed his feelings. Every night he placed the diary in a drawer where his wife picked it up and read it. They never discussed the contents, and neither one ever overtly admitted the diary's existence to the other.

Most examiners found little, if any, physical basis for Dirk's symptoms and concluded that they were emotionally caused. One psychiatrist felt that both the short-term and long-term prognoses for Dirk's recovery were poor indeed. He was in no financial distress, his wife was working, and eventually some compensation money was paid him. Dirk appeared to enjoy his domestic routine. He had become habituated to drugs, but did not seem concerned about his addiction.

Bobby was another target of name-calling and fun-poking by his fellow workers, after he injured his back at work while dumping a heavy can of waste paper, when he stooped over and felt his back pop. He saw physician after physician and used a back brace and tried physical therapy. He continued to work, though attempting to obtain a medical excuse that would have allowed him to terminate. After his endless complaints of pain, some effort was made to lighten his workload. This adjustment produced vehement reactions from his fellow workers,who, he says, got "rowdy" with him and called him names such as "goof off." They even went so far as to complain both to the union and to the supervisory staff that he was shirking his duties. His coworkers' skepticism and hostility were major factors in his leaving work, and because these attitudes made him feel unwelcome, they further diminished his chances for an early return to the plant.

Harassment by Consumers

The effects of harassment by consumers are especially dramatic in situations where workers think they are in fairly "safe" occupations and do not expect attack. Unlike policemen or prison guards, who know they work in a dangerous

atmosphere, these workers are in positions usually considered nonhazardous.
An insurance adjuster, an apartment manager, a bus driver, all were happy with
their jobs, but for each of them job satisfaction was disrupted by a force external
to the work group, that is, by harassment from a consumer.

Joe, a friendly, client-oriented, white insurance adjuster, was mugged in a
black neighborhood. Immediately he became withdrawn, depressed, and phobic
about blacks, and had to leave his job because of his inability to function. Hating
all blacks because he was attacked by two persons who happened to be black, he
ruminated about the wrong done him. Whereas he once considered himself no
more vulnerable than anyone else, after the attack he considered himself a potential victim for every hostile or deranged person in his environment. He bought
a gun, a large dog, and extra locks for his doors. He avoided certain neighborhoods at all times. And he became a bigot: whereas previously he had thought
that black people were basically good, he began to believe that they are evil,
and expected to be attacked by them or by anyone who seemed unconventional.

Joe developed a true traumatic neurosis. We can call it a neurosis because
he recognized that he was being unreasonable. He realized that not all blacks
represented a threat to him, but in spite of this awareness, he became intensely
uneasy in the presence of any black, and extended his fear of blacks to fear of
what he labeled "unpredictable" persons. On a bus or a street corner, if he
found himself near a person who seemed to be behaving strangely or who was
dressed in unusual fashion, Joe became anxious and wanted to run. If someone was walking behind him and he was not certain who it was, he had to turn
around, even though he might be in a relatively public place. Joe withdrew
from persons, his interests were diminished, and he was profoundly irritable.
Formerly social, in the sense that he enjoyed being with women and in small
groups, he spent time only with his dog, in whom he invested all his emotional
energy.

Joe is an example of someone whose illusion has been shattered. Joe never
thought of himself as vulnerable. He knew he was a friendly person and simply
expected that all others would be friendly with him. Reassured by his success
and by his good relationships with others, he felt that if he did not bother anyone else, he himself would not be bothered. Uncrystallized in his mind was a
notion that people who found trouble had gone looking for it. He knew that
he did not go looking for trouble; therefore, he would not find it. Much to his
surprise he found it anyway, and the incident destroyed his own built-in
probability system. Whereas formerly it was utterly improbable that anyone
would attack him, now it had become highly probable that he would be
attacked by almost anyone. Although he knew consciously that this was not
so, he felt and responded somatically as if it were.

This case also demonstrates how social and racial attitudes are determined
by personal experiences. Joe considered himself a liberal and voted as such;
his response to most social issues might have been labeled liberal. He was

prointegration, antiracism, in favor of help to the poor; afterwards he was racist and segregationist and would have carried a gun except that he feared arrest.

Brian, sixty-five-years-old and white, was a bus driver in a large city. He had liked his work, for he enjoyed helping people and particularly liked to drive through town and see the sights. On one occasion when he refused to accept a transfer from a black patron, he was attacked viciously with a knife and was severely lacerated. He never fully recovered. After a time he went into a severe psychotic depression. He later purchased a gun and shot himself in the head. Between the shooting and his death, Brian spoke with doctors and police officers and told them that he had purchased the gun with which he shot himself to protect himself from "coons."

A crucial question in the worker's compensation hearing held to determine the eligibility of Brian's widow for death benefits was establishment of a causal connection between the patron's attack on Brian and his later suicide attempt. We cannot draw legal conclusions, but the causation issue is of concern to us in our discussion of the effects of harassment on the victim. The rider's attack was thought to be an important factor in his suicide, along with Brian's lifelong unstable depressive personality and a tendency to unrealistic thinking.

Lee, sixty-one-years-old and white, was not affected in quite as extreme a fashion as was Brian, when he too was assaulted by a member of the public. Lee was manager of a 200-unit apartment complex in a large city; the occupancy was 80 percent black. He had held the job for five years and felt well accepted by the tenants. He described himself as well liked and successful. However, three incidents within a two-month period radically changed his view and caused him to leave his job. The first was a hold-up. When he returned early from lunch one day, he found four young black men waiting in front of his office. They asked him about renting an apartment. He was suspicious and explained that apartments were available only to families. They insisted that he show them the model apartment and when he was hesitant, finally shoved a gun in his back and ordered him to open the door. They ordered him to open the safe, and he tried, but he was so nervous that he was unable to open it. They pulled out two guns and put one at either side of his head, until he finally managed to open the safe. One of them hit him on the chin with his fist, and another started beating him with a pistol. They made him lie on the floor as they escaped. Lee said he was terribly frightened and called the police. When the police finally arrived at the apartment where he was waiting, he collapsed. Lee believed that only one of the four men was ever caught and that nothing was ever done to that man.

Shortly after that incident, someone stole seven matched sets of drapes from the storeroom. Lee believed that whoever took the drapes must have been an insider because no one else would have known the matching system. He mentioned his suspicions in front of the woman whom he suspected; on that very night, the drapery room was again entered and the remaining draperies were taken. At this point Lee began receiving threatening phone calls. The voice at the other end of the line said, "We are going to get you, white pig." He became increasingly anxious and made sure that he was never alone either in his office or at home.

In the third incident, he was accused by the woman with whom he had had the drapery problem of molesting her daughter at three o'clock on the previous Saturday. When the woman discovered that Lee could not possibly have been in her apartment at three o'clock on the previous Saturday, she instructed her children to change their stories to claim that it was after dark. According to Lee, he was never out of sight of someone during that whole day, and when he arrived home before dark he had a rather lengthy conversation with a neighbor. He did not leave home after that. The case against him on this morals charge is still pending, but Lee is confident that the case will be dismissed because his alibi is substantial.

The combination of pressures from these incidents was such that Lee felt he was "not up to working." He resigned and spent his days at home. He continued to take a small amount of medicine "for his nerves." His wife said he was quite irritable, and Lee reported that his major problem was that he became terribly frightened of blacks, even of his friends who were blacks, and he "went to pieces" when he saw a black. Lee hoped to get another job, but was concerned that he might be unemployable because of his age.

Harassment by Friends

Not all our patients were harassed because they were unacceptable or were making trouble for someone, so that someone wanted to get rid of them, to get them out of the system. Some were harassed because people wanted them in the system, wanted them to be friendly, and because they were not, their coworkers felt rejected.

One case was almost analogous to the kind of harassment that parents receive from their children when the children want more attention. Such harassment is easy to misperceive and to misinterpret. One psychiatrist who saw the harassed person superficially believed that his coworkers were harassing him because he was a foreigner. A more extensive study of the problem showed that this was not the case, and the worker himself did not think it was.

This man had worked in his organization as a packer and wrapper in the distribution section. He was a union man and was well paid for his efforts. He had the opportunity to work overtime if he wanted to earn more money. He was highly respected by his coworkers, many of whom were born in other countries, and he was highly respected by his superiors who offered him a supervisory position.

Then, he suffered a traumatic event, when a coworker dropped dead. The circumstances of this event were such as to produce an unquestionable traumatic neurosis in him. He became terribly anxious, hypochondriacal, depressed, and withdrawn. He went through an odyssey of medical treatment with possibly excessive prescriptions of medication, further medical treatment, and finally psychiatric treatment.

During the course of all this treatment, he became very concerned with himself and withdrawn from others, not only from his coworkers but also from his wife and children. He tended to want to be alone and to avoid all activities, in view of his concern that he too might have a heart attack. As a result, whereas formerly he had joked and kidded and talked with his coworkers and was generally considered by them to be a happy person, now he rejected their overtures. They were generally concerned by how he felt, because they knew that something had changed in him, but when anyone inquired about it, he would be gruff, and when his gruffness was not effective, he would demand to be left alone. When one coworker asked him what was wrong, he challenged him to a fight.

A psychiatrist who examined the patient had described it in this way. "My examination of the patient has revealed some interesting problems relating to this man's employment. There is no doubt that the incident concerning his coworker's death did trigger the anxiety, but a great deal of the anxiety turns out to be work-related, too. He works with a group of men who like to tease him, particularly concerning his minority status and accent. The picture has become much like the Mexican bullfight, the patient being the bull and all these men the picadores, each in turn becoming a matador for a while. Although my patient started out being fearful and intimidated by all this harassment, he now has the courage to face these men and work out his problem with them."

But the author found that the patient himself had complete insight into the problem at work. He was able to report the exact details of how his coworkers tried to be friendly, and how he did not want to be friendly because he feared they would discover how upset he really was. He felt that it was better to reject them and suffer the consequences than to open up to them and have to tell them about his internal misery; he especially feared that he might cry if he told them. His coworkers continued to try to "kid" him out of it, but were unable to.

Work organizations find it difficult to tolerate persons whom they cannot integrate. There are two kinds of persons who cannot be integrated; the first is the person who does not fit and is a troublemaker. The second is the one who will not permit himself to be integrated. In the latter case, members of the group react with various efforts that might be considered the equivalent of flirtation and seduction, and the target may respond to these efforts as if they constituted harassment.

4 Work Pressure as Harassment

"Work pressure" describes the continual pressure exerted to maintain maximum worker productivity. The private sector in our economic system is based on maximization of profits through high productivity; today, labor costs are often the single most significant cost. Each manager is driven to produce more so that the company can compete economically. "Get the most out of the worker" is a pervading maxim in industry, despite some recent efforts to stress the importance of bearable working conditions as a prerequisite to long-term cost reduction. The government also puts a premium on worker productivity, and employees in government bureaucracies are expected to meet quotas to "get the most for the tax dollar." Police officers, for example, prove themselves productive according to the number of tickets written or arrests made. The work loads of high school counselors and of social workers have been increased to accommodate the budget rather than to serve the people concerned.

Work pressure, then, is the residual tension inherent in a production system. Work pressure has been defined primarily as externally imposed work demands [84]. Work pressure is threatening because the employee realizes that he may lose rewards or control over his environment and that punishment may be imposed if he does not measure up. Punishments include threats, reprimands, transfers to lesser jobs, dismissal, potential lowered self-esteem from attacks on one's ego, and disruption of friendship patterns. This definition of work pressure focuses on the objective "induced force" of management productivity demands.

Job pressure can be conceptually defined as "the resultant psychological state of the individual which exists when he perceives that conflicting forces and incompatible demands are being made upon him in connection with his work; at least one of the forces or demands is an induced one; and the forces are recurrent or stable over time" [28, p. 49].

Work pressure can result from role conflict and role ambiguity [79]. Role conflict refers to incompatible demands between worker and occupation; it undermines interpersonal relations and weakens mutual trust, respect, and attraction. Role ambiguity is itself the result of a discrepancy between the amount of information a worker needs to do a job and that which is available. The missing information includes proper definition of the job, its goals, and the permissible means of implementation [79].

Job stress can also be related to role conflict and role ambiguity. A certain percentage of workers are unclear about their job responsibilities; many were also unclear about their coworkers' expectations and their supervisors' evaluations.

Both quantitative and qualitative "role overload" can contribute to work pressure. Because of excessive demands, a worker may not be able to finish a day's work in one day, and because of the pressure to finish, the quality of his work may suffer.

One can speak of "goodness of fit" between a worker and his environment [47]. When the fit is optimal, the worker's skills and abilities match the demands and requirements of his job. When there is misfit, work pressure results in job dissatisfaction, depression, and physiological strains.

Another theory of person-environment fit sees individuals responding to identical job situations in very different ways. Five common dimensions of job-related strains are: (1) subjective reaction to specific situations (anger at the boss); (2) chronic psychological responses to job stress (chronic depression); (3) transient clinical-physiological changes; (4) physical health status; (5) work performance decrement [108].

Not all investigators have found stress to be damaging. On-the-job stress can be healthy when it indicates an acceptance of responsibility [140]. Damaging or unpleasant stress is "distress." There can be positive meaning in job stress and the responsibilities of a job have been referred to as a "social corset" holding the personality together [89].

Most workers accept some degree of job pressure for production or results. Each job has a range of such pressure. On the low end, the worker is aware that he is not earning his keep; on the high end, he believes that he is not being rewarded adequately. The worker might gripe about the high end, but if he accepts the average output required, he will not consider himself pressured. An unwritten agreement is assumed, and both worker and management are aware of it.

If a new managerial team with new standards of productivity raises the average productivity (or in some cases lowers the average productivity), the worker's balance is disturbed; he feels the contract has been changed unilaterally, and he senses the new demands as unacceptable work pressure. For some workers, greater work pressure is harmful. In our cases, the harm frequently resulted as much from the anger and the sense of helplessness that came with the unilateral change as it did from the additional energy expended by the worker. Emotional conflict about the demand limited the concentration available for the job and made the job a truly pressuring and impossible task.

Emphasis on production, along with devices for exerting the pressure to achieve it, is not unique to the work setting, nor is it simply the result of cost-benefit analysis [152]. Such pressure is apparent in every part of the social system in which we live, whether the family, the school, or the working place. We expect people to have more friends, to have better friends, to get better grades, to achieve higher honors, to produce more products, and ultimately to "make the first team."

Results of Work Pressure

Children have been known to commit suicide, under pressure for performance in school, in social groups, on the athletic field, or in development of personal characteristics. Many adults also commit suicide when they cannot establish a perspective or realize that they need not respond to pressure, when they cannot select goals for themselves that satisfy their own needs rather than those created by some externally imposed standards. A number of persons commit psychic suicide through a self-inflicted assault on their ego or sense of self-esteem. They believe that they should be able to produce at the demanded level and that their failure is a sign of inadequacy. Instead of judging the work quota unreasonable, they judge themselves inadequate. Others resist evaluating themselves this way initially, but constant criticism and negative evaluation by superiors erodes their self-esteem, and eventually they become even less productive [69].

The following example illustrates suicide brought about in large measure because of work pressure. This patient was not psychotic in the ordinary sense; he seemed able to function normally. The victim recognized that he was under pressure from a system from which he could not escape but in which he could not remain.

This middle-aged man worked as an insurance claims adjuster. When he was younger, he had been a lineman for the utility company, doing outdoor work that he enjoyed. Two factors, however, caused him to change jobs. First, the company moved its center of operations. Because he liked the area where he was and because his wife's relatives lived nearby, he chose not to accept a transfer. The second element in his refusal to transfer was his self-image: he hoped that someday he would have a white-collar job. While growing up, he had never considered himself "blue-collar material." His wife also imagined her husband a "professional." Consequently, he did not move with the utility company, but remained in the same town and took the job as an insurance adjuster.

His first employer was a gentle, paternalistic man who helped him learn the field and do the work. Some time later, following the merger of two insurance companies, his work situation changed abruptly. Workloads and production were carefully scrutinized. He was expected to accomplish a given amount of work in an alloted time. From that point on, he felt that he never caught up with his backlog of pending cases. He was especially desperate because with the merger he had lost his original supervisor, who had always helped him when his caseload was too heavy. As a result, he felt pressured, anxious, and tense, began drinking more as his depression increased, and withdrew from his family.

At one point he consulted a psychiatrist, explaining that he considered the workload excessive even though he knew that others were able to cope with the same workload. He recognized that it was his own personality that found it difficult to tolerate the burden. Despite his increasing discomfort with work backlog, he continued to work as an adjuster for five years. Then, he began to feel that there was no way out, that he was too old to change careers. He had debts to pay and a family to support. Even though his wife was a superb manager, he felt that any decrease in income would certainly put them in a difficult position. He could not get "out," and increasingly he found that he could not stay "in." He shot himself.

Stress and Work

Stress is a fuzzy, general term that describes a number of different phenomena. Subjectively, we label an experience as stressful when we are aware of a reaction in ourselves. Ordinarily, we use the word stress to define unpleasant reactions, to describe events that seem to have strained us in some way, that have caused us to mobilize our emotional resources, at least temporarily. Thus, bursting into tears, breaking out in a sweat, having a profound eruption of gastrointestinal movement, having one's heart race or beat irregularly, or blushing might all be defined as stressful experiences because they produce perceptible reactions in us, unpleasant reactions far greater than what we would have experienced ordinarily.

Ordinarily we do not think of a pleasurable experience as being stressful, but subjectively we experience the same bodily reactions and the same sense of strain when we are observers of an athletic event in which we have become very involved and in which the score is close. The critical pass, run, or man on base will produce a racing pulse, gastrointestinal hypermotility, sometimes loss of sphincter control, and many other physical symptoms. This must also be considered stressful because it strains us and produces reactions that are far greater than the ordinary. Although we cannot say that such reactions cause heart attacks, we know that sudden death and myocardial infarctions are reported regularly in the press as occurring at exciting athletic events.

One must assume that any term that (1) refers to phenomena experienced by all and (2) is so difficult to define, must be so broad and must refer to so many different types of phenomena that its major usefulness is that it defines one end of a polarity. In this sense, one can compare it to the term beauty when contrasted with ugliness. Scientists have not tried to define beauty, but philosophers have. Aristotle defined it as "that which when apprehended, pleases." Although aestheticians have tried to improve upon that definition, few have matched its simplicity. None has evoked the level of agreement to the appropriateness of the definition.

We might paraphrase this definition to read, "stress is that which when apprehended, disturbs." With that definition we can deal with the problems of work pressure and harassment as stress phenomena. We can differentiate between harassment and teasing and between harassment and joking relationships. We can differentiate work pressure from hyperproductivity on the part of a person who wishes to increase his salary or his standing in an organization. Work pressure becomes a demand that is evaluated as stressing and straining the individual because it asks him to push himself to the limit of his capacity or even beyond. Hyperproductivity represents a worker testing himself to see how much he can produce in order that he may receive the gratification of praise and money and the kind of self-appreciation that comes to the person who breaks a record.

Stress can be either constant or intermittent. For example, the air traffic controller in a busy airport during the daytime hours is under constant stress. He might perceive this as stress, or his blood pressure or pulse might react as if they were being stressed. On the other hand, a police officer in a patrol car might find 90 percent of the day dull and boring. He might even find himself dozing, until his radio sends him off to a confrontation with an armed person who could injure or kill him.

Stress can be constant in the sense that the conditions remain the same, but the individual worker might perceive them only intermittently. Prison guards, for example, have reported that they catch themselves getting sloppy about security measures. Being in an environment of constant danger, they tend to become numb, and after a while adapt to the danger and act as if it did not exist. Then something happens, a guard is injured, there is a near miss, there is an attack on the worker himself, and the fear, the expectancy, and the stress rise again.

Some sense of arousal, pressure, or potentially harmful excitement may be acceptable to a worker. For some, it is exactly what they want in their jobs. Such is the case of the race car driver in the world of sports. In a recent film, a race car driver was asked why he enjoyed driving. He replied that the joy, the fun, and the excitement of racing had to do with the probability that one would be killed at 141 m.p.h. and that one would lose the race at 139 m.p.h. This need to test one's ability and oneself causes individuals to put themselves in, to seek out, and to remain in positions of acceptable stress.

Unacceptable stress usually is imposed from without. A man who left a job as a salesman for one of the larger firms in this country did so with the statement that "No amount of money compensates for that pressure." In that instance, the pressure was expected but not accepted.

We react differently to events for which we are prepared and to those that come as a surprise. Unexpected stress is the most disturbing and seems to produce the most profound reaction. Unexpected stress is built into suspense films. A body drops out of a closet. A car goes over a hill, and there is no road at the end. A door is opened, and a monster is on the other side. The audience, lulled into a sense of security, is shocked. Hearts pound and palms sweat. But when the moment of suspense has passed, slowly the palms dry, the heartbeats slow, and the audience laughs.

How very different, when the unexpected stress is genuine, or when it happens in an environment where one does not expect any shocking event. A driver is sitting quietly and dreamily in his car waiting for the light to change, when the car is struck from behind. He hits the steering wheel, bounces around, and flys to the other side of the car, and is aware that there is blood coming down from his head. The stress of that moment is profoundly greater than the one produced by a suspense film. One might expect the consequences to last longer, and indeed they do.

Sometimes expected stress turns out to be very different from what was predicted. Thus, we all know that some day we will be ill, that if we live long enough we might have cancer or heart disease, or suffer some physical trauma. When this happens, it should be expected stress, but in fact, it is predicted rather than expected. In other words, we assume that we will feel or experience some kind of reaction when we learn that we have cancer or heart disease, but in fact we cannot imagine what our real reactions will be. The response at the time an illness is discovered mobilizes fears and concerns that have long been covered over and that are rekindled by the actuality of the illness.

Harassment as Stress

In work situations, we deal with all kinds of stress, constant and intermittent, accepted and unaccepted, expected and unexpected. The variable of personality is as important in situations of harassment and work pressure as it is, for example, in the case of a rear-end accident. One man's experience and emotional symptoms may be the exact opposite of another man's. Pain in the neck and back, nightmares, weight loss, loss of interest in sex, withdrawal, and crying easily, may be symptoms that last for months and diminish only gradually, even though a settlement for the injuries has been made long before and there seems to be no reason for the psychological symptoms to persist. Another man who is rear-ended might get out of his car somewhat shaken, but by dinner time be quite recovered. He might even have a second such accident, subsequently, with exactly the same response. One cannot talk about stress alone; one must talk about stress and the susceptible person. In relation to harassment, one also has to consider the susceptibility of the person.

At work, at school, and in military life some harassment and work pressure are expected. We do not like them, and yet unpleasant as they are, we would not say they are stressful until the pressure or the harassment reaches a certain level. If all the members of the group are being treated in the same way, there is no special sense of stress except by the highly susceptible individual. For example, a paranoid person will always feel stress. The obsessive-compulsive person will always feel stress. They both are at full alert, for quite different reasons. The former is afraid that he will be attacked from the outside; the latter is afraid that he will be attacked from the inside, that he will break out and lose control.

Different aspects of stress disturbed our worker/subjects at different times and to different degrees. Fear is always stressful, and our subjects were afraid of being harmed physically and socially. In the case of the prison guards and sometimes the school teachers, there was the experience of being attacked and the fear of being attacked again. The prison guard who said, "All I know is that I'm going to walk in there in the morning; I don't know that I'm going to walk out at night," was describing this fear. The teacher who was physically attacked, or the one who was threatened with attack, or the one who was threatened with having her wig pulled off thus revealing her baldness, were all afraid of some form of physical harm.

Others were afraid of social harm that might come to them. They were concerned that the harassment represented the beginning of an effort to reject them, to get them out of the job, whereupon they would suffer social losses. There was always the fear of the loss of that social-psychological element, respect. The harassed person always feared the loss of his position, the loss of his status the loss of his standing with his coworkers and with his family.

The conflict about how to respond to harassment was in itself stressful. The harassed person ruminated about the indignities done him and about various possible responses. Depending on personality, some would argue with themselves about whether to respond violently or to take the harassment and hope that it would pass, while others devoted most of their waking and some of their dreaming hours to playing out in their minds how they would retaliate, how they would insult, how they would put down, and how they would eventually triumph over the aggressor. The latter were in a state of constant agitation; sometimes their spouses would catch them talking to themselves, putting their thoughts into words. It must be remembered that those subjects who could resolve the conflict easily either attacked or withdrew; generally speaking, our subjects were the ones who stayed on the job and remained in conflict. In many of our subjects, harassment produced stress by rekindling memories and feelings of helplessness. It brought remembrances of attacks by parents, by siblings, or by schoolmates, and these were relived in the subjects' minds. There was also stress that came with anger about the aggression or harassment. Although some accepted the harassment as a matter of course, as having come to them because it was their "turn," others were outraged. They would have liked to express this rage physically, by beating, maiming, or killing their attackers. Others raged because they felt that there was no justice, that the system provided no recourse for those who had been harmed.

Depression was also a cause of stress. Frequently, there was a profound agitated depression associated with the worker's sense of loss. Everything had been going well, but now his fortunes were reversed. He might feel that in some way he had been selected, that he had bad luck, and that it was very likely he would continue to have bad luck in the future. Formerly, he had been on a winning streak; now, he was on a losing streak and nothing good could happen to him.

The harassed person experienced stress because of the feeling of isolation from support. Although he might never have thought about it explicitly, he had a sort of fundamental notion that there were people around who would support him when he needed them, who would come to his aid if he were in trouble, that they identified with him enough to join with him if he were attacked. Instead, the worker experienced a walling-off effect. His coworkers were reluctant to discuss his problem with him and did not want to become involved. Only rarely did they rally to his support. This produced a sense of isolation in the victim that was especially difficult for these workers because they did not feel they could abandon the struggle; they needed to go and fight, even if they fought alone.

Ultimately, they were caught up in what must after all be the most stressful and difficult situation of all, where they could not win no matter what they did. If they fought, they were marked as losers because they disturbed the system. If they did not fight, they were marked as losers because it was obvious that the harassment was deserved. In either case, they were marked with the judgment that those who have ill fortune probably deserve it.

This "pariah effect" operates in both high- and low-status work situations, but it operates differently in each. Persons who work in high-status situations or have high-status jobs are aware that their position is always somewhat insecure. There are always others trying to make their way into such positions. Even when the worker has tenure of a sort, as does a civil service worker or a university professor, his position or his status may still be uncertain because he is vulnerable to attacks on his power and his influence, if not on his job itself. Although it might not be possible to displace him, he can for all practical purposes be put on the shelf.

The lower-class worker is less concerned about power and influence and more about being able to keep his job, about being in a channel that will make it possible for him to be promoted to an easier, better paying job. He is more concerned about being sufficiently favored by his coworkers and supervisors than that he will not be harassed by being given the undesirable jobs or being pressured into working harder or faster or being criticized for the quality of his work. Any superior has a great deal of leeway in how he treats his workers. Given the same level of performance by a worker, the supervisor can react with praise, acceptance, or criticism. Each worker tries to maintain a realtionship with his supervisor that keeps him closer to the praise and further away from the criticism.

Work Pressure as Stress

Our work pressure cases contained many of the same elements of stress as did the harassment cases. There was a sense of unfairness, that it was not right that so much should be loaded onto one individual. In some instances, the workers felt that they were the only ones who had to work so hard or of whom so much was demanded and that their coworkers had a much easier lot, and this thought was galling. There was a feeling of helplessness, that if the worker protested or resisted or refused, then he would be fired. If he did not, then he was exploited. There seemed to be nothing in between. There was also a fear of job loss. Some workers felt that the increased pressure was a testing procedure to determine who would survive and who would be dismissed. Other workers felt they were being set up, that they were being presented with a test they could not meet so they could be discharged.

There was always the individual's doubt about his own adequacy. The worker wondered whether he could meet the increased demand and tolerate the greater pressure. Even when he felt that the workload was excessive, he still wondered if he was not a failure because he could not cope with it. The fear of ever-increasing work pressure was also present in some cases. Some of the workers saw the requirement for increased productivity as a prelude to increasing demands for greater and greater productivity, demands that would increase until the workers were no longer able to keep up, and they or their health would break. There was also concern about what would happen when, with advancing age, their strength, stamina, or adaptability diminished, and, even without increased demands for greater productivity, they might be unable to meet the already burdensome requirements of the job. Finally, there was a fear of being rejected by the work family, which carried with it the same kinds of fears that they had had earlier about being rejected by their own families.

Both harassment and work pressure are stressful because they signal change. In most instances, the harassment was a new event in the person's life. Whatever the working conditions had been before, the worker had not seen them as containing harassment or excessive work pressure. At some point something happened that made him feel he was being harassed and subjected to excessive pressure. This awareness is stressful because it signals change, and change is frightening. Change always carries with it some risk. If there is a probability that good things will come out of it, there is also the probability that bad things will come out of it. In those cases that were identified as work pressure and harassment, the workers predicted that bad things would come of change.

Most of these cases contained elements of both harassment and work pressure, each covering a wide range of forms of behavior. Work pressure is a conglomerate of tensions arising from the job and the work environment itself, rather than from specific incidents of harassment. Work pressure is inherent in the job; harassment is not.

The following are examples of individuals who felt both work pressure and harassment.

For twelve years, Jane had been a secretary in a large organization, where her work was generally "fine," until the pressure began to mount and she became extremely nervous and depressed, and developed severe diarrhea. A "vicious female" in her department made life difficult for her. Jane claimed that everyone was afraid of that woman, even the supervisors. Jane was not aware that the woman was her enemy until she learned that this woman gossiped about her, telling everyone that Jane was having an affair with the man with whom she rode to work. Jane could not cope with this kind of person because she did not have the courage to stand up and tell someone off. When attacked, Jane usually was taken aback and only later thought of what she should have said. Jane believed that the woman's gossip about her was the result of resentment because Jane was chosen to demonstrate the use of the MTST typewriter.

A second problem followed Jane's promotion to a middle-level supervisory position. She was on a senior list, and if promoted again to the senior status, her salary would have been substantially higher. She considered it outrageously unfair when she was "bumped by an employee from Mapleton" who had resigned but was subsequently rehired. Because she had been "bumped," Jane was to be transferred back to the transcription pool, and she could not bear the thought of having to work with the "vicious female" again. The only course of action she felt open to her was to resign.

A substantial contributing factor to Jane's unhappiness was her stressful domestic situation. Shortly before resigning from her job, she separated from her second husband. At the time of her first marriage, she had been disowned by her family for marrying a man of a different race. Her father had been extraordinarily domineering and strict, entirely work-oriented. He permitted no dating when Jane was a teenager. After her first marriage, her father did not allow her to return home. Jane's second husband had severe psychological problems and her relationship with him was described as pathological.

The combination of domestic stress and office pressure was too much for Jane. In the midst of all her troubles at home Jane felt that she could hold on as long as she did not have to work with the "vicious woman," but she knew she could not handle returning to the transcription pool. When she was forced to do so, she became depressed, developed gastrointestinal symptoms, and, in effect, gave up. At home, Jane felt that she was calming down and wanted to look for other, part-time work in the near future.

For six years Alexis, a fifty-six-year-old specialized nurse, felt that her work was too much for her. She referred to her supervisor as "NG" meaning "No Good," and continual pressure from this supervisor exacerbated her lack of self-confidence. She said she was "going to pieces and losing my mind," she was so nervous and upset. En route to a meeting, Alexis had a bad fall in the corridor and was hospitalized for a week. A few days after she returned to work, her supervisor transferred her to working with emotionally disturbed patients. She complained that she was not well enough "to handle that type of a patient." She was extremely frightened by what she viewed as hostile patients, one of whom, for example, had recently been released from jail and came in to see her with an 18-inch knife in his pocket. She was "scared to death of him." On another occasion, a woman who apparently was a paranoid schizophrenic patient (and very large, 6'2" and weighing 275 pounds) behaved threateningly during an interview with Alexis, grabbing her and shaking her back and forth. Then the woman put her arms around Alexis and squeezed her until she choked. After that, Alexis felt she was "going downhill" at a rapid rate. She said she looked horrible, her hair looked horrible, and she had constant pain in the back of her head, neck, shoulders, wrists, and hands. She could no longer be as active as she liked to be. Eventually she took an extended leave of absence and was placed on antidepressant medication.

Alexis felt the aging process prematurely and acutely, but one of the most striking aspects of her case is the insensitivity of her employer in the face of her repeated requests to be allowed to continue in the kind of work she felt capable of doing. Given the other factors involved, one concludes that to some extent the employer's intent was to "break" Alexis, to create a situation in which Alexis would leave. However, Alexis did not just quit and go away quietly. One might conclude that a more reasonable employer would not have transferred her in the first place or would have listened to her requests to be transferred back.

Forty-three-year-old Hilda was, until recently, the private secretary to the sales director of a large corporation. She left her job because "I couldn't stand the pressure." For some time she had been "going downhill" physically: she was tired, she could not speak coherently, her memory failed, she developed back trouble, and she became increasingly nervous. "I was so ding-y I would go to the grocery store and almost cry because I couldn't make decisions. The only time I drove my car was to the doctor's and to the grocery store. I always got lost trying to find places. Right now I can't stand too much pressure, I can't stand too many demands at once; when there are too many demands at once, I can't think."

She attributed her problem basically to her conscientiousness. She had always taken personal pride in her job and wanted to do well. She felt that she worked well without being pushed, yet she was being pushed at work. Her boss was personable, but other secretaries had asked her how she could stand the job, when her boss yelled at her instead of using the intercom system. Her workload was extremely heavy. She alone did 90 percent of the work in reordering the filing system. No one helped her, and no one even said, "Thank you." She had to do double duty for three weeks while another secretary was on vacation. The volume of incoming phone calls was enormous. But the most distressing aspect of the job for Hilda was the congestion in her office. Her desk was located in a passageway that had heavy walk-through traffic, and she shared this "office" with two other sales secretaries and the telephone-order woman. Even worse than the traffic were her lackadaisical officemates; it annoyed Hilda to have loafers in her area.

Hilda internalized the problem because she could not bring herself to complain about the situation. "I don't like to make waves. I have always been the doormat type." She left, staying at home and spending her days doing housework and participating in sports clubs. She would like to find a less stressful, part-time job. Hilda could not fulfill the demands of a full-time job in a busy office where she was expected to perform multiple tasks for many different people. She is a tense, perfectionistic woman who needs to feel appreciated. Because she did not receive the praise that would have made the job demands tolerable, she left.

Jack had done construction work for twenty-five of his fifty-five years. He developed an ulcer, in large part because of job stress. He had been distressed by overwork, no vacation, no employee benefits, and employer intolerance of any kind of illness. According to Jack, a salary dispute brought on his ulcer. He had been promised a raise as of January 1, but when he received his check, it was *less* than the previous week's. Jack had thought the bookkeeper made a mistake, but when he inquired, he was told that the boss had ordered that he be paid the lesser amount. Hurt, Jack threatened to resign. When his employer arrived, he assured Jack that he would get the raise. Jack continued to work but felt miserable. He thought he was getting the flu. He felt worse and worse and for several days stayed home in bed. When he did not improve, he went to a doctor, was hospitalized and immediately given a blood transfusion. It was then that the ulcer was diagnosed.

He left work and spent his time at home doing odd jobs around the house and dabbling in art. He got better physically, but remained deeply hurt that his employer never called him after he became ill. Jack lived off his savings and planned to retire in the country.

Change

Persons who claim psychological disorders resulting from work pressure seemingly are unable to integrate change. These cases fall into several clusters. The first is composed of persons who themselves brought about a job change that increased the pressure on them intolerably. The second includes those persons who were unwilling targets of change. The third comprises the "victims" of change that was brought about in various ways, and this group differs in the method by which it protests change, that is, by means of the industrial accident.

Kent and Wynn, both middle-aged males (fifty-four and sixty) working in civil service jobs, typify the "faded dream" pattern. Both went from years of self-employment into jobs in the public sector. When they had worked on their own, they had never been great successes. In their switch from self-employment to working for others, their expectations for security and freedom from stress were high, but they largely met with disappointment.

For eighteen years Kent had owned his own business. He sold it because his family had grown and "the business became more and more hectic every day." He applied for his most recent position as a building inspector because he wanted to work only a forty-hour week. Part of his new job involved working alone, confronting violators of the local building codes. He soon found that that, too, was hectic. He could not tolerate intentional violators and had repeatedly requested a transfer from his department but was always refused.

Kent had been on this job for four years when his symptoms began. He began to suspect that his wife had a lover. The next minute, he would have the "crazy notion" that his wife was a homosexual. He began to come home at odd hours during the day to "check on her." He told his brother-in-law that if he caught his wife with a boyfriend, he would kill her. His mind was in a "terrible turmoil," he became a "bundle of nerves." At times he thought he would be promoted to supervisor at work; at other times, his mind would imagine a conspiracy between his wife and his department to "eliminate" him. One night he became so enraged with his wife that he tried to choke her. After a fit of uncontrollable crying, he was hospitalized and treated with antidepressant medication. He tried to return to work but had a breakdown in the office and had to stay at home, where he spends his days doing minor repairs, playing bridge with friends, and studying the Bible.

Kent was diagnosed as suffering from involutional psychosis with a combination of depression and paranoia that frequently occurs in depression-prone persons such as Kent, for whom things must run perfectly. When Kent discovered that he had traded one rat-race for another, his response was psychotic.

Wynn's reaction to the "end of the honeymoon" was a histrionic episode. He had been self-employed for twenty years, but during an economic slump had been forced to change jobs. At first there was only one other man in his department. They divided the work equally, but after several years, Wynn claimed to be "snowed under" when his coworker started "sloughing off his half of the job. If I couldn't do the job right, it really got to me. I'm a perfectionist." Wynn felt the pressure increase unbearably. He was terribly nervous and could neither sleep nor eat.

The day before he left his job an episode took place at home that he remembered only faintly. His wife came home from work and found him in a dazed, semiconscious state, halfway between the bedroom and the bathroom. He remembered getting out of bed but nothing further. He was hospitalized but had only a "foggy notion" of that period of time. Later, the problem was diagnosed as a respiratory illness, possibly complicated by over-medication.

Wynn had decided some years ago that his job was making him nervous. His supervisors said that, if anything, the workload had decreased, but Wynn felt greater pressure. He took increasing numbers of tranquilizers during this period, over-medicating himself on several occasions so that his job performance was

impaired. Wynn attributed all his problems to job stress; however, it is likely
that a changing relationship with his wife and children, as well as the effects of
aging, contributed to his distress. Unconsciously perhaps, Wynn concluded that
he could no longer work, and he reacted in the only way available to him—with
hysterical symptoms of a physical ailment.

Bill himself brought about a job change that resulted in an atmosphere he
found intolerable. After ten years in his position as department chief, where he
was highly respected and extremely successful, he requested an evaluative survey
of his entire program. He expected the results to be positive and had requested
the study because he believed the program so successful that the survey would
serve as a basis for increased budget requests. It never occurred to him that the
results would be anything but good. The survey was a disaster. The evaluation
team focused only on the negative aspects of his work. The study attacked him
as unqualified, stressing his lack of formal education instead of his great
experience. The survey so undid him that it brought on severe headaches,
memory loss, numbness in arms and legs, and respiratory problems. His diabetes
became uncontrollable, and within six months he was declared disabled and left
work.

Bill then stayed home while his wife worked. He seemed comfortable with
the role reversal, but his psychological state was mixed. Relieved to be free of
the pressures and conflicts of a highly demanding job, he also was depressed and
apprehensive about the future. Intellectually he was unimpaired, a bright,
energetic man with great native intelligence that allowed him to rise to a high
position with virtually no formal education. His energy and conscientiousness
forced him to great self-demands. He always expected to exceed minimal job
requirements; pushing himself to do more and to do it better, he achieved more
than most people would have in his circumstances.

After the survey he was unable to tolerate actual or perceived criticism.
Although the criticism has faded, Bill cannot return to work because he is so
sensitized to failure that he feels incapable of trying to perform in his old role.

Neither Wade nor Faith could integrate the externally imposed change in
their work environment that came about because of a change in state administration. Both worked for agencies whose funds were cut back. The consequent
reorganization included an increase in workload. Wade reacted with outrage at
those who had cut back the funds, and outrage led to psychological incapacity.
Faith was extremely angry because there was more work to do; her unconscious
reaction was "Because there is more work to do, I cannot work at all."

Wade had been a department supervisor in a state agency for a decade.
Until the change in the state administration, Wade was functioning well, loved
his job, and even volunteered ten extra hours a week in a related agency. With
the different state administration came a new director. Wade was immediately
thrown into conflict with this man, chiefly over changes being made within his
department. At the same time the new administration merged departments.

Wade felt pressured to make impossible agreements with other agencies; he lost half his staff, yet his workload was doubled. Because of these extradepartmental politics, Wade felt less and less capable of doing his job.

Shortly before the reorganization, he and his wife had begun a training course in transactional analysis to become group therapists. With the troubles at work, Wade became increasingly dependent upon his psychiatrist. When that relationship became unproductive, Wade attempted suicide by rapidly drinking a full bottle of vodka. He was found in a coma and hospitalized for some time. Then, his superiors began pressuring him to resign or transfer because they regarded him as incapable of carrying out his duties. He refused a transfer because he believed it to be a demotion. Wade resigned under pressure and was hospitalized with a psychotic depression.

Wade had been unstable throughout his life. Under a variety of stresses, including aging, changing marital relationships, increased responsibility at his job, and overwork, he began decompensating. Instead of dealing with his feelings, juggling all his work and family problems, as he had in the past, he felt overwhelmed. He could not concentrate, he could not suppress his anger and his fear, he felt that he could not cope with his problems and would never be able to. His depression became more acute. While Wade's personality predisposition was important, job pressures clearly were a significant precipitating factor in making him snap. He could not adapt constructively to changes in his work environment and refused to accept political reality. Overwhelmed by his own loss of control and outraged by his own impotence in the face of these changes, he reacted psychotically.

Faith is a person whose unconscious controls much of her life. Her reaction to increased job demands was an unconscious refusal to work. For seventeen years she had been a hospital worker, enjoying her job and functioning well in it. Sudden personnel cutbacks required her to do more of the heavy work. She was angrily and vigorously mopping the floor when suddenly she felt something snap in her back. The pain was unbearable, and she was hospitalized in traction for ten weeks. Although she returned to work, the pain in her back made it impossible for her to function, and shortly thereafter she quit her job.

She spent her days at home knitting and reading and engaging in various sedentary hobbies. Her husband had divorced her three years before the accident, and she lived with her two children and her dogs. The divorce had a profound effect on her, and she was still sad when speaking of it.

Faith's status was more hysterical than depressed. She seethed with anger at what the new administration had done to her.

In the following cases workers protested a change in job demands because they were not consulted prior to the increase in workload. The sense of personal affront more than the greater workload itself brought on the anger.

Forty-seven-year-old Charles had been a service representative for three years. His problem began when he was converted from a service representative to an orders representative "without being consulted." This change resulted in an increased workload, but more importantly it meant that he was no longer working directly with people. Instead, he was required to remain at his desk for forty hours a week. He said that many coworkers resigned because of such changes, but he vowed to stay on, awaiting the promised return to his former job. He finally broke down, crying, and could not handle the work. He left his job and sought psychiatric help, but even when he was no longer working, he became anxious when he had to talk with other people or make a decision. Any demand unnerved him. Even balancing his bank statement could produce stress symptoms. His routine was to get up at 7:00 a.m. and take care of his four-year-old child while his wife went to work. He spent his days doing housework and watching television, not leaving the house very often. He received $191 per month in disability payments, and his wife earned approximately $300 a month. When he was working, Charles earned almost $900 a month.

Charles' history was marked by extreme educational, occupational, and geographic mobility. He attended seven schools at the college level, eventually receiving a law degree and an MSW. He had had ten jobs in four states and, in addition, spent three years in the armed services as a bomber pilot during World War II. He was married twice and was experiencing some problems with his second wife.

Following are excerpts from Charles' autobiographical statement about "Factors leading to present situation." "I finally went back to school and studied social science courses sufficiently to get myself a job as a social worker. I really enjoyed this work and was very effective."

"After three years my duties were suddenly, without my consent, changed . . . This created frustrations within me . . . It became impossible to adequately meet my clients' needs. Essential paper work piled up . . . There were human problems which could not be pushed aside by me. I could not refrain from helping clients who asked, on the excuse that my paper work was piling up . . . I was frantically trying to carry on when the administration laid off one of my coworkers placing one-fifth of her work on me . . . I was in such a dilemma and under such pressure that I felt I was going beserk and found myself yelling at clients when they called. (The last thing I would consider doing.) Finally at about 10.00 a.m., with my desk piled high and the phone ringing and my supervisor (who was very considerate) was telling me there was no replacement for the laid off worker available, my brain seemed to shut down and I began to bawl and could not stop . . . I have continued to the present to have a bizarre set of symptoms and crying spells when I think about my present situation or the above stress I was under."

Charles became irritable, tense, and overwhelmed when his job required him to spend full time at his desk. He fell into a disabled state of mind. His symptoms were hysterical: he was overwhelmed and believed he could not function.

Lee also felt overwhelmed by a job change to which she had not consented. Whereas Charles internalized his feelings, Lee externalized her outrage. For three years she had been in a job similar to Charles'. Suddenly, new administrators came in, and twenty-nine-year-old Lee found that she had to work extremely long hours in order to keep pace with the changes. For eighteen months she worked ten hours a day. Then, within several days, her mother died and her father nearly died. She was gone from work for two weeks to attend to family matters and upon returning was told that she would be "pulled off my job." Her supervisor told her she would thereafter handle emergencies. Lee believes that this change was "punitive," since she was caught up with all her work before she left the office and thus was thought to have "free time." She told her supervisors that her nerves were such that she could not handle emergencies. But, as usual, "no one paid any attention," and she was transferred.

Later in the day she "freaked out"; that is, she hyperventilated and panicked. She wanted to run, but she did not know where. She stayed at home for several weeks in an attempt to recuperate. When she tried to go into the office, her panic symptoms increased. A strike further complicated matters, and she never returned to work, spending her time doing housework and caring for her nine-year-old daughter. She lived with a boyfriend, twelve years her senior, and his sixteen-year-old son. As a hobby Lee rode motorcycles.

Psychiatrists have concluded that the change in Lee's job duties was a major cause of her neurotic panic. A number of factors combined at that moment to upset her: the death of her mother and the near-death of her father and an unstable domestic situation because she had recently moved in with her boyfriend. The change in work assignment angered her because her supervisors did not heed her warnings. She felt she could not face a new situation in which she might have less freedom in her work than she had had formerly. When her vocal protests were ineffective, her protest was illness and departure from work.

The Industrial Accident as Protest

The escape valve for work pressure in the following group of cases is the industrial accident claim itself. The claim became a vehicle to protest the injustice of changes with which the claimant could not cope. These patients were conscious of their motivations, to varying degrees.

Alice, age twenty-nine and a secretary in a large corporation, made three claims for industrial compensation in as many years. In the first two claims, she complained of gastrointestinal problems and a skin rash. The third claim arose from a fall at work, when she slipped on a rain-soaked sidewalk enroute to the trash cans. Each time, psychiatrists noted that Alice reacted with somatic symptoms to situations of emotional pressure. The pressure she felt on her job was a result of her own inability to maintain an equilibrium. The basic problem lay in Alice's own personality: she was unable to tolerate change.

Alice's repeated claims must be viewed in the context of events in her office during this three-year period. She began working in a small department store where she was responsible to one individual. Later, the work load in this department increased but, paradoxically, the other full-time secretary was transferred out, and a two-person job became a one-person job. Eventually, as the workload increased, her secretarial position was abolished and she was transferred to the clerical pool. This change in assignment infuriated her.

Alice said that when she joined the clerical pool, her attitude deteriorated: "I just don't know who's going to stab me in the back next." Although she was physically removed from her old department, her major social ties remained with the people there. She attended department birthday parties and after-hours social activities. She felt that she "had let down the fellows" in her old department by doing something that caused her to be transferred to the clerical pool. She was unhappy with her supervisor in the clerical pool because she thought she was not wanted there. Originally she had refused the job, but was persuaded to take it when the supervisor sent her a memo stating that he genuinely wanted her to take the position.

Her relationship with her new supervisor went from bad to worse. She exchanged a volley of memos with him in which she complained about the lack of supervision and the heavy workload. Finally, she received a memo informing her that she was to be transferred to another department. This upset her and she walked out. She contested this transfer because she felt she could work with her supervisor, but the supervisor vehemently disagreed with her assessment.

Alice has been analyzed as a rigid-compulsive personality who cannot tolerate change. Under stress caused primarily by her own internal conflicts, her anger intensified in the face of change. This in turn heightened her somatic reactivity, and she was increasingly unable to reconcile herself to new developments.

Tim believed that he had been unjustly treated by local civic leaders who forced him to resign, in effect firing him, from his position as city manager. Four days before he was to resign, he suffered a fall as he rushed to City Hall in response to a bomb scare. This fall led to more than a year of therapy; despite his repeated requests, surgery was refused. He occupied himself with managing a few apartments, a more than full-time job.

During the past twenty-five years Tim suffered numerous ailments, most of which had significant emotional overlays. During World War II he suffered injuries to his eyes, ears, and back. The back injury occurred when he was "blown to the tops of the palm trees by a mortar shell." Following that episode, he suffered a three-week period of amnesia. Psychiatrists concluded that the amnesia could only be emotional in origin. The second incapacity occurred following the death of his mother, when he became totally paralyzed from the waist down and could move no part of his body. This paralysis lasted for a week and a half. Tim says it was cured by a two-hour visit to a chiropractor. Since the war experience, he had had recurrent muscle spasms and several times had back surgery. He suffered from a stomach ulcer, of which he "cured himself," and a hearing problem.

One year after his accident and his retirement, Tim was still an extraordinarily angry man. His accident occurred just after he had, in effect, been fired from his job. He was angry at every doctor he saw, and could not understand why physicians disagreed with him about the nature of his symptoms. He has never been able to see himself in a bad light, nor could he admit to a psychological problem. One could reasonably conclude that Tim has gross hysterical conversion tendencies. He refused a $2,700 settlement offer because to settle the matter would be to give up all claim to further treatment and attention.

Linda was a forty-five-year-old hospital employee, unhappy in her job, who claimed to have been sexually attacked one night on the hospital grounds. The truth of her story is at the heart of the dispute over her workers' compensation claim.

Linda claimed that as she walked between two buildings, she heard someone behind her, and assuming that some nurses were following her, she paid no attention. She was struck from behind and knocked unconscious. When she came to, she was being attacked sexually. She said she did not open her eyes until the attack was over, nor did she report the attack to the police, to her employer, to physicians, or to her husband, because she was so embarrassed. Only much later did she inform anyone of this occurrence.

The accident occurred at a stressful moment for Linda. She had just returned from department evaluation sessions, at which she had been roundly criticized. She felt the "evaluation" was unjust and was very angry about it. Her evaluator commented that she was moody, that she refused to treat patients warmly, and that she openly complained about her work. Linda also felt that her neatness rating should have been much higher, but because the supervisors generally were women who had been on the job for twenty to thirty years, they wanted everything to continue as it had been and felt threatened by someone who disagreed with them.

Several days after the alleged attack, Linda was fired. Her supervisor had come to her home to ask her to resign because her "personality was bad." Linda refused to resign because the request was unjust and responded, "Go on and fire me if you want to," and they did so.

Unemployed, Linda spent her days caring for a fourteen-year-old son and two-year-old granddaughter, whom Linda regarded as her own child. She continued to fight the denial of workers' compensation benefits. Possibilities of reemployment were slim because of child-care problems.

Linda's case is that of a worker who felt that she was literally attacked from two sides. She was overwhelmed by both attacks. She could not tell anyone about the sexual attack until much later. In one sense, each attack made her more vulnerable to the other. She might have been able to deal with one assault, but she could not deal with two.

Another case of the same type involves a patient who did not really complain of increasing work pressure although his physical deterioration was manifested in a psychological reaction against work.

Marvin had been a police officer for twenty-nine years and had always liked his job tremendously. Over the past four years he had felt increasing work pressure but was unaware of the reason. Recently he had had a continual feeling of nausea and had suffered sharp chest pains, attributing these problems to two unpleasant investigations: a bloody battered-child case and a tussle with a teenager who was on drugs. He felt worse and worse and finally took an early retirement.

Psychological testing revealed a marked impairment in intellectual function. Marvin appeared to be suffering from an organic brain disorder, and stress resulted from his diminishing intellectual capacity to handle normal work demands. Because Marvin was unaware of these changes in himself, he was less able to handle the pressures of his job. It is understandable that he would prefer to retire instead of taking a leave of absence.

In contrast to Marvin, Debra has been diagnosed as chronically psychotic. Fifty years of age, Debra worked as an office clerk for ten years. The problem that caused her to leave work developed when she was required to lift heavy books during an office move. She did not want to do this, claiming that it bothered her back. She complained to her supervisor, who paid no attention to her. She went home and told her mother. The next day she became confused and did not remember anything. She was taken to a psychiatric institute for examination and was referred to a state mental hospital. While at the mental hospital, she apparently went into a coma and was retained in the hospital for three months. After her release from the hospital, Debra returned home to live with her elderly mother and sister. She did virtually nothing but light housework all day long. The three women were in no financial distress. Although Debra said she would like to work, she felt incapable of doing so, because her memory was failing.

Debra had suffered a previous mental illness, twenty years before. Her mother stated that that episode also occurred when her daughter was overworked, but both mother and sister insisted that neither illness was mental; in both cases, they blamed a physical symptom.

Psychiatrists have judged both episodes to be schizoid. The more recent illness was thought to be a catatonic schizophrenic reaction, a disorder of the thinking process. Debra exhibited the prototype symptoms. The catatonic schizophrenic patient becomes concerned that any act or spoken word or thought may produce dire consequences. For example, he might believe that if he moves his arm, he will kill someone. He is afraid to eat or drink because those acts might kill someone, including himself. In Debra's case, the move from one building in which everything was in order to another building new to her upset her equilibrium and took away her ability to predict the work situation. Her subjective experience of work pressure and change was severe. Where another person might experience only a sore back because of moving the books, Debra experienced a disruption of her personality structure.

The question is, what brought about this schizophrenic reaction. Debra and her mother and sister believed the cause was overwork or unhappiness with work. Psychiatric opinion attributed the episode in part to job pressures. The change from her normal clerical routine to moving books may have disturbed Debra's tight, rigid pattern of existence. To that degree, the work change contributed to her decompensation. Other factors were involved as well: a recent anesthesia during dental surgery could have contributed to a loosening up of her feelings, and a probable overdose of medication might have had the same effect. She undoubtedly experienced some internal change unrelated to work that affected her thoughts and feelings and was the prime contributing factor to her schizophrenic episode.

In another case, the patient's long-standing hysterical personality led him to perceive intense work pressure. Vince, forty-eight, had been the head janitor in a large office complex for eight years. Before that, he owned his own business. He left his custodial position because of job pressures highlighted by accidents and conflicts with the administrator.

His problems began almost as soon as he started work, when he was knocked out of a tree and a limb struck him in the front teeth. As he told it, "It flung me twenty feet through the air into the neighbor's woodpile." He woke up standing on his head in "a lumped up mess." As a result, he said, he developed chronic sinusitis and, in his words, became "addicted to nose drops." Shortly thereafter, he was struck on the back of the neck with a piece of heavy equipment. He claimed to be paralyzed from his neck through his arms to his hands, finally being cured by a chiropractor. Vince felt that his supervisor never filed an industrial accident form because he did not want the organization's safety record to be affected. The form lay on the supervisor's desk for a year and a half. Vince had a similar paralysis the year before, when he was working very hard in quite hot weather.

Finally, during a violent argument with the administrator, Vince lost control of his emotions. After the argument, he thought he was dying. He lost all feeling in his legs and toes and developed chest pains. A visit to the hospital revealed no physical symptoms. A further conflict with the administrator developed when Vince, who is white, was asked to assist a crew in unloading an art exhibit by various black artists. Vince resented having to interrupt his work to participate in the unloading. When he arrived at the appointed spot, he discovered the other crew was not there. In an argument several hours later over whose mistake it had been, Vince developed chest pains and was hospitalized in intensive care for four days. Because of all this turmoil, Vince left work, suffering from nervousness and uncontrollable anger.

His medical and social histories reveal chronic instability, including the remarkable fact that within the last twenty-three years he had made 382 office visits to his physician. Vince's social history shows constant conflict in school. Indeed, he left high school during the tenth grade after a "run-in" with a guidance counselor over a search of his locker. He held a variety of odd jobs over the years and was involved in one battle after another at work, even ending up in court after contesting a union election. His marriage, in contrast, has been stable. He and his wife have been married for twenty-five years.

Psychiatric analysis shows that Vince had a long-standing personality problem. He had been analyzed as a hysterical personality with traces of a paranoid personality. This basic personality predated his custodial job, even though he claimed that work pressure caused his problems. Vince tended to see himself as blameless, good, and able, thinking that all his problems resulted from the mistakes or malevolence of others. His physical symptoms fell within a hysterical syndrome. They were consciously dramatic, attention seeking, and dependency inducing. His need to be noticed and to be important forced him into situations that turned out to be more than he could handle.

Harassment on the job may be a by-product of work pressure either as it exists intrinsically in the work or as caused by the inadequate perceptions of the worker because of his inherent personality structure. Some of the actual causes of work pressure are those created by new managers, by excessive emphasis on production, by disregard of the needs of the workers, by the tediousness of the task involved and resultant boredom, by lack of management appreciation of extra effort and application, and by the effects of the aging process that the worker has not recognized. Either because of the reality of the situation or because of the distorted image of it that the worker has, an industrial accident often comes as a protest to what he sees as injustice and lack of personal appreciation of his efforts. Personality must always be considered as a prime factor in a worker's perception of job pressure. Hyperconscientiousness, rigidity, and sensitivity, among other factors, must be given consideration in dealing with claims of harassment.

5 Harassment by the System

The victim of work pressure believes that the demands of his job are excessive—more than could reasonably be expected of anyone. The person suffering only from work pressure generally is better educated than the person who falls prey to harassment, and his complaint is almost always quantitative rather than qualitative. There is too much work, not too hard. Qualitative complaints arise when there is what we have called "harassment by the system," when the worker complains, not that he is overloaded by the work or that someone is "out to get him," but that he "can't stand working in this kind of atmosphere," with constant surveillance and constant checking. It would drive anyone crazy."

This is the worker who, after being out sick one day, is chastized by his superior for his absence. When the worker says that he was using sick leave, the superior replies, "Yes, sure we have a sick leave policy, but we also have a policy that people are expected to come to work." Or, the minority employee who in spite of his capabilities is never promoted, not because he is personally unpopular, but because the system is structured so that only whites get good positions. It is the systemic unfairness or pressure, then, that outrages victims of this type of harassment.

A Culture of Harassment

The components of harassment are ubiquitous: people, interaction, a confined situation. Joking, teasing, horseplay, and harassment are forms of interaction that can be seen at all social levels and in all group activities.

In some forms they are congenial, supportive, and preludes to closer relationships of sex or friendship or both. But in a situation of tension in the environment, or between individuals working to keep pace with job demands, where one worker is seen as weak or dependent, the outcome can be less pleasant—illness, hatred, violence, and sometimes even murder or suicide.

For harassment to occur, the harassment elements must exist within a culture that permits and rewards harassment.

Even though a number of potential harassment elements coexist, however, harassment does not necessarily follow. For example, a newspaper story compared the attitudes of and toward police in Japan and the United States, pointing out that Japanese police are polite, closely related to the neighborhoods in which they work, and highly respected by the citizens in their neighborhoods, in contrast to the situation in the United States. Almost never, apparently, is there an instance of harassment of the police by citizens nor of citizens by Japanese police. To the extent that that report is accurate, we question why there is such a disparity in police harassment levels between the two societies. Certainly fifteen or twenty years ago there was far less harassment of police in American society than there is today. A key ingredient among many that determine the level of harassment in police-community relations is the "culture"—that is, the extent to which there is a pervading sense of "permission to harass" on the part of police and on the part of citizens.

The same holds true of relationships between supervisor and worker and among workers. Without this sense of permission, the individual who undertakes to harass another will himself become the victim of ostracism and another kind of harassment by his fellows. Any social group needs allies to function, whether it is a benign group such as a charity, or a malignant group such as a vigilante group. Harassment in the work setting requires at least acquiescence by management. In some cases in our sample, supervisors in fact supported and participated in harassment; they had fist fights with their workers or made passes at women employees. Occasionally we found that even when a superior knew of a lower-level supervisor's harassment of employees, he was unwilling to intervene on the theory that to put an end to it was to undermine the supervisor's authority. This fine line between harassment and authority is illustrated by the experience of a secretary whose boss approached her at the water cooler one day and patted her buttocks. She reacted angrily. Although recognizing his authority to give job-related orders, she did not recognize him as a higher-status figure or as a personal authority figure who had permission to interact with her in that manner. If she had smiled at his sexism instead of telling him to stop it, their whole relationship might have been a different one, for she would have accepted his authority along with the harassment.

Supervisors and workers alike recognize that the intimidation inherent in the harassment process is an efficacious way of controlling workers. The use of harassment in order to keep workers subservient was cited by the *Campus Voice* (June, 1976), a publication of the California State Employees Association for workers in the California state university and colleges. The headline was, "Harassment Defended as 'Tool of Management.' " One supervisor of building and trades who had been hired from the outside three months earlier was charged with being "sarcastic, egotistical, and cold in his relations with his employees." It was said he had told his subordinates that he had been hired to "clean things up." According to the report in this paper, the supervisor admitted to the charges and said, "My attitude is exactly that. You're absolutely correct." He noted that his behavior "is just a tool of personnel management. I used it to get everyone's attention, and I don't think I need it any more so I'll stop." It was noted by one of the aggrieved that he had actually stopped a week earlier when the complaint was filed.

Harassment by Fear

Everyone must cope with fear. The woman in the doctor's office waiting room who has discovered a lump in her breast, the middle-aged man who feels a constriction in his chest, the passengers in a hijacked aircraft, the victims of a flood, all suffer the physiological concomitants of fear. They suffer relatively little conflict, however, because they can make no decisions until the moment of crisis passes. Eventually, the fear subsides. Very different is the fear of those who are surrounded by hostility and hatred, such as the prison guard or his technician counterpart at a mental hospital. Indeed, the prisoner and the guard are both prisoners, both in constant jeopardy from the other, neither trusting the other [50,151], each viewing the other from a narrow and hostile perspective [51]. Whereas at one time the role of the guard was explicitly defined and agreed upon, not only by the corrections system but by the general public as well, today the guard may be additionally discomfited by the ambiguity brought about by the prisoners' rights movement and the reevaluation of the criminal justice system. These view the prisoner not as an object but as a human being who does in fact have rights.

One might say that the guard obviously has a choice of whether or not to "go in there," whereas the true prisoner does not. Does the guard really have a choice, though? He generally has little education and few skills, and does not want a production-line or construction job. He earns a reasonable salary, has fringe benefits, has an investment in a retirement program, and a certain degree of status. How can the average guard realistically leave? Is he not as trapped as his charges? To the extent that he is a prisoner, he suffers many of the same reactions seen among inmates: depression, irritability, paranoia, and psychophysiological disorders. It is no surprise if he eventually "breaks" and seizes the opportunity provided by an assault or accident to claim disability as an escape from intolerable tension.

One of our noteworthy cases of this type was Lyndon, who had worked as a state prison guard for four years. Prisoner unrest had grown there, as it had nationally, and during several violent riots the prison guards were in great danger. After one such rebellion, two inmates threw coffee at Lyndon. In a reflex action he returned their "fire" with another cup of coffee. His superiors said this behavior was unbecoming to a prison guard, and as punishment they sent him to work in the prison laundry. When he returned to guard duty, because the inmates realized that he had a breaking point, they continued to taunt and provoke him by gestures and cat-calls. Lyndon came into conflict with his fellow guards and supervisors on another occasion, when, while he was relaxing in the guards' room, a fellow guard opened the door for a prisoner to deliver a package. Lyndon was tremendously upset because he saw this as a dangerous violation of regulations, to admit prisoners to the guardroom. He was particularly frightened because of the many recent prisoner take-over attempts. Despite his complaint to the sergeant, Lyndon felt that no punishment was meted out to the guard who had admitted the prisoner. This began a tug-of-war between Lyndon and his colleagues, most of whom thought he was much too concerned with rules in view of the minor danger. Lyndon developed severe nervousness along with chest and stomach pains. When these symptoms were not alleviated by medication, he decided to leave guard duty to work in a calmer television repair job.

Willard was a correctional officer in a state prison in charge of the most severely psychotic inmates. He had worked in mental institutions and prisons for some time and was accustomed to frequent outbursts; violence was a daily event in his wing. In fact, one of Willard's predecessors had been killed by the inmates. Three-quarters of his charges had been convicted of one or more murders. Although he shared his fears with his family, Willard did not request a transfer because he felt no one listened when employees complained. He was attacked by an inmate and seriously beaten. Immediately after the attack, friends and coworkers visited him frequently at home to see how he was faring. But he could not bear to be with people, and gradually his visitors sensed this. He withdrew from society and barely got along even with his wife. His history revealed that this was Willard's second marriage, and it was as unstable as his first, in which his wife divorced him for his repeated infidelity. Domestic quarrels led to police intervention on numerous occasions. His work history shows that he had been involved in many unsuccessful businesses. An impulsive man with a hysterical personality, Willard could not function in the volatile, fear-ridden prison atmosphere.

Another of our subjects, Bert, had been a psychiatric technician at a mental hospital for eight years when he was seriously beaten with a steel bar by several inmates who tried to steal his keys. He was working in the locked adolescent security ward with patients considered unmanageable in other wards or prisons. Bert said these patients, all with histories of violent social difficulties, should more appropriately have been in prison for the criminally insane rather than in a mental hospital.

After rest and treatment for his injuries, he tried to return to work, but when he entered the ward and heard the patients "screaming and hollering," he began vomiting and could not bear to be in the hospital. He has not returned to the ward since then because he is afraid for his life. He says that God spared him from death because he had to care for his children, but he is not at all certain that God would do so a second time. The sole support of his three children, he arranged his finances so he can return to school and then obtain a higher-level position in a health field. He continued to suffer from headaches and nervousness and became addicted to medications prescribed for those conditions. He was distraught because of his stagnation since the attack. He realized that further education would be difficult but he was determined to obtain it so that he would not have to return to the frightening mental hospital.

Why People Remain in Unpleasant Jobs

One of the most common reasons workers stay in unpleasant jobs is that they accept unpleasantness, dissatisfaction, and a certain amount of misery as part of the job. They believe all jobs to be miserable and, therefore, as long as this one is paying and is not unbearable, they remain.

Many workers will leave if conditions change for the worse. They accept the usual working conditions as a baseline and appreciate any improvements; they resent worsening conditions and react by complaining or resigning. Obviously, how readily individuals resign from their jobs is related to the availability of other jobs or alternative support systems that are commensurate with the rewards of the job. It would not be unrealistic to expect that if unemployment compensation came within 5 or 10 percent of salary, many would choose the unemployment stipend.

There are other reasons why workers stay on in unpleasant jobs, even if the job gets worse and the fear of being unemployed and unable to maintain their standards of living is minimal. Some workers stay because they believe they have a right to the job. Although most workers believe that a job is the property of the owners or of the government (in the case of state, municipal, and federal jobs), some believe that the worker himself in a sense "owns" the job, and these do not permit themselves to be easily displaced. Thus, one worker—whose employer decided that she could not provide the kind of leadership and initiative required by the position and who tried to have her dismissed— brought her case to a grievance committee of coworkers, and she won. When interviewed, she said, "He wanted someone he could get along with; I felt I had as much right to my job as he did to his. I was willing to get along with him; so, I saw no reason why he should not have to do what was necessary in order to get along with me."

Other workers stay in unpleasant jobs because they believe resigning will mean that the owner, the harasser, the supervisor, will have won a battle against them. For them, resignation is a personal defeat, and they could not tolerate defeat. Feeling that they had given up some of their dignity as human beings, they would hate themselves for their cowardliness. Rather than have to face themselves, they stay on the job and suffer.

For others, resigning would leave them in doubt about whether they had been right or wrong. To resign would be in some way to agree with the aggressor, to admit that he was right, and they were wrong. In private industry, such a worker is fired, files an industrial claim, and sometimes continues to fight for many years. One man after five years was still ranting about the indignity done him by one supervisor, remembering every detail of the aggression. He had kept careful notes, adding to them as he recalled other incidents of injustice. In employment situations where it is not this easy to fire a worker, for example, in civil service jobs, some of these workers will prevail, after a very long period of time. They may win and be given another job where they are happy. One secretary, after being transferred from the job she loved, tried two other jobs and on each felt that the employer was harassing her in order to force her resignation. Finally, she was given a job in a department where she felt comfortable. She was content and happy and pointed out to the author that what she had said was true. It was not she but the job; when the right job was given her and she was properly treated, she could indeed perform at the high level indicated by her current performance ratings.

Some workers stay on a job even when it is miserable because they enjoy the fight. In the same way that some individuals after ridding themselves of a sadistic, brutal, or stormy spouse, are bored and depressed when they marry "a nice one," some workers feel better when they are fighting than when things are going well. Some are paranoid, assuming that the world is conspiring against them and they must deal with each conspiracy. Any change in their working conditions represents such a conspiracy, and they must fight it to the limit.

Characteristics of the Harassed, of Harassers, and of the Job

Characteristics of the Harassed

We cannot describe a composite or model harassed person. Many different kinds of people are harassed; many different characteristics coalesce within an individual to make him feel harassed. Two persons may share a common personality characteristic, yet one of them may be harassed and the other not, depending upon additional circumstances [36]. Not all persons who exhibit the characteristics discussed in this chapter will be harassed or will perceive harassment at work, but there are clusters of traits that we observed repeatedly in our subjects.

Among these patients were individuals to fit almost every psychiatric diagnostic category. In some there was organic impairment of the central nervous system; others had functional psychoses, neuroses, and personality disorders. Psychosis generally refers to cognitive or emotional disturbance of such a degree that the victim is unable to recognize emotional or external reality, so that the person is out of touch with reality. The person with neurosis does not lose contact with reality; he usually is a fully functioning being but has a characteristic anxiety. He is fully aware that his behavior and experience are not based on a logical event or reality. There are numerous kinds of neuroses, including freefloating anxiety, phobias, obsessive-compulsive neurosis, depressive neurosis, and conversion reactions. Personality disorder refers to a characteristic mode of behavior in which anxiety is rarely experienced and in which responses are inappropriate, disruptive, or unacceptable to self or to society [24]. This person is not aware that he has any sort of problem; he complains of interpersonal problems but rarely of intrapersonal problems. Like those who have neuroses, persons with personality disorders seldom are out of touch with reality. Generally, those in our harassment population suffered from either neuroses or personality disorders. Only an occasional patient was psychotic.

The harassed victim generally tends to be conscientious, literal-minded, and somewhat unsophisticated. Often, he is an overachiever who tends to have an unrealistic view of himself and of the situation in which he finds himself. He may believe he is an ideal worker and that the job he is going to get will be the ideal job. As a result, he has great difficulty in adjusting not only to the imperfections of the situation but to the imperfections of his own functioning as well. Whereas most of us might in such a situation come to the conclusion that we were not as well adapted as we thought we were, the harassed person often does not see the lack within himself that contributes so significantly to the work problem. Since he cannot see himself as being less than ideal, he tends to blame others for his own inability to perform at the level he had expected of himself. He does not recognize his own very real limitations of intelligence, or of ability to understand and analyze a situation and to plan a strategy and devise tactics for dealing with the situation. Although believing himself something of a superman, he does not understand that a superman must have certain attributes that include physical strength, intelligence, judgment, and resources other than work.

In the cases that follow, the focus is not upon the power or status relationship between harasser and harassee, but upon the nature of the activity itself. While each case may illustrate many points made earlier, one, or at most a few, significant features have been emphasized in each case.

Subjective Harassment

Matt was an excellent example of a person who experienced subjective harassment, and perceived and suffered great injury, although an observer can find little or no external evidence of harassment. Subjectivity refers only to perception and does not necessarily imply fabrication. It was only in retrospect and after the suggestion of a psychiatrist that Matt himself saw a connection between his physical problems and his emotional distress. Initially, Matt had associated his reactions with the pneumonia he had had two years ago. Only much later did he begin to attribute his problems to his work under a particular supervisor.

For eight years, Matt had been a $13,000-a-year investigator for a local government. During the quarter century before that, he had made at least $50,000 a year as a self-employed professional in Europe and in several Eastern states. Because of family obligations, he moved to the West Coast, where he was unable to continue in his profession. After three years in his government job, a new supervisor was brought into his department, and with him, Matt claimed, came confusion, mismanagement, turmoil, and petty politics. Matt became embroiled in conflict upon conflict, each associated in some way with this supervisor. One conflict arose over what Matt regarded as a completely fabricated unsatisfactory efficiency report from the new supervisor. Matt requested that this report be removed from his personnel file, but this was never done. Matt also believed that he was harassed because of certain investigations he had carried out in the course of his job. For example, he had uncovered a scandal involving a local judge and his mistress, who had committed welfare fraud and allegedly had had an illegitimate child by the judge. An investigation of a political party had led to a burglary of Matt's house and anonymous calls and letters. In addition, Matt believed that he might unwittingly have antagonized the district attorney's office, because he was accused of falsely representing himself as a member of the district attorney's staff.

In each case, Matt perceived an effort by his supervisor, in league with others, to "bug or harass" him. Regarding his supervisor as inexperienced and sick, Matt felt degraded by an association with such incompetence. He viewed himself as extraordinarily competent and claimed to have been harassed primarily because of this competence, by superiors who were incompetent.

From the time of the arrival of this supervisor, Matt experienced continuous physical problems, including great weight loss, nervousness, and an inability to sit still. Psychological tests revealed that Matt was experiencing a significant impairment in intellectual function, partially as a result of aging, perhaps exacerbated by what he felt was a lower-status job. Physical impairment, plus a spiraling depressive reaction, led him to see only the negative aspects of other people's performance and only the positive aspects of his own. What Matt regarded as unfavorable responses to his complaints of harassment only increased his anger and depression.

The following case of subjective harassment illustrates the histrionic patient playing out a role she forces herself to assume to add excitement to her life.

While at work on the assembly line, forty-year-old Bernadine fell off a chair and landed on the floor, striking her right hip sharply. The plant nurse sent her home to rest. Over the weekend, Bernadine began vomiting blood. She had her children telephone the nurse, who told them their mother had a bleeding ulcer. She also told the children to remind Bernadine to return to work the next day. Bernadine reported to work and saw the nurse, who again said her problem was ulcers rather than the fall and referred her to her private physician for treatment. Her doctor, however, believed the bleeding was caused by her industrial accident. When Bernadine relayed this opinion to the nurse, they quarreled about the diagnosis. The nurse told her, "You are just trying to stir up trouble."

With this exchange began a steady decline in Bernadine's physical and psychic state, marked by continual encounters with the plant nurse, unproductive visits to ten different specialists, an unsuccessful disc operation, and the histrionic highpoint of a bizarre suicide attempt when she threatened to swallow all the medicine she had, but was persuaded not to by the insurance company claims adjuster whom she had telephoned to announce her planned suicide. While talking with him, she swallowed instead an heirloom heart necklace from her grandmother.

As time went on, Bernadine required more and more medication for pain; not only did she take far more than the prescribed dosage, but in addition begged for medication from almost anyone who would give it to her. Increasingly, Bernadine felt that it was the plant nurse who was her nemesis—determined to harass her, withholding medical treatment, and discrediting her pain and suffering in the eyes of other medical personnel. A year after her fall, still experiencing pain, Bernadine left her job. Thereafter, she suffered from headaches and a burning sensation on her scalp. She said she was "tired of it all. I want to be new—I want to be something—I want to be put in a hospital."

The youngest of eight children, Bernadine had been born and raised in a small midwestern town where her father was at various times a deputy sheriff, a mail route operator, and a lead miner. Her mother worked in a shoe factory. Bernadine remembered growing up as a pleasant time. She recalled a traumatic event at the high school senior class picnic when she visited a "haunted house" and it collapsed on her, fracturing several vertebrae. She could not walk for seven months, but described the whole event as "beautiful."

Bernadine had three children from four marriages, the first three of which ended in divorce and the fourth in annulment. She divorced her first husband after he was sent to prison, the second after he locked her daughter in a closet in a fit of jealousy, and the third because he drank too much and stole her money. Then, because she "loved to take care of people" and thought she could "make him happy," she married a man she knew was a "psycho." She got an annulment after three weeks, when he was diagnosed as psychotic.

Bernadine's hysterical personality is seen first in her increasingly frenzied search for a doctor who would respond to and thereby lend credence to her perceived ills. It is also revealed in her relationship with the plant nurse. Bernadine refused to stop fighting until she had proved the nurse wrong and demonstrated that she had indeed suffered serious injury as a result of the fall. The nurse's response was to assert that Bernadine had a long history as a continual complainer and was babying herself, a response that was combative rather than supportive and understanding. Bernadine's treatment became a cause celebre both in her own mind and to others. A group of her friends at the plant rallied to her, in her fight against the nurse, and complained to the boss about what had happened to Bernadine. Finally, it seemed that Bernadine could win only by the ultimate drama of her planned suicide.

Carlos was another who blamed those around him for his own failures, believing that his competence had gone unrecognized. Forty-one years old and a confirmed bachelor, Carlos was born and educated in South America, where at the age of twenty he received a degree in mathematics from a national university. He wanted to go to medical school and become a psychiatrist but could not because his father, a wealthy cattle rancher, refused to pay for any more schooling. Carlos then embarked on a series of business ventures, all of which met with defeat. He became involved with a woman who was much younger than he, whom he described as a "borderline psychotic." She committed suicide. After the failure of his business ventures and the suicide of his girl friend, Carlos came to the United States, hoping to find success. Initially, he did obtain federal funding to attend a community college clerk-typist trainee course, but after that he met only frustration. After several years of searching, the only job he could find was as a messenger in an office, and he accepted it because he needed money, although he believed the job to be beneath him. He had only problems on that job. He believed he had not been treated with respect and deference, and was angry that he was not promoted to the position of clerk-typist for which he had been trained. He did not believe that his inability to read or speak English—after five years in this country—was relevant to his nonpromotion. These "injustices" have made him violently, even obsessively, angry. He believed he was the victim of relentless teasing, although he could not describe exactly what was done to him. Whether the teasing and horseplay in his office was any greater than in other offices is not clear; however, for Carlos that teasing was highly personalized, and he saw himself as the sole target of most of it.

He had numerous plans for revenge—to try to raise $30,000 to begin a competing plant in Spain or in the Canary Islands, in order to destroy his employer by producing a better product at a lower price.

Carlos could be categorized as having a paranoid personality. This characterization is based on his tenacity in continuing in a job where he was miserable, on his litigiousness, and on his grandiosity. This is the personality he brought to his job and that has been with him for many years. This personality was certainly a central factor in his perception of harassment. Culture and status changes also operated to frustrate his ambitions, so that he felt victimized at every turn.

Forty-eight-year-old Ricardo also used an instance of physical harassment and claimed resultant disability as an "explanation" for his unachieved dreams of becoming a soccer hero. Ricardo did not work for seven years following his accident at a packing plant. His story is remarkable because of the duration of his disability and because his social disability developed to such an extent. Ricardo was involved in a scuffle with his supervisor and was pushed to the ground. He was not sure whether he was unconscious, but he was taken to a hospital, where he said he remained in a "coma" for several weeks. He had extensive treatment for numerous pains in his neck, head, ears, legs, back, and arms.

Ricardo, his wife, and eight children lived on welfare, following this "accident." He spent his time at home reading the newspaper, watching television, and reading. His only interest was in soccer, and he wrote a book proposing improvements in the game. He enjoyed teaching young boys to play soccer and worked with several sports clubs, in an effort to get a large gymnasium where Latin American boys could play soccer year round. Soccer had been the love of Ricardo's life for as long as he could remember. He tried to play professional soccer in Mexico, but could not qualify as a member of a professional team. He worked at various odd jobs in Mexico, and eventually came to the United States where, after tedious periods of unemployment and underemployment, he located the packing plant job.

Ricardo experienced a massive psychological reaction to what appears to have been a minor physical incident with his supervisor. His "coma" and the subsequent spread of symptoms throughout his body, followed by total functional disability, are certainly psychological rather than physical reactions. While Ricardo perceived the incident with the supervisor as an attack, it might more properly be viewed as a manifestation of his psychiatric state. His disability represents a histrionic statement that he is disabled.

Being knocked down by his supervisor produced a conflict for Ricardo. There had always been tension between him and other workers. Perhaps in his own mind he had always thought that if he were attacked, he would be much more aggressive; when an actual "attack" did occur, his only response was to go into a "coma." From that point on, the course to disability was relatively simple. He began with a compensated injury and progressively saw himself as more and more disabled, because the alternative to disability was a return to the same unskilled, unprestigious, boring labor, which did not coincide with his self-image as a sports hero. His sense of the grandiose took over, and he truly believed that he would write a book that would influence soccer on an international scale. He believed that he had an insight into this sport that others did not have. Thus, the harassment incident permitted him to pursue a career for which he believed himself to be destined.

The Noninsightful

The outstanding common denominator among a certain group of patients was their lack of insightfulness. The expression does not denote a value judgment, but means that few, if any, of these patients can make predictions that time proves valid. Thus, they cannot predict other persons' reactions to them; they cannot predict the outcome of a protest; they cannot, or for emotional reasons they do not, predict the consequences of their acts. This inability leads them into disappointments. Their statements produce reactions far different from what they had anticipated, and when mired in the resulting predicament, they cannot understand how it happened. Because they do not see the problem, they panic, and in their panic, compound the difficulty. Panicky reactions produce increasing questions about their competence and more desire to remove them from the organization. Many appear unconsciously to want no insight, because with it would come an understanding of their own role in creating discomfort at work. Although their problems most likely would not be entirely their own fault, many cannot tolerate acceptance of any responsibility for their acts.

His noninsightfulness also means that the harassed person is not a systems thinker. Rather than perceiving the world as a vast set of systems in which he is one component interacting with other components, he focuses on the functions of the separate parts. For example, he concentrates on the personality of an individual supervisor, on an idiosyncrasy of a single coworker, on only one aspect of a directive, and misses the context in which the people operate or in which the events occur. He is like the person who cannot abstract a proverb such as "people who live in glass houses shouldn't throw stones," who comment on the glass, the house, the stones, but does not understand the broader message about retaliation.

So, too, with the behavior he considers harassing. He sees the one act—the transfer, the teasing remark, or whatever—as the central element, with an importance far beyond what it would have for another worker who could put it into perspective. We know that such behavior occurs commonly in persons who are anxious or who feel threatened. Some of these patients had been so traumatized in the past that they were sensitized to attacks and hurts. Others were chronically anxious and scanned the environment for danger. Still others, seeking to justify their failures, were blinded by their ever-present belief that the world was against them. Some were unable to synthesize the elements in their environment because of low intellectual capacity.

Many of these noninsightful persons were unable to express their feelings directly and tended to focus on their bodies. For many in our population, the first reaction to harassment was physical symptoms.

People Who Cannot Break Away

Although most of these patients were terribly unhappy in their jobs, many stayed on for years and years. Their alternatives were few, but they also were temperamentally disinclined to experiment. Their remaining on the job was related to their noninsightfulness. By making unrealistic assessments of their value to the organization they came to expect better treatment, advancement, and recognition. Misleading personnel policies compounded these initial misperceptions, saying to the worker, "You can go right to the top." Our patients did not realize that very few can, in fact, ever get close to the top. Many organizations mislead people into thinking they practice participatory management with each employee playing an important role in decision making, when in fact very few employees have any voice in decisions. Organizations commonly suggest that they are one big happy family whose members love and protect each other, which also is not true. But in our patients, noninsightful people who were not systems thinkers, the realities went unperceived, and the results were perceived as injustice.

Most people can determine when they have found a "good" job, in view of their limitations of education, skill, personality, or physical abilities. Our patients often did not directly confront this. Somewhere in their awareness, they might have known that they could not do much better, but even if they recognized this, they hated to admit it. One sees a real ambivalence in these workers who hung on to a job they disliked. They stayed out of necessity, sensing that there was no place else where they could do as well, yet feeling underappreciated and underutilized in their present capacity.

A part of this ambivalence arose from the comfort they derived from playing familiar, if painful, roles. To be "put upon" or "done in" is a sympathetic position for many people. They use this stance to explain to themselves and to others their failures in a hostile, cruel world. They fear that if they stop being put upon and are moved on to become "winners"—to borrow a term from transactional analysis—they will be in great danger. Becoming "winners," they would upset the status quo, would themselves change, and would face a series of choices involving the development of, or denial of, their own potential. Change, for them, introduces the probability of making mistakes, the most threatening of all courses. Yet, along with this almost enjoyment of being "put upon," they resent deeply the associated anger and isolation. At the same time, they will sometimes confide that they have imagined what a better life would be like.

Ambivalent continuation in an unhappy job often occurs when the employee is the subordinate partner in a relationship where the dominant person is sometimes cruel and frequently degrading, yet occasionally demonstrates some affection and support. In the work context, a person may be subjected to numerous affronts by his employer and still find pleasure perhaps in the employer's indications that he will care for him in his old age, or that the worker will always have a job with him, or that the worker is, in spite of everything, a valued friend who would not be picked on if he were not so close to the boss. Such maltreatment might continue for a period of years, while the employee works for a salary far below the prevailing wage. Suddenly he is injured. Although not seriously hurt, he is frightened, and with this minor injury he takes it for granted that he will "collect" on all the love his employer owes him for twenty-five years of nonstop, low pay work. But the boss has no use for a worker who cannot or will not do the work he had done before. The boss fails the employee's "test of love." Without the expected "payoff," the worker feels defrauded and depressed.

Paranoid Problems

The Diagnostic and Statistical Manual of the American Psychiatric Association describes the paranoid personality as follows:

This behavioral pattern is characterized by hypersensitivity, rigidity, unwarranted suspicion, jealousy, envy, excessive self-importance, and a tendency to blame others and ascribe evil motives to them. These characteristics often interfere with the patient's ability to maintain satisfactory interpersonal relations. Of course, the presence of suspicion of itself does not justify this diagnosis, since the suspicion may be warranted in some instances [40,p.42].

Many subjects described in this book would fit that picture.

The paranoid person lives in a world that seems very dangerous to him. Paranoia has been described as a communications disorder, the paranoid person reacting differentially to a social environment, which he perceives as symbolically organized against him [94]. That is, he believes that he is treated differently from the way others are treated. Paranoia thus is not as centered in the individual but is a reciprocal interaction between the individual and those around him.

External circumstances can create a paranoid disposition, even in the absence of any special psychopathological personality structure. For example, radical changes in norms and values, displacement, strange environments, isolation, and a separation from those with whom one has a common language all may provide external circumstances that foster paranoid thinking.

Paranoid diagnoses usually are based on social interactions, including hostility, aggressiveness, suspicion, envy, stubbornness, and jealousy. The paranoid person tends to disregard the views of others and to disregard accepted group processes as well. He might resort to formal means to solve problems—such as filing a lawsuit—where others in the group would resolve their difficulties by informal negotiation. From the viewpoint of the group, the paranoid's behavior is ambiguous, uncertain, and untrustworthy. On the other hand, the paranoid often believes that group members are hypocrites and feels that the group is avoiding and excluding him. Feeling excluded, the paranoid person becomes more arrogant, insulting, and presumptuous, and the group in turn either humors him or expels him.

Although a particular person may fit the description in the *Diagnostic and Statistical Manual,* no two paranoid persons are exactly alike. The quiet paranoid keeps his suspicions to himself, and though inwardly seething, he does not display these feelings publicly, although he might discuss his thoughts at home with someone he trusts. The quiet paranoid's coworkers generally see him as introverted, not suspecting the hostility and suspicion that lie underneath. At the other extreme, the reactive paranoid person is ready to fight at any provocation. No one in the organization doubts that he is an unusually hostile person, although they might not label him paranoid.

The difficult and troublesome employee, in whatever environment he may find himself, creates dissension. "This dissension is the 'trademark' of the condition and must be present, if the diagnosis is correct. It is the 'sine qua non' of the paranoid individual" [133,p.54]. This would certainly be true for the reactive paranoid. He will always fear that he is being treated differently from others and will blame his employers and coworkers for discrimination.

Closely related to paranoid thinking and behavior is an individual's method of handling humor. Commonly, the paranoid person is unable to deal with humor, especially if it even remotely concerns him. He is quite capable of laughing at the humor in a movie, because he recognizes that the actors are not focusing their joke on him. However, he may very well be upset by the laughter of the people next to him in the theatre, thinking that they are laughing at him. The paranoid may even be unable to laugh at the action on the screen, although realizing that it is not aimed directly at him, because he thinks it is intended to ridicule someone *like* him. That is, he has ideas of reference. Paranoid thinking is, of course, not the only personality characteristic that contributes to an inability to handle humor. Noninsightfulness and passivity, alone or in combination with aggression, are characteristics that also have this effect.

The ability to participate in humor requires a recognition of the difference between humor that is benign and that which is malignant. The paranoid person has difficulty making this distinction, because he cannot identify or cannot trust the cultural cues, such as a body gesture, a facial expression, a prefacing statement, that indicate whether humor is friendly or hostile. Nor can the paranoid person easily change his mind once he has classified the humor as either benign or malignant. The humorist may, for example, begin the joke by appearing deadly serious, with no clue, for a moment or two, that this is all in fun. Then the little smile or twinkle says, "Hey, this is a joke." Often, the contrast itself is what makes the incident funny, and to appreciate the humor, the listener must pick up on the nuance. But the paranoid person cannot make this change. He is outraged because he has been "put on." To be fooled even for a minute is threatening to him, because it means that he could be wrong. Most of us can tolerate our own errors and are not destroyed by being wrong. For the paranoid person, however, to err even slightly means that all his knowledge, all his cognition, and all his understanding mechanisms are open to question. He is resentful whenever he begins to doubt his own cognitive powers. Thus, in this humorous situation, he will very likely ignore the second signal, if he senses it at all.

The inability to read interpersonal cultural cues and to know that no harm is intended is often coincident with the inability to send these cues. Often the paranoid is so concerned that others will be upset by his humor that he cannot be funny; he is nervous, his timing is bad, he cannot send out *his* cues that would reassure others that his joking is benign. As a result, even when he tries to "play" with his coworkers, he often is rejected because they find it too difficult to tell whether he is kidding or serious. Empirical studies have shown that if one is able to express hostility, covertly or overtly, one usually appreciates hostile humor [30]. When one is unable to express hostility and has trouble differentiating hostile from nonhostile humor, one is unable to appreciate hostile humor. One empirical study found that when negative affects or inhibitions were aroused, their subjects were less able to appreciate aggressive humor [144]. Understandably, in the presence of hostile humor, this type of person would readily become upset.

The Rigid Compulsive

The rigid, compulsive individual is a second personality type characteristic of harassed workers who file a compensation claim. Many rigid, compulsive people are superb workers who do quite well at detailed tasks precisely because of their rigidity and compulsiveness. They can, to some degree, accept other people's different work habits, but they cannot themselves deviate from their own self-created standards. The protagonist in Thurber's "The Catbird Seat" was a rigid, compulsive man who functioned well in his job as office manager in charge of accounts and procedures in a British textile firm. However, the boss became enamored of an American efficiency expert whose modernizations wreaked havoc on this man's quarter century of "order," and he thought he could no longer function. His first resolve was to kill this meddler, but upon reflection he decided that making her appear the fool was a much better way to handle the situation.

Our patients, however, are rigid, compulsive employees who cannot change their patterns enough even to mock those within the system who distress them, much less to enable themselves to work within the system. They find it difficult to work with those who have values, behavior, or work styles different from their own, because they expect others to behave according to their own standards and values. This expectation stems not so much from authoritarian tendencies as from the rigid, compulsive person's own vulnerability: when his coworkers do not act as he does, he begins to question his own actions. Whereas many persons would think of reevaluating themselves if challenged by alternative styles of thought, the rigid, compulsive person cannot. Because he is too frightened by the threat, he becomes anxious and depressed, or else he tries to change others.

When the rigid, compulsive worker tries to bring others "into line," we see the first step in a disruption of the working system. A group of people who have been working together at some kind of regular pace, perhaps sloppily, perhaps pilfering from the organization or taking extra time off, but working together, cease to do so. The question then becomes, what to do with the rigid, compulsive disrupter. Generally the group's first response is, "Don't rock the boat." To a few people that plea is effective; they adapt and stop trying to disrupt the system. For most rigid, compulsive persons, however, this is a reaffirmation of their belief that they are right. They read the statement as "Yes, you have caught us doing something wrong. Please stop that complaining or else you'll expose us." At this point the rigid, compulsive person may go to a higher authority, who then must decide what to do with the disrupter and his complaint. Most often, in our experiences, the decision is that things cannot be changed to suit this one person, even if he is right. The superiors reason, "Something must be done with this guy," and they start to isolate him. As colleagues begin changing their relationships with this employee so that his work is less pleasant, he starts feeling harassed.

A fascinating aspect of some rigid, compulsive patients is the unconscious discrepancy between their evaluation of their own behavior and the behavior of others. For example, although outraged if a coworker steals something or wastes time, they themselves often do the same things. This is not hypocrisy. They are simply unaware of the similarity between their own and others' acts. The discrepancy points up the vulnerability felt by rigid, compulsive workers and their need to protect their sense of being in the right. Admitting to such behavior in themselves would upset them and put their own faculties into doubt, just as a pointed or humorous comment from coworkers would challenge them, so willing are they to believe a negative appraisal about themselves and so desperately must they defend themselves from such an attack.

Grandiosity

Another quality that surfaced repeatedly in our sample was grandiosity. For numerous psychological and sometimes physiological reasons, people can believe that they are much more than what they really are. The person who has never demonstrated in school or in work or in artistic performance any particular intelligence or talent, yet who believes he has special knowledge or insight into solutions of complex problems with which he has had no experience, might be called grandiose.

These people are not delusional. They do not believe that they control or are controlled by external systems in which others are participants; they do not believe that there are plots or forces external to themselves; they do not postulate a control system whose existence most members of their own society would doubt. Honestly believing in their special ability, strength, wisdom, or intelligence, they attribute their lowly positions to prejudice, nepotism, or "the system" itself. While it is true that most work systems do discriminate, these are people who objectively appear to have relatively little ability, yet who claim victimization and act accordingly.

It was formerly thought that grandiosity resulted from brain damage caused by infection; for example, central-nervous-system syphillis. Most grandiosity, however, has a psychological origin. When the mind accelerates in the manic phase of manic-depressive psychosis, the individual may be unable to judge his capabilities and may overestimate them. Conversely, in the depressed phase, he tends to underestimate himself. In other patients, grandiosity develops out of early childhood experiences. Those who have had all the attention of the significant adults in their lives focused on them, who have possibly demonstrated some few skills and have been constantly told how great they were, might come to believe that they really are the greatest. "Some are born great, some achieve greatness, and some have greatness thrust upon them."

For still others, grandiosity is a defense against extremely low self-esteem, mobilized when they feel depressed. They conduct an argument within themselves: "You're not very good. You *are* good. You're the greatest. You're the worst." When the positive side wins the argument, we call it grandiosity, an inflated notion of one's worth, or high self-esteem. When the negative side wins the argument, we call it depression, low self-esteem, or an inferiority complex.

Our patients demonstrated several varieties of grandiosity. Those who are overtly grandiose are easily identified, the "Emperor Norton" who lectures from the soap box, announcing to the multitudes the order of the day, for example. More complex are those who are secretly grandiose. A woman is working happily at her job; her office mates think she is perfectly adjusted. Deep down she feels far more self-important than she appears to be, far above the level at which she seems able to function. If for some reason she suddenly feels pushed into a corner, the secret grandiosity may become overt. She begins to talk about her real worth and reveals a gross overestimation of her own abilities. When that happens, her colleagues attack, through ridicule or by direct confrontation. "You are not as good as you think you are. As a matter of fact, you are not very good at all." Or, they attack by exclusion. Whereas formerly they permitted her in their circle, now they think she is too strange or too crazy to be one of them. Then the same process occurs that has been described in paranoid and the rigid, compulsive persons. The victim becomes depressed. Some may leave work. Others stay and fight because they can do nothing else in the face of the challenge to their self-esteem, yet their grandiosity makes them deaf to employers' or coworkers' explanations of why they are treated in a particular manner. Eventually, some of these come to us with physiological symptoms and a complaint of harassment.

Passivity and Dependence

Many of our patients needed to live and work in an environment with a constant supply of love and approval from those around them. We all seek approval, but these dependent people felt a particular need. They could not function in a neutral state, where approval or love was neither given nor withheld. Because they were totally unable to tolerate disapproval, they tried hard to please and generally avoided expressing aggression [70]. Although eager enough to work for approval, they often found themselves at a loss, because they needed immediate approval from a supervisor that they had not yet done enough work to earn. Such individuals seem to operate in a unique time sequence. They need to be "paid" by the minute and on the minute, in the currency of immediate, cognizable rewards, a pat on the head, or a "positive stroke" to assure them that they are still loved and appreciated. If payment is delayed even for some very brief period, they become first quite anxious and then depressed. One consequence of depression is harder work in an attempt to gain approval. A second consequence is a loss of efficiency, which in turn brings less and less approval. Of course, the patient does not see the relationship between his own drop in productivity and the supervisor's increased demands for more work. The frustrated worker responds with yet a greater need for approval, and thus begins the familiar cycle culminating in a claim of harassment.

Quite often the kind of worker just described finds a "happy marriage" with a supervisor, in which a symbiosis is established. The worker receives love, approval, and rewards. In return, he provides the supervisor with affection, respect, and status. A kind of "inhibited exhibitionism" can be seen in this kind of relationship, where one person parades as harmless, generous, inept in order to reassure the other. A personnel change can destroy the efficiency and self-esteem of the dependent worker in such a relationship. A new boss comes in who is unprepared or unwilling to play the game. The worker resents both the departure of his approving boss and the replacement. In several extreme cases, our patients could not deal with the sense of loss and anger at being deserted, feelings akin to those experienced by children when a parent dies.

One young man simply did not understand that bosses come and bosses go. When the old boss left, therefore, he was angry with the new boss for coming and regarded him almost as an assassin. He approached his new supervisor with a profound ambivalence, to which the latter responded defensively. Our subject was convinced that his new boss was going to be punitive toward him, though the boss was not even aware of this man's feelings.

It is change itself that is difficult for dependent persons to tolerate. Many workers know that while the new supervisor will initially sweep clean with a new broom, if they hang on for several months, things will quiet down. New standards will be relaxed, and they will be back where they were under the old supervisor. But the passive person who needs love cannot wait that long because he lacks perspective. The very thought that the new supervisor might deprive him of approval, affection, or attention for even a short time is enough to cause depression, anxiety, and in the aggressive-dependent person, acting out. Thus, change often brings about the following sequence: A new supervisor arrives with no opinion or a low opinion of the worker in question; there is an increasing demand by the worker for approval and reassurance that the old relationship will survive; rejection by the supervisor plus requirements of greater productivity or responsibility further upset the worker; finally, he makes a claim of harassment or work pressure.

The kinds of personalities seen in our patients have been studied by other authors who have observed their on-the-job difficulties in the military service [75]. The passive-dependent character is the boy in man's clothes, who has difficulty making decisions, shuns responsibility, and expresses his need for attention through medical symptoms. The passive-aggressive character is "the man you don't like." This person expresses his hostility by staying just within the boundaries of the rules; because he is constantly testing them, he engenders hostility in his superiors, who therefore assign him to undesirable jobs. He argues with his superiors about job assignments and then does the chore inefficiently. If reprimanded, he is quick to state that he has actually done the job, and looks for a way to blame someone else for his own failures and consequent suffering [145]. Feeling picked on because he has been assigned to such lowly tasks, he frequently takes advantage of minor illnesses to express his passive-aggressive hostility toward all authority. He may even imply that his sickness is a direct consequence of ill-treatment. The passive-aggressive person pursues this tactic through frequent trips to sick bay, with many return visits to complain of ineffective prescriptions. Passive-aggressive personalities are frequently retired from the military service on the basis of such disabilities, and they are a common personality type in court-martial prisoners in the service [138].

A person who elicits teasing is the overreactive sulker, unskilled in interpersonal relations, who is dependent, has a poor self-concept, and fears having to defend himself [147]. Since his potential ability to strike back is negligible, he is an excellent target for teasing and harassment. By an aggressive use of face-work, some people arrange for others to hurt their feelings so that the offender will feel guilt and remorse [52]. Although he does not use the term "passive-aggressive behavior," the tactic is exactly that. We noted this often in our population; our patients could not abide the uncertainty of an undefined relationship with the people around them. Very subtly, they provoked a confrontation until underlying hostility exploded. After that, it was impossible to work together.

Foolishness

There is a bit of the fool in each of us, and from time to time everyone but the most rigid person has played the fool. In most social situations, one can be a fool for a brief period and then resume one's former role without any permanent stigma. At work, though, when an employee tries to slip into the fool's role for a short time, he often finds that such role playing has serious consequences because his peers may force him to remain the fool. Functionally, he has become the focal point for group cohesion [36]. As a result, the unwilling fool may claim harassment by his coworkers.

The traditional fool has been described at length in the literature [83]. He is known as a crackpot, fanatic, simpleton, butterfingers, yes-man, and sucker, to name only a few designations. Deviating from conventionally expected conduct, the fool usually is subnormal in intelligence, sobriety, or competence, and is thus viewed as an ineffectual being. Because of his extreme exaggeration or deficiency, evidences of weakness or irresponsibility, and perceived offenses against propriety, the fool is generally on the periphery of any group. Rarely is the fool happy with this position.

A fool who was both ostracized and supported by his colleagues in Air Force basic training was, on the one hand, the company scapegoat who became the object of numerous projections of deviance from normal behavior. On the other hand, because through his antics he could deflect or forestall depredations against the rest of the company, the group accorded him a special positive status [36].

Those of our patients who were cast in the role of fool rarely were appreciated. They were rejected and laughed at, group behavior that only served to exacerbate tendencies toward deviance. It was clear that the fool's behavior often was conduct that group members were unable to accept in themselves, so that the identified fool became the target for dislike. There is a masochistic mechanism that causes some people to behave in self-effacing ways [92]. This, in turn, elicits and provokes others to treat them in punitive and contemptuous ways. In a sense, the masochist is training others to act superior in his presence.

We are well acquainted with the negative effects of harassment, but we must not overlook its positive aspect. The victim of harassment is not naturally courageous or self-determining, and the decision to fight his tormentors is a drastic step. Like the timid soldier who becomes a hero for his bravery in combat, the harassee may be surprised at his own resolve, for he never imagined that he could respond firmly to attack. The soldier knows that he will have to fight only once, for after battle he will be hospitalized or dead. The workers' resolve, though, is tempered by his knowledge that the fight must continue; consequently, his defense often brings with it anxiety, nervousness, withdrawal, and somatic symptoms. Nonetheless, for both soldier and worker, this resistance may produce the strongest and proudest sense of self they have ever felt. We have observed that the self-image of the worker who has resisted harassment stays with him, and he refuses to be beaten down again.

Hypochondriasis

Hypochondriasis is the result of subjective work pressure experienced by the type of person who does not express his conflicts emotionally but who instead focuses on his body. Victimization by external forces is felt; the person turns on his own body, which in turn registers the protest.

Pete, who was thirty-two-years-old, has spent the last twelve years doing hospital work. Within the last three years he had been injured in the chest twice while attempting to restrain violent patients. After each injury he was off work for several months. Each time, upon returning, he felt increasingly pressured to do a kind of work that was revolting to him—restraining patients. Eventually he became so upset that he suffered continual chest pain, upset stomach, diarrhea, and headaches.

The psychiatric diagnosis was that Pete suffered from hypochondriasis. He was not malingering nor was he organically ill. Pete has a "fix" on his chest area, psychological and not organic in origin. The psychological basis of his hypochondriasis is his resistance to restraining people. Pete is a soft and tender person.

To restrain violent people goes very much against his personality. The kind of work he prefers involves nurturing and supporting people; in fact, his favorite part of nursing is postoperative care, when the patient is helpless and needs attention and comfort. It was therefore extremely difficult for Pete to be punitive toward his patients. Chest pains became his vehicle for saying he would not and could not be a policeman.

The Target and the Harasser

The target in a harassment situation at work usually sees himself as a hard worker who has been wronged by the group, by the system, or by bad luck. The target sometimes sees his harasser as compulsive, bullying, bigoted, although despite these characterizations, the harasser may be at the same time a secretly wished-for friend. An instructive method of studying the relationship between target and harasser is to put their relationship on a sliding scale of increasing emotion.

We begin with the ambivalent love-hate relationship, in which the forces of attraction plus anger and repulsion are at work. While the target is attracted to the harasser, he is also angry with him for being cruel and rejecting. Although the target has the opportunity to avoid his counterpart, he arranges things so as to establish contact with him. The target quietly reproaches his harasser. Then he confronts him directly for his cruelty, and the cycle of rejection and demand begins anew. The harassee may regard his tormentor with clear anger. Although the target does not, for example, reject the harasser on grounds of race or sex, he does reject him because of his values, because the harasser mistreats other human beings, or because he has become part of a system that has dehumanized the target. Sheer hatred toward the harasser may be felt. The target sees the harasser as a type, the white man who has always persecuted the black man, or, conversely, the black man whose only purpose is to seek revenge against the white oppressor.

Although we have not in most instances examined the alleged harasser, we have a considerable body of data revealing his opinions of the harassee. Our sources are varied and might be said to be "biased" views of the employer, but bias is as irrelevant on this side of the problem as it is on the harassee's side. Although we must assume that there was bias in each witness's or participant's report, nevertheless, there was enough in common among the descriptions so that a picture of the accused was etched. In some instances, there were several persons who accused one superior of being a harasser. We had no evidence there had been collusion among them; this person was well known to all the citizens in the work community. We are not concerned with the validity of the views but with what they tell us.

Many case records included interviews with the claimant's associates: the alleged harasser himself, the claimant's previous employers, his present and previous coworkers, and his neighbors, and some of the interviews were tape recorded. We also referred to the testimony these people had given at previous administrative or court hearings. In the case of a police officer, we have descriptions from his chief, from several sergeants under whom he worked over a period of fifteen years, and from numerous coworkers. In selected cases we conversed directly with the parties involved. On one occasion, when an employee claimed harassment on a racial basis, we talked with the general manager of the plant and with the claimant's direct supervisor. The general manager granted that the accused harasser was indeed a racial bigot; on the other hand, he also described qualities of the claimant showing how he created and exploited opportunities to interact with the bigot.

Based on data from these sources, we know what some alleged harassers think about some harassees. This material is not exhaustive, but it is instructive. The predominant comment is that the harasser does not understand the claimant or why he could be making such an irrational allegation.

The harasser is not the mischievious little boy who really knows that he did wrong and then says, "How can you accuse me?" Instead, he really does not understand what has happened. Another common view of harassers is that while there was some provocation which the harasser understands, such as teasing, job change, or pressure, he certainly does not believe it sufficient to explain the claimant's profound reaction. Many other people in the same situation, he says, have experienced the same treatment and did not react that way. Or, he believes the claimant is overly sensitive and cites numerous examples of the claimant's overreaction to relatively minor slights that other people would not even notice. Another group of accused harassers sees the claimant as paranoid, pure and simple, a person who constantly searches for and finds persecution. Frequently, the harasser thinks the claimant is a "goof off" and an opportunist. The harasser sees the claim as a way to dodge work. As evidence, he cites a bad work record, repeated criticism for low-level performance, and opinions of coworkers that the claimant shirks his responsibilities. On rare occasions, the harasser's analysis was that the claimant was a troublemaker who could not be integrated or with whom no negotiation was possible.

Characteristics of the Harasser

We can learn about the characteristics of the harasser from the same sources that indicate his view of the harassee, from the individual himself, his coworkers, his superiors, and his subordinates. Most accused harassers do not see themselves as such, nor are they seen this way by their nonharassed coworkers, who most frequently maintain that the so-called harasser is simply doing his job. He is demanding compliance with the rules of an organization, he is trying to maintain production standards, he is attempting to ensure the safety of members of his organization. Rarely does anyone but the claimant criticize him. Rarely is there any evidence of harassment aside from the claimant's allegations.

In a number of cases, however, the accused harasser does project a far less complimentary image. People describe him as a bigot because of his frank, overt expressions of bias. He believes in his own right of free speech, even if this includes discomforting a subordinate or a coworker. He believes that blacks or Jews or women should have to prove themselves if they want positions equivalent to those given to majority group members. Left to his own devices, he would be sure that no one of "undesirable" origin or gender would reach managerial or even highly paid craft positions. He may not even be aware that he appears as a bigot, assuming as he does that his point of view is correct. Another type of harasser is motivated by a need to demonstrate power. Like the bully who believes that unless he knocks down at least one person a day the others will no longer fear him, this harasser reassures himself of his power by intimidating someone else [147]. While he fools some of the people some of the time, others see his insecurity and realize that he hates to be crossed and will react violently when contradicted in any way. He seems able to function only so long as those around him agree with him.

Numerous authors have studied aggression as it relates to humor. As indicated previously, harassment is often cloaked as humor. People who attack and punish others by means of humor achieve a token gratification [96]. They hurt and master others by means of humor because more direct expression of aggression is not available. Some people have an "affective set" or a predisposition to act aggressively [115]. Their enjoyment of disparaging humor indicates a repressed need for destruction; it reflects their underlying aggressiveness, egocentricity, and derogatory world view.

The "maladjusted male," as defined by self-ideal discrepancy scores has been found to enjoy hostile wit under nonstressful conditions [122]. This is the man who represses hostility, but manages to express it by displacing it into the form of hostile wit. Hostile wit is predominantly a male reaction. The sadistic personality whose self-respect seems to stem from the provocation of fear in others uses potential insult, derogation, or punishment that can be successful in provoking guilt [92]. The sadist and the masochist may exist symbiotically because hostile, punitive people often seek out rebellious and distrustful counterparts, and some establish durable relationships. Our population contained several such examples.

The harasser himself usually is subservient to authority [2]. He dares not cross anyone above him and cannot tolerate opposition from those below him. He believes firmly that rank has privilege. One of the "privileges" he enjoys is picking on his underlings. Consistent with this, he maintains that those who have not yet earned the right to peck should accept being pecked. He thinks of himself as a benevolent person and he often is paternalistic. He would describe himself as being firm, but just, as a person who knows how to dish it

out and how to take it. That description is apt because he does take whatever
his superiors hand out, and he also transmits it to his subordinates. He is not
the kind of person who has good peer relationships. His closest relationship is
probably with his wife, by whom he frequently seems henpecked. It is the
kind of benign henpecking that he smiles at, but it is not simple indulgence
that makes him tolerate it. It is as if he recognizes this as a control system, as
the same kind of dominance with love that he believes he bestows on others.
His children see him as either a doting or an oppressive father, often one child
seeing him as oppressive and another as benign and giving, which is exactly
how his employees would categorize him. He sees himself as being a simple person and is not aware of conflict. He would describe himself as being very clear
about his values and his beliefs, what is right for him to do, and what is right
for others to do.

He cannot understand complexity in others. He cannot understand why
all people are not like him and why all the people with whom he interacts are
not like each other. Complexity and diversity frighten him, so he rejects them.
He has a testing procedure by which he determines whether "a man is a man"
or not, although others might not agree with his criteria. For a man to be a
man, he must be able to take it from his superiors and he must not sympathize
with those who cannot take it from superiors. Once he is convinced that a
man can take it, the harasser-type adopts him, protects him, and promotes him.
Characteristically, he is not indecisive about the quality of human virtue; if
someone disappoints or crosses him, he gets rid of him. He cannot tolerate the
sense of helplessness that comes with finding that he cannot get rid of the person whom he had judged wanting.

Teasing may be projection and may serve as a release from feelings of inadequacy [131]. Projecting one's own deficiencies onto one's rivals exposes
them as ridiculous and thus discharges one's own aggression. Having thereby
denied his fears, the harasser can utilize his feelings of inadequacy for aggressive
purposes, for the destruction of his rivals. The success of the intimidation serves
as reassurance that his original fears were unnecessary. At the same time, his
exhibitionistic impulses are gratified.

One case history in the literature describes a man who became a scapegoater
out of his need for a displacement activity and for sublimation of an unconscious conflict [17]. The subject needed appreciation and identification with
the "underdog." He scapegoated his real reasons for quitting his own job (desire to take a better paying position in another city) onto a coworker ("I can't
work with him"), in order to avoid his real conflict with his wife (who did not
want to move). The subject's guilt feelings, stemming from his relationship with
his wife, may have reinforced both his prejudice against his coworker and his
ability to scapegoat onto him.

A curious feature of the harasser's parallel insecurity and assertion of dominance is the apparent need to be part of a group, any group, so he can join with

a few similarly situated persons to keep others out. The notion of this vague and negative group becomes important only when a new person appears. The newcomer must be tested before he can be admitted to the group or, better yet, he must be excluded in order to reaffirm the existence of the group.

Harassers, as we have seen, share many qualities with their victims. Their behavior and self-images cover the same range. Most often, the harasser has no insight into what he is or what he does. He thinks his behavior is natural and acceptable and is surprised and hurt when criticized. Some accused harassers know perfectly well what they were doing. They know not only that they were causing pain, but also that if they caused sufficient pain, they might damage or destroy the victim. Unfortunately, we could not learn enough about other areas of their lives to assess whether they had generally sadistic personalities, or whether the harassment was a specific reaction to the individual victim. But after studying harassers and studying their victims, it seemed that there was never a victim who would not have made an excellent harasser.

"It's Not the People; It's the System"

Fear is certainly not the only component of a system that leaves people feeling harassed: John came from a large eastern city, the youngest of five children of a Protestant minister. He was black. After an average high school career, John served in the Army in Korea, and upon discharge moved to California, where he worked as a mechanic in a large industry. After six years at the plant, he began to experience what he called harassment by plant management concerning his job performance and his attendance. He claimed to have documentation of his good record and believed that the claimed inadequacies were false. On one occasion his supervisor berated him, saying that he had no mechanical aptitude and should resign. When John refused, his supervisor threatened to fire him. Another time, when John asked a foreman where a particular tool could be found, the foreman pointed to a row of eight cabinets, smiled, and said that it would be found in one of those. The supervisors would take notes on his performance as he worked and made a habit of literally "overseeing" his work from a balcony.

Over a period of two years John made repeated requests to the proper authorities that his complaints be investigated. All the while, he became more nervous and exhausted. He began to hate the very thought of going to work. Although he got up earlier and earlier, he invariably would be delayed and would have to race to work at eighty miles-an-hour. By the time he arrived, he was even less eager to confront his supervisor's daily unpleasantries. Finally, while awaiting the results of a hearing on the attendance issue, he decided that whatever the outcome, no job was worth being so upset. He left the organization, rested and looked for work, having decided that he would live on a minimum budget, if necessary, in order to work in a pleasant atmosphere.

John stated explicitly that he was not harassed because of his race. His fellow workers all were accorded the same treatment. The system was designed to harass the employees, he said, so they would fear losing their jobs and hence be more submissive to the foreman's demands. He did not want a job in another department of the same organization because the system of harassment permeated it. Built-in tensions were too much for John's personality, and he resolved the problem by leaving the job. While he acknowledged that because of his temperament he might have reacted more acutely than other people, he added that many others felt just as he did. Some even suffered severe physical problems as a result of harassment, but they were unable to leave work because of family and financial obligations.

In another case, a former participant in the harassment system became his own victim. Dan had been a claims adjuster with an insurance company for seven years. Then, he suffered what he thought was a heart attack. He was hospitalized, and after several weeks returned to work. Continuing to experience anxiety, he saw a psychiatrist. His on-the-job conflict with company policies and personnel became so intense that he quit his job and for three years worked only intermittently for various other companies, visiting the psychiatrist weekly. His biggest problem was with the company. He felt that he was treated unjustly while employed as a claims adjuster; the handling of his own compensation claim following his departure was equally unfair. By nature a self-styled "compulsive fighter," he was always in one disagreement or another. He was threatened by the company's aggressive stance in the face of his claim and became angry every time he thought about his case. The relationship with the   rance company became a profound symbolic conflict. Dan recognized this, but could not change it. He viewed the company as a nemesis out to degrade and defeat him. He was intent on "beating the company," and in response, the company scrutinized every aspect of his claim with great care. Neither party was likely to alter its position, under these circumstances, and each continued to be a thorn in the side of the other. The harassment process thus become cyclical and cumulative.

7 Dealing with Harassment at Work

Recognizing and Preventing Harassment

Harassment cannot be eliminated but it can be reduced in frequency, intensity, and duration. This can be done by establishing in the work place a culture that exposes, discourages, and censures harassment. Intervention, either by government or by an employer, should have the effect of attenuating the harassment process and limiting whatever social support it has.

The increasing number of worker's compensation claims made for psychological injury due to harassment indicates that workers will no longer sit by quietly and permit themselves to be victimized. Some will leave the job and find other work, some will stay and rail at the injustice of the system or at their own weaknesses and inadequacy, but many will make claims and those will be costly not only, as we have seen earlier, to the worker himself but also to the employer and to the public.

Harassment creates social problems, including unemployment, alcoholism, and excessive drug use, upon which family disruption, psychosomatic illnesses, and mental illnesses may follow. The families of harassed workers, especially their children, come to see the work system as a hostile one. They see work as unrewarding and the workplace as a place where one might be physically and psychologically damaged. They see the person who avoids work as in some way more intelligent, better off, sharper. They become determined not to be caught in the traps they see their parents caught in. Sometimes this works to their advantage, because it motivates them to seek more education and training. However, some of these youngsters become disenchanted with the society in which they live and skeptical of the justice of the system; some may even turn to crime to avoid their parents' fate.

The harassed employee tends to take more sick leave and become accident prone. He drinks more. Absenteeism rises among this group. Work attitudes become increasingly negative. As one worker said, in reference to the equipment with which he worked, "I've come to feel if you can't screw it up, steal it; if you can't steal it, smash it." The employer and society pay a high price for both the loss of productivity and the damage that is done to their equipment, either deliberately or through lack of care.

To reduce the incidence of harassment, all supervisory personnel should be trained, if only minimally, to listen to those working under them. All supervisory personnel should be urged, encouraged, and, if necessary, pressured, to treat their employees as human beings. This does not mean that they must coddle their employees. They can still make whatever demands are necessary for production. But foremen must be taught to recognize harassment among workers and to intervene in a manner that does not mark the victim for further attacks but helps both the aggressor and the victim see what is going on. The foreman needs to know how to listen to a worker in order to learn what is troubling him. The same might be said of spouses and parents who harass, but there is more hope for foremen; they are less involved and have less invested than parents and spouses, and therefore can more easily learn to listen. The process of learning to listen is the same for supervisory personnel and workers as it is for students of nursing, medicine, and law. Texts, demonstrations, and experiences in which they can observe themselves talking to people on video tape are all helpful aids to improving their techniques.

Supervisors and those who work in personnel must learn to tell the difference between a reaction that is situational, that is, resulting from the preceding events, and one that demonstrates a profound disturbance of personality. The first problem might be dealt with by the supervisor; the second is more serious and would require professional help, if only because anyone involved with the disturbed person might have difficulty in helping him.

Because coworkers are also a source of harassment, educational programs are needed to inform even unsophisticated workers about the elements of job satisfaction and job misery. Workers should be shown that support of their fellow workers, kindness to them, understanding of them, and cooperation with them is not softness or weakness but is both humane and sensible—that they themselves benefit, because a work environment that is pleasant for others will be pleasant for themselves.

Educational programs, by the usual public techniques such as advertising in newspapers or on radio and television or by posters, can inform the public and the consumer about the importance of being friendly or at least civil to the person who serves him. Courtesy can be made a positive value. The consumer can be informed and reminded that the courtesy he gives will make the person serving him more caring.

Management must be made aware that some individuals and groups are more susceptible to harassment than others [134]. The employer must facilitate the integration of minority groups and women into positions in which they were not formerly accepted. The entire working force must realize that what is not harassment or teasing for a member of the in-group may be just that for a nonmember.

Management should periodically consider the question of worker morale, a part of which depends on the state of the relationship among workers and between management and workers. Although the purpose of the organization is not to perform a therapeutic function for its workers, but to serve as the site of some kind of production, both workers and management can, without impinging on the production process, learn to behave in a way that will reduce the pressure on individual workers and make the time they spend at work happier and probably more productive. In the same way that safety engineers check for physical hazards of overhangs or unscreened machinery, management should check for social and psychological hazards.

Although both management and organized labor tend to be apprehensive about groups forming at the site of work and functioning in an organized way, such groups working on safety matters, both psychological and physical safety, could do a great deal to reduce both kinds of hazard. Feedback concepts, special councils, and cracker-barrel meetings would be useful for this purpose [45].

Each organization will, of course, have to devise its own structures and mechanisms to fit the personalities and needs of the participants; however, the functions of the group will generally be the same. The purpose will be to help those involved in harassment to change the nature of the interaction to something less destructive. When they see a harassment situation developing, individuals within an organized group can intervene to abort it. This kind of group can serve to make its members more aware of each other's humanity. It might bring them closer together and as a result make for increased group cooperation, both at work and elsewhere. It could help those workers who cannot fit into the organization to leave. The group could suggest individual help for the troubled worker. Disturbed workers and families could be referred to therapists, to clarify problems, to defuse problems, and to study solutions. Such groups could have professional consultants to help them structure their recommendations.

Grievance procedures should be established through which the harassed worker could apprise his superiors and coworkers of harassment. A large number of grievances relate to specific individuals and these grievances have to be aired; mild disagreement or tension should be enough to invoke the grievance mechanism [9]. If the requirements for a grievance are too rigorous and the worker feels that "little" grievances will not be considered, eventually the little problems will grow into big problems and will reach a point where it is impossible to discover their origins and causes, and the worker and those around him will have become so angry that compromise and resolution will be impossible. If early expression of feelings is allowed, such crises can be avoided. "Beefing" and catharsis serve the function of reducing the internal pressure [4]. As pressure is dissipated, the number and intensity of problems decrease.

One of the reasons harassment flourishes among workers is that they have few common bonds other than sharing contiguous space for eight hours a day. Both labor and management should work to increase the social interaction among workers. Stronger bonds outside of work, relationships among families, and membership in an athletic or social group tend to decrease the likelihood of destructive harassment. Workers should be encouraged to establish a rapport outside of work that can reduce friction on the job. Such social bonds might serve to channel the energies of even the hostile individual into a friendlier relationship.

Supervisors and managers must become aware of their responsibility to treat their workers as individuals, to be flexible under stress, and to make work as gratifying as possible for their employees [32]. Once harassment is brought to the attention of supervisors and workers, all parties must be helped to cooperate to prevent occurrences. All levels of management must watch for increases in harassment. Complaints should be dealt with immediately.

Ultimately, everyone bears some responsibility for harassment. Employers and supervisors must learn that harassment and work pressure are not an effective way to control employees and maintain productivity. There are rewards that are far more effective—money, recognition, the opportunity to participate in one's work planning.

Psychological Health-and-Safety Engineers[a]

Study after study has indicated that industrial accidents occur with greater frequency among those who are unhappy in their work. Delayed recovery occurs more frequently among those who do not want to go back to their jobs or among those who are angry because of the way they were treated after they claimed to have been injured. Psychological health-and-safety engineers must be trained to examine the work environment for psychological hazards. Included in a list of such hazards would be depressed workers who are unlikely to protect themselves properly, who might be unable to cooperate with other workers in their tasks and in that way create tension for those who depend on them, and whose very presence makes others uneasy because they do not know the cause of the behavior and reactions of the depressed person. The hazards list would also include the counterphobic person who has decided unconsciously that it is unlikely that he will be injured or that anyone else will be injured as a result of his actions.

From the viewpoint of harassment, two types of person should be identified; the first is the one who cannot tolerate quiet and tranquility, but who must keep his environment turbulent: the one who will "horse around," plan practical jokes, tease and, if he finds an appropriate victim, harass that person. It is equally necessary to identify the person who will be the victim. This person is especially sensitive to seemingly benign comments and as a result is a menace to himself and to those who work around him. He needs help; he is as dangerous as an unscreened machine.

The psychological health-and-safety engineer needs techniques for identifying

---

[a]The California Workman's Compensation Institute made a study of attitudes underlying litigated claims for benefits, which was presented in a Report to the Industry in 1975. The findings of this study are referred to in this chapter with the citation CWCI.

the highly pressured work situation and the highly pressured worker. In most instances the two will be found together. Both supervisors and employees recognize this configuration. However, some individuals are especially susceptible to work pressure. For example, some compulsive individuals need to plan ahead and to achieve perfection; they cannot accelerate in the face of a new demand. They have to do things at the same rate and in the same way they have always done them. They cannot adapt to new demands or to special demands for acceleration. In a sense, they are always working at full capacity. Such persons experience as pressure any change in the quantity of work presented to them or in the work environment itself. Some refuse to change and, although they resent the pressure, they do not feel guilty about being unable to meet the demand for increased performance. Others are placed in conflict by the new workload and become profoundly upset, directing their anger against their employers and coworkers in the form of suspicion and hostility.

Some workers can perform at a very high level both qualitatively and quantitatively as long as they like their bosses and feel appreciated in return. Given a new supervisor or a new administration, however, they might react angrily to exactly the same kinds of demands that were made on them by the previous administration, finding fault, becoming uncooperative or developing somatic illnesses, so that a minor physical event such as a twist of the body will be enough to cripple them.

In a review of well over a thousand cases of delayed recovery from industrial accident, we found many distinctly different types of reaction to work pressure and to harassment. The psychological health-and-safety engineer cannot eliminate all psychological hazards any more than a safety engineer can eliminate all physical hazards. Realistically, he can reduce the number of such hazards by attending to them as he discovers them in the work environment and by helping those who are especially susceptible to these hazards to find a place for themselves that has a lower probability of being psychologically noxious.

Understanding Delayed Recovery

Most illnesses and most trauma have a certain predictable course. When a patient does not recover within the expected range of time, the physician will look for the cause of the delay. The patient's biological profile, psychological profile, and ultimately social situation will be reexamined in the search for an explanation for the failure to follow the predicted course. Some of the patients in this sample were referred to us because the degree of trauma did not seem to explain the extent and duration of the disability.

Why did such work-related trauma produce delayed recovery? After all, such occurrences are not unique to work settings. An argument between friends or spouses can be traumatic too, as can criticism from one's parent or child. Ordinarily, we do not expect such effects to persist for months and years. How does one explain the apparently excessive duration of symptoms in such cases?

Workers who find routine tasks burdensome and challenging tasks impossible might well believe their environment to be hostile. More commonly, workers experience stress because of interpersonal conflicts. On-the-job uncertainties can exacerbate normal stress into distress, producing pathological manifestations [65,140]. Pressures in the workaday world have been thought to provide a plausible explanation for even the most severe symptoms [6,82,95,106]. Unquestionably, stress produces unpleasant subjective discomfort as well as objective change, especially behavioral modification. Why do some persons react to stress with a prolonged illness—either psychological or physical—with delayed recovery extending far beyond what would be predicted, while others either continue to work or react with a briefer period of illness?

Those whose recovery is delayed have been considered highly suggestible [12], often grasping one sentence from the doctor, whether accurate or not, often out of context, and using it to frame their views of their illness. A doctor's casual, "That's a bad one," or "You could have been killed," or "You're in bad shape," serves as permission to take an extraordinarily long time to recover because their case is so serious. Delayed recovery results from the inadequacy of the personality prior to the accident, the desire for compensation, the influence of suggestion that may come from a doctor, a nurse, or a boss, and the reinforcement of the suggestion by legal advisers and medical experts [114]. Well before the trauma, many were depressed, had shown signs of slower motor functions, and had experienced changing of endocrine activity. Some authors have claimed that delayed recovery always creates a suspicion that the patient has discovered some neurotic satisfaction with illness [59]. Numerous writers have considered secondary gain a most important factor in delaying recovery [46,102,103]. Significant secondary gains are money and what money may symbolize, that is, righting of a wrong, or even an unconscious gift of love, security, or friendship. Revenge, too, has been seen as an element of secondary gain [59]. Seeking secondary gain, the patient loses self-esteem and then finds it all the more necessary to justify the pursuit of secondary gain through illness.

The complex process of secondary gain represents a judgment by the observer. The disabled person who works hard at painful physical therapy is assumed to do so because he or she wants the benefits of health. The patient who lies motionless in bed, not eager to engage in a painful rehabilitative process, often is judged to be seeking the benefits of illness. We assume that secondary gain is an unconscious process, that the patient is not aware of this motive. Secondary gain is thus different from malingering, the almost-conscious plot to defraud.

Many workers who experience delayed recovery are in fact seeking restitution for a previous physical injury or psychological hurt. In many cases, the worker had had a previous injury for which he was not compensated or for which he was compensated so little that he felt he had been cheated. He saw himself as having "lost out" on just compensation, largely because he was inexperienced. At the time, he did not know exactly how to assert his rights. He may have feared loss of his job if he stayed off work to recuperate. Initially, the worker had some sense of loyalty to the employer and believed that loyalty to be reciprocal. However, during a first illness he discovered that he was a valued employee only so long as he was a healthy employee, so he would go back to work, sometimes before he was ready. During the months and years that followed this experience, he came to see himself as having been cheated. By the time a second trauma occurred—physical or psychological—he had become quite prepared to fight, and fought those who did him wrong the first time—the employer and, often, the insurance carrier.

The urge for retirement, in the broadest sense of the term, is a strong force in delaying recovery [23]. Disability becomes a channel that leads to an early retirement. Provision has been made for early retirement in certain occupations, such as for police and airline pilots, fields that require physical strength, agility, alertness, and quick reflexes. However, there is generally no such possibility open to the laborer, for example, whose work consists of moving heavy objects from one area to another. For this kind of worker, there is no institutional provision for respite, and age and fatigue become motivations for "early" retirement through a delayed recovery from injury or illness.

Many a worker still has dreams of changing occupations—of starting a business, of converting a hobby into a part-time or full-time occupation. Lacking capital, he has no way to start such a new enterprise. When an on-the-job injury occurs in the form of physical or mental trauma, the worker may come to see this as a natural point for transition to the dreamed-of occupation. He may fantasize a large cash settlement that could facilitate his transition into the new field. When this sum of money does not materialize, he may grow bitter and feel increasing anger, as he thinks of his suffering and his thwarted aspirations on the one hand and the pittance offered as compensation on the other.

Therapeutic Considerations

The purpose of workers' compensation laws and of the agencies established to implement those laws is to help the injured person recover and regain as much of his function as he can, as quickly as he can, so that he will return to work or, if that is not possible, at least he will live as comfortably as possible. The workers' compensation system is, therefore, a part of the therapy. Every person involved in the workers' compensation system has a potential for being a therapeutic or antitherapeutic agent [CWCI].

Underlying Assumptions

Certain premises must underlie any therapeutic approach. First, when treating a patient who claims he is harassed or the victim of work pressure, one must always assume that the patient is honest, that he believes the story he is telling is the truth, and that he is claiming disability in good faith. Granted that his story is told from his subjective viewpoint and possibly with conscious and unconscious notions of gaining some advantage as a result of the traumatic event, still, one cannot proceed if one sees the patient as one's adversary.

The patient may be naive, and his concept of what is wrong with him may be very different from the physician's concept. He might have a notion of physiology based on "common sense" rather than actual knowledge; his idea of where nerves go and what they do might boggle the mind of the sophisticated therapeutic helper. Nevertheless, one must start with the notion that he is telling the truth as he sees it, and one must respect his concept of what happened to him, of how it affected him, and of how it produced changes in him. One must not, however, set up a therapeutic regimen based on the patient's ignorance or misconceptions.

The second underlying assumption is that the patient's goal is to return to work. He might not want to go back to the same job; he might want compensation and rest now; but most of the people with whom we dealt in this group of harassed workers did not want to spend the rest of their days sitting around doing nothing. Most of them had an idea that they would return to work some day.

These premises suggest that the psychotherapeutic process should begin early. Many professionals in the field of workers' compensation and compensation medicine fear the initiation of the psychotherapeutic process, because they believe it will prolong the illness, that it will reinforce the patient's notion of his injury and his impairment and encourage disability. Their concepts of what takes place in psychotherapy are based on the same kind of ignorance that often structures the patient's notion of the mechanisms of his illness. Most professionals in the compensation field have never participated in the psychotherapeutic process; their ideas of what it is like and what occurs in that process come from caricatures or from the unusual, dramatically positive or dramatically negative result. Presuming that the patient's only goal or objective is to bilk the compensating agency and ultimately his employer, or to retire early, these professionals are pessimistic about any intervention that aims at restoring the patient's ability to work. They apparently believe that psychotherapy merely prolongs disability, that the patient will use psychotherapy as an excuse for not working, and that as long as he is getting free psychotherapy (paid for by the insurance company), he will continue with it forever.

This has not been the experience of the author. It is his belief that if there is a problem, it should be treated immediately; if there is no problem, it will not need to be treated after the patient returns to work. Many of the patients in this population who would be rated by most therapists as unlikely candidates for psychotherapy improve remarkably with exactly the same psychotherapeutic approaches as do their richer, more educated counterparts. If helped early enough, they do not leave their original place of work, but instead study their work problems and return with a different attitude and approach to their coworkers and employers. For some, of course, the harassment situation, the industrial claim, and the litigation surrounding it make a return to work impossible, if only because the system is such that it cannot reintegrate the worker once he has left.

In all the cases treated, we observed a remarkable reduction during the course of treatment in somatic symptoms, drug usage, and visits to other physicians. In no instance did we find an abuse of the psychotherapeutic relationship or the free care. The problem with most of these patients lay in convincing them that they were not imposing, that it did make sense for them to come, and that they should maintain a given frequency of visits, even if they were not sure what they were going to be talking about when they came to see the therapist.

Recognition of the Problem

In dealing with harassment patients, a physician must first take the time to make a proper diagnosis. One must recognize that one is dealing with a problem of harassment and not solely with a physiological problem. For example, there is a difference between the patient who comes to a physician complaining of stomach pains as a result of work pressure and the patient who comes complaining of stomach pains as a result of harassment. The patient who feels pressured and overloaded by work might well be in a crisis that will respond to reassurance about his symptoms and medication that will modify his anxiety. The patient who feels he is being harassed will not respond in this way, but will be angry and resentful and trapped, and will spend his time ruminating about the wrongs that are being done him. He will not respond to an approach that does not explore and deal with this problem. Thus, the person examining or investigating the patient's physical or mental problem or his claim must permit and encourage the patient's expression of dissatisfaction with his work.

Physicians traditionally have shortened and simplified the complete diagnostic process because it is enormously expensive and, if utilized in all cases, would push the already high cost of medical care beyond reach for almost everyone. The physician operates on the basis of probabilities, selecting the treatment that seems to have the highest probability of matching the cause. Selecting a treatment for the symptoms, even if he does not know their cause, assumes that this treatment represents a therapeutic test. If the symptoms go away, the treatment and the symptoms must have been related. Physicians are not so naive that they ignore the curative effect of time and the natural healing forces that exist in a human being. This kind of treatment works in a very high percentage of cases, but in

the small percentage in which it does not work, the outcome can be
tragic.

For a patient who has a work-related problem, treatment with tranquilizers,
pain medication, or other kinds of physical intervention dealing with the somatic
manifestations of a social or psychological conflict misses the point of the
symptoms. The doctor who treats the patient's problems as solely physiological
only aggravates the symptoms. As the patient becomes more and more frustrated,
he will develop more and more symptoms. The physician resorts to further physical
interventions and soon, in a relatively high percentage of the cases, he will have
created an iatrogenic disease. In work problems, as in other social and psychological problems, when the physician focuses on communication between himself
and the patient that is medical and biological, he ignores what he should be
treating.

The Physician's Role

Physicians often are reluctant to become involved in the complex of problems
revolving about harassment or work pressure, even when they sense that there is
a work-related psychological problem. Physicians are action-oriented and solution-
oriented. They see the world of work as one over which they have no control.
They can influence the patient's diet, exercise program, or activity-rest ratio but
not his work situation. As one physician said in his report, "In order to get this
man back to work, we would have to change United Airlines."

Although physicians as a result of their education and through their exposure
to numerous publications are fully aware of the function that emotions play in
producing illness and in delaying recovery, they also recognize that the exploration
of the patient's total situation is very time-consuming, and both medical economics
and the rhythms of their own practices cause them to focus on the immediate
problem the patient presents to them and to limit their treatment to this
problem [26].

Although there are no accurate statistics on the effectiveness of this approach,
it probably works reasonably well in most cases. It does not work well in cases
where the patient comes with physical problems that are the result of longstanding,
continuing emotional or social irritants. Therefore, the physician who focuses on
the medical rather than on the social and psychological aspects of harassment
cases ignores what he should be treating and treats manifestations, not causes.

Initial Contacts

There is ample evidence to indicate that the initial contact with the claims system
professional and with physicians is significant and often determines whether the

claimant is going to engage in a costly, time-consuming process of litigation or is going to trust the people who are treating him and participate in the treatment process they design. The author makes no virtue of passivity in the applicant or in the patient. However, an examination of many cases where the patient doctor-shopped, makes it clear that patients did so largely because their initial experience with a physician left them dissatisfied and distrustful of the physician's intentions, concern, or skill.

Empirical data demonstrate the determinative nature of the initial contact with the claims system professional or with a physician. This initial contact affects the claimant's decision as to whether or not to litigate. Litigants who selected their own physician gave a higher rating to the quality of medical treatment they received and also constituted a small proportion of the litigated sample. Litigants in workers' compensation cases (not necessarily limited to harassment or work-pressure cases) indicated that they would have changed their doctors if they had known they could, primarily because they felt that treatment was inadequate or that the physician had an indifferent or biased attitude. Positive attitudes were based on the same factors [CWCI].

In the course of our examinations of harassment and work-pressure patients, we inquired about medical treatment and often, even before we inquired, patients told about their medical treatment and their satisfaction and dissatisfaction with it. In talking about their contacts with the compensation system generally, those who were dissatisfied complained either that no one listened to them or heard them out fully, or that those who listened were skeptical of the validity of the facts they presented and of the symptoms of which they complained. They felt the person to whom they were talking was not fair or sympathetic. They described how the professional gave them advice that was impossible to follow, and they complained of being rushed.

Fully a quarter of the sample of patients in both the harassment and the work-pressure groups and among other patients complained about their treatment by their physicians or by agents of the compensation system generally.

There is a lesson in this. The professional, whether physician or claims adjuster, should not move in too quickly to try to solve the patient's problem. First, he should listen and listen sympathetically. Sympathetic listening does not require agreeing that the patient's complaints are valid or related to his work but requires keeping an open mind and hearing all of what the patient is trying to say. The professional must have some sense of timing about listening. Obviously, he cannot listen for hours and hours. He must learn to recognize that magic moment when the patient feels that he has communicated his problem, his fear, and his anger, and is now ready to listen to and consider advice. It is all-important that the professional permit the patient to express his anger, to register his complaints, and to explain his symptoms. He cannot help the patient until that has been done.

After the patient has ventilated his feelings, the professional can start by

stating his position to the patient. He can explain that he is not partisan, that he
is there to learn all about the patient's situation, and that he will try to understand
all aspects of the patient's problem. In that way, the professional can explore
not only how the job might have affected the patient but how the patient might
have affected the job. He can learn about and help the patient learn about work
behavior that might provoke harassment, talking about this only after the patient
is convinced that the professional is not an apologist for the system, but is there
to help the patient.

For this reason the professional must be very careful about any advice he
gives during the initial contact. His advice should be conservative, cautious, and
possible for the patient to follow. Advice should be couched in terms of action,
not in terms of feeling. The professional should never say to the patient, "You
shouldn't feel that way." The patient cannot help how he feels. He can advise
the patient on how he might proceed from that point on.

How to Approach the Patient

The physician approaching this kind of patient must understand all the details of
the case. For example, it is very easy to come to the conclusion that a patient is
merely acting out, is concerned with secondary gain, and is not in need of medical
care. Although it might indeed be true that a portion of the patient's problem
represents behavior designed to discomfort the employer or other supervisors, it
might also be true that a larger part represents a true physical manifestation
resulting from the work conflict.

When the patient complains of being harassed, whoever is listening to him
should immediately accept the fact that it is going to take longer to deal with
this patient than with one who comes in with a simple physical symptom. The
same is true with the patient who complains of work pressure. Although the
physician or the claims adjuster might at that moment feel that he, too, is
harassed and under tremendous pressure, that the whole world is under tremendous
pressure, he should not respond by indicating to the patient that his condition is
not unusual. Workers have a very clear sense of how much is an acceptable burden
of pressure, and each worker has gone through ranges of pressure, of mild to
moderate harassment, and knows what the tolerable limits are for him. He knows
that in this instance the pressure or harassment has exceeded those limits.

If the person who has made the initial contact with the worker does not
have the time to do so immediately, he should set aside time for the worker to
explain his problem fully. Not only must the worker be permitted to explain in
great detail all that happened to him on his job, but he must be helped to explain
it. From time to time, the harassed or pressured worker will interrupt himself in
the middle of a sentence or the middle of a thought and say "What's the use." At
that moment, he might feel that no one can understand or that he cannot explain;

he needs the help of a professional to carry him over that critical obstacle so that he can continue.

The physician and all others who are trying to help the patient must determine what emotional reactions actually exist. Frequently, one sees reactions that are intense but temporary: violent anger, painful insomnia, debilitating anorexia, massive depression, sudden impotence, and severe frustration. Although the patient may report that he "thinks a lot" about what happened to him on his job or what is happening to him on his job, unless the physician asks a question like "How much of the time do you actually think about it?" he will miss the fact that in many instances the patient thinks of nothing else. He ruminates about it, going over and over the same hurt, the same incident, the same fear.

Some patients go through a crisis of work pressure or harassment with nothing but the psychological symptoms. They will deny any physical discomfort except the concomitants of rage and depression. They themselves are aware that their symptoms are entirely psychological, and they assume that sexual dysfunction, loss of appetite, and insomnia all are the result of the disruption of their psychological balance. Others use somatic language, complaining of pain and dysfunction. Some patients complain only of simple disability. Their statement is, "I can't work." At times the physician or claims adjuster finds it difficult to understand or to believe the statement, because it is not supported with other symptoms or other experiences. The patient does not explain why he cannot work. In reports, these patients are deemed to have "functional" or "emotional" overlay or to be malingering. The patient's somatic language must be attended to as carefully as is his psychological language. Patients who complain of physical symptoms tend to believe they have them. If one examines a large number of patients, one will note they might have very different emotional reactions to their physical symptoms, some being very concerned and others relatively unconcerned. But the person to whom they are relating or describing their symptoms must take each of those symptoms seriously, because there might indeed be an anatomical or other physical basis for them, and the patient will not be satisfied until he is certain that the helping person has heard about that symptom and has heard enough about it to know whether it is serious.

When emotional factors are involved, when one has a sense there is a "functional" or an "emotional" overlay, it is important not to overstate or to describe in frightening or ominous terms the severity of the disease process. The concerned patient already believes that he might have injured himself irreversibly. If the physician, in an effort to be agreeable or to frighten the patient into a medical regimen, agrees with the patient's appraisal that he might be in very bad shape, then the groundwork is laid for a long-term subjective disability and sense of illness. Of course, the patient must be given some perspective on the time needed for recovery, in order to relieve his anxiety about his illness and to forestall demands for radical and dramatic treatment. One can tell a patient that he might have pain or discomfort for several months or perhaps for years, without indicating to him that he will be disabled. In giving him this perspective, the physician can also warn him about the danger of analgesic medication, which, although it might relieve his symptoms radically, might also prolong his illness by creating dependency on the medication.

Given proper perspective, the patient should recognize that he will have to endure some aches or pains for a long time to come, but that he can attempt to relieve them by judicious use of non-habit-forming analgesics or the very cautious use of habit-forming analgesics. There can be no question that even when the physician uses the most cautious of approaches, gives the patient a perspective, warns against the use of analgesic medication, cautions against radical intervention, some patients will ignore his advice and seek a quick cure or relief from symptoms. However, based on a review of the cases in this sample, we must conclude that the number that would take this course would be far fewer if the physician warned his patients of the dangers inherent in medical treatment.

There are other important reasons for taking sufficient time with the patient. Physicians frequently are rushed by the pressures of their practices. They tend to make comments like, "That might be very serious," referring to a symptom or to an observation the patient has made of his own physical function, and then drop it. Or, in referring to a work-pressure situation, the physician might say to the patient, "If you don't quit that job, you will not live to see your grand-children grow up." In some ways that statement resolves one part of the patient's problem, namely whether to continue working at the offending job, but it does not help the patient understand how he might be able to continue working at his job or how he is going to support himself if he leaves it.

In an effort to be agreeable, or because most authoritative persons are not aware of the impact of their words on those who come to them for help, physicians and others frequently accept the patient's estimate of his symptoms and agree that they are as severe as the patient believes. Sometimes, in an effort to frighten the patient into accepting treatment or rest, authoritative persons will overstress the severity of symptoms. Thus, careless words such as, "Your experience might have aged you ten years," or, to a forty-year-old woman, "You have the arteries of a seventy-year-old woman, I am surprised that you are alive," are more than diagnoses; they are sentences. It is not surprising, therefore, that we often see cases in which the patient's subjective state is still one of illness, while his objective state, as nearly as the expert external observer can determine, is already one of improvement. Therefore, whether a patient claims harassment or work pressure, or any other kind of injury, caution in expressing diagnosis or prognosis is as important as the subsequent treatment.

Some physicians go to the other extreme. Patients in crisis need support. One cannot ask them to "tough it out." A mild tranquilizer can be specific for tension and discomfort, and if the physician takes the time to explain to the patient that this is to help him through a crisis that will pass, and that the medica-tion will not remove the symptoms but will simply make him more comfortable, then the patient and the physician have formed a partnership that will endure long after the crisis has passed.

While being supportive, the physician must avoid becoming the patient's friend. Some physicians ally themselves with the patient against other physicians, especially against those physicians who found no objective signs of illness. Some physicians ally themselves with the patient against an insurance carrier that did not agree on the presence of a disability. Because he wishes to ingratiate himself with the patient, or because he may come to conclusions and make statements before he has had an opportunity to take a good history, talk to colleagues who treated the patient in the past, or examine the record, the physician often finds that altering his course is most difficult. The patient will not permit it. Having been told he definitely has a given illness or that he has been injured in some specific way, the patient wonders what has caused the physician to change his mind, and the conclusion he often comes to is that the physician is in collusion with the insurance companies. In order to avoid this outcome, the physician must be cautious, not committing himself to a course of action he is not prepared to pursue to its conclusion. Otherwise, the physician may feel trapped in the promised course of treatment, and the patient may be subjected to a pattern of more and more medication and sometimes even physical intervention, as a demonstration that the physician is convinced of the existence of an illness.

At the same time, the physician must not reject the patient. He can offer to do what he can for the patient, even though he cannot reverse the symptoms. If the patient is dissatisfied with the quality or the intensity of the treatment and wishes a consultation from another physician, no effort should be made to discourage him. It is part of the physician's obligation to the patient, however, to explain to him that there is no magic in medicine, that the physician has done everything possible to help him, and that more radical intervention might be harmful to the patient. Of course, the physician should not object to a request for consultation and should indicate he is willing to take the patient back after such a consultation. Further, he should offer to call or write to the other physician to whom the patient is going.

The physician should carefully record all interventions so that any physician who treats the patient has complete information, particularly about drug dosage. Patients underestimate quantities and often are not accurate about how much they take.

For several reasons, physicians would do well to talk with the important members of the family, as well as with the patient. Relatives, especially those who live with the patient, need support and an opportunity to tell the physician what they believe is happening and what they think needs to be done to help the patient. As he listens to family members, the physician or other helping person will learn a great deal about the family and about the pressures on the patient both for recovery and for remaining ill. In one conference with a husband, who was the worker, and his wife, the wife monopolized the conversation.

She described his problem and the damage done to him, indicating that he would
never be able to go back to work. During this entire conversation the husband sat
by with a slight smile on his face. Litigation had been going on for several years,
and it was obvious to the examiner that this scene had been repeated many times.
In fact, other medical reports described the same tableau. When the examiner
indicated that he would really like to hear the answer from the husband, the
husband reported that he could not remember, but when the examiner pressed
him, he was quite able to remember dates and the like. The examiner concluded
that this was not a case of malingering but that the wife had become the spokes-
person for both of them, and the husband had come to see himself as the mindless,
voiceless cripple.

　　In other instances the family members will express anger and skepticism
about the degree of the worker's impairment. In both instances relatives may
try to project their own notions onto the physician. From time to time, a relative
will want to talk privately with the physician, which he should allow, but he
should be careful about such discussions and should give no information except
in the presence of the patient. Neither should he exchange confidences with
relatives. If he does not adhere to this rule, he will discover that remarkable
distortions occur when one talks to anxious relatives separately, for each one of
them "hears" a different evaluation of the patient's condition, a different treatment proposal, and a different prognosis.

The Return to Work

Physicians are not usually trained to deal with a patient's social and economic
problems and often recommend measures that are actually antitherapeutic.[73].
To avoid this, physicians should hesitate to recommend that a worker leave his
job because of harassment or pressure. Our findings indicates that prescribing
rest when such conditions or complaints are present is often the worst thing to
do, for the worker may interpret the prescription as a statement that he cannot
cope with the noxious conditions. The suggestion might touch one part of his
ambivalence; although the worker might want to leave his job, he might also fear
leaving and want to stay on the job. Permission to leave supports one side of the
conflict, but as soon as he leaves, he might be unhappy with the consequences
and regret giving up the job or not making an effort to cope with the work
problem. He might come to realize that the harassment was only one part of the
work situation, and other components of it were pleasant and rewarding, or he
might become aware that his alternatives are few and that other jobs will probably
be more difficult and perhaps even less rewarding. Examining his alternatives in
the light of a decision already made, he might become quite depressed. He will
be angry with both himself and the person who made the recommendation.

Furthermore, during a prescribed period of rest, the worker might well build up or magnify in his own mind the pain of the work situation. As time goes on, he might become embarrassed about the prospect of going back to work and, consequently, develop "work phobia" [131]. He might hate to face his coworkers, imagining himself on his first day back at work, facing snide remarks. He might imagine that he will be assigned especially loathsome and difficult tasks. Many workers become angrier rather than more accepting of their work situation the longer they are away from work, and even a brief rest might push someone into a channel of disability for the remainder of his life.

Therefore, one must always consider what the possible results of the recommendation to "take a rest" might be. The physician must ask himself what the goal is. Is the worker going back to work at the same job at some time in the future? Is he to rest for a week or two and then start looking for a new job? Is he to litigate a compensation claim and start seeing himself as disabled? Is he to take on the disabled role, in the belief that he is not the same man he was and will not be able to work until he returns to being the same man? The physician then faces the challenge of making him the "same man."

For these reasons a worker should be kept on the job as long as possible, unless the physician believes that continuing on the job will result in an outburst of either external aggression or internal aggression, such as gastrointestinal problems, insomnia, anorexia, or an overwhelming nervous reaction manifesting itself in a tremor. When the patient is treated on the job, with the support of the physician his anger might subside, and he might establish a reasonably good working relationship with the person he has considered to be his attacker. To emphasize that he is part of the support system, the physician should encourage the patient to have "stick-to-it-iveness," suggesting that he would be proud and happy to come to grips with the situation and would come to see his coping with it as a victory.

Sometimes, when workers go back to their old jobs, they are treated with more understanding and respect for their rights than they experience formerly and they then function well. There may have been changes in the organization, since most organizations are reasonably dynamic in change of structure and turnover in personnel. A new supervisor or new coworkers may well convert what was a very unpleasant working situation into a pleasant one. Some workers do return after a prolonged absence and do reasonably well. We saw the ones who did not do well. A substantial number had made a serious effort to return to the jobs they claimed caused their problems. But their unpleasant associations may have triggered anger and psychophysiological symptoms. Profoundly worried about returning to work, they might have feared being singled out for further ill treatment. They certainly continued to have difficulty facing coworkers, friends, family, and, most of all, themselves. Illness can represent a way of coping with such failures, and the doctor is in a special position to encourage patients to find a healthier response [142].

The return to work after "a rest" often confirms the existence of a harassment situation. Supervisors and coworkers sometimes seem to welcome a chance to continue their former treatment of the worker. They may be angry with him for having been "disabled" while they continued working. They are not certain who won the struggle for dominance, but they are prepared to try again.

Often, the harassed worker had become a very serious problem for the whole job system. Since he had been the focus of tension and conflict among his coworkers, they breathed a sigh of relief when he left and dreaded having him come back. Some workers, indeed, have a personality style that tends to undermine group morale [145].

In any except transient laboring jobs, the return of a worker means that someone who filled his position will now be displaced. The person who is to be displaced resents the return; other workers have identified with the replacement and resist a change in the status quo. It is not surprising that they tend to be cool to the returning worker.

The physician who recommended that the patient leave work may find after a time that the patient has become embittered, with more symptoms than before, with no place to go, and with a profound dependence on and anger toward the physician.

Rehabilitation

If the physician decides that the worker definitely will not be able to return to his job, then he should immediately begin to discuss the search for another job or the possibility of rehabilitation.

Rehabilitation has its own pitfalls. In this instance we are talking about job retraining rather than basic rehabilitation. Our subjects were not so physically or mentally damaged that they would be called disabled. In all instances they were capable of doing the work required by their old jobs; it was the job environment they could not cope with. Rehabilitation in this case, then, is retraining to give the workers new skills and the chance to find work environments where they will not feel harassed.

Rehabilitation is a program or a formal regimen in which a person engages in certain educational and work experiences, with financial support, at least in part, while he is going through the program. While in this program, he does no other work, and moonlighting is kept to a minimum.

The rehabilitation process is based on a number of premises. The first is that work is good and that the absence of work in one's life is bad. It is good to support oneself; it is bad to be supported by society. This premise is based on the work ethic and its subtle extensions. The second premise is that there is a job somewhere that this particular person can do; all one has to do is match the job and the person. By extension, this premise assumes that a trained person, especially one trained specifically for a given job, will find such a position more readily than someone who does not have such training.

The third premise is that the transition can be made at almost any age. Rehabilitation counselors are generally very realistic people, but just as physicians are deterred from giving up on dying patients, so rehabilitation counselors are hesitant to say that there is no place in the vocational market for a particular person. Of course, rehabilitation counselors and physicians do give up, but the culture requires that they act as if they do not.

The decision to rehabilitate should be based on a careful evaluation of the possibility of returning the worker to his old job. If such an evaluation has been made, and if it has been decided that this would be impossible or inadvisable, then the worker's desire for a new job must be considered. Some of the workers examined had very clear notions of new jobs they wanted, and some of these new jobs were relatively realistic. One person, for example, who had done sales work in the past, wanted to go into sales again but wanted training in a special area that would qualify him to sell for a firm with which he had some assurance of getting a job.

The worker's fitness for training is very important. In order to learn a new vocation, one has to have a certain ability. The trainee must have intellectual resources sufficient to the task, and the kind of personality that can learn from others. Moreover, he must have the physical and, more important, the psychological stamina required to go through a program. Many people give up early in the course of a training program, whether learning to play golf or tennis or learning new job skills. If a person does not have the psychological stamina to go through the process, he will soon become discouraged, drop the whole project, and think the less of himself afterward. It is a disservice to a person to start him in such a program when the probability of his completing it is low.

Social stamina, too, is needed to make this kind of change. There must be a tolerant and supporting social system to encourage and sustain him as he goes through changes in pattern. Studies indicate that a disabled person's family obtains "tertiary gains" from the illness. A striking example of this was a woman who had two insurance policies, both of which paid for her hospitalization. As a result, each illness produced a windfall of 60 percent of the hospital costs. She and her husband depended on this money to pay for some of their living costs when she was not in the hospital. One might imagine that the husband would not be psychologically supportive of her recovery.

For rehabilitation or retraining to succeed, there must be support from external agencies; there must be a training facility that can help the person to acquire new skills and a market for his services. Training someone for a job as, say, a computer programmer or plastics specialist when there are no such positions in the job market is wasteful of the community's resources and the individual's time. The outcome is always demoralizing for the worker and his family.

Among our patients, a few had relatively realistic notions of new jobs. Some

hoped to return to school and acquire an education that would give them greater
freedom of choice. A substantial number had decided to retire and live on
whatever benefits were available to them. Others intended to continue a fight for
justice against their oppressors, and they did not want their energies diverted into
what they felt were less constructive activities.

Motivation is all-important to a worker's potential for rehabilitation. Without motivation, the best facilities in the world are wasted. Efforts to "inject"
motivation, as by pep talks, usually fail. It is easier to get people back to work
through such injections of motivation than it is to keep them there.

In most cases, it is better to keep the person on his job than to try to train
him for a new one. Psychotherapeutic intervention should be utilized, the
employer should be encouraged to make any needed changes in the job, the
family should be mobilized to support the worker in his effort to remain on the
job. Whenever possible, the claim should be settled. Regardless of how litigious
or nonlitigious the patient is, the presence of a claim affects the field in which
he exists. It diverts his energy and does not permit him to focus fully either on
retraining or on returning to his job. If these approaches have been unsuccessful
in keeping the patient at work, then conservative rehabilitation plans should be
made, plans that have the highest probability of returning the person to gainful
employment even if the new job does not fulfill all his dreams and wishes; the
job he had before did not do that either.

Retirement

The physician, and all those planning for the patient's future, must at some
point consider the possibility of retirement. Many harassed workers have already
made retirement plans. This alternative should be given full weight and not dismissed as bad just because the physician believes that one should not retire until
one dies. Many of our subjects derived little or no satisfaction from their work,
and the quality of their lives would indeed be improved by retirement. Their
material requirements were such that they needed comparatively little income.
Living in a mobile home in an area where taxes and other living costs are low,
the worker might well be able to get along comfortably enough on what little
pension, savings, social security, and odd-job income he might have available.
All this must be taken into account when planning for the patient's future.

Psychotherapy of Harassment

Harassed or pressured patients are frightened persons: they have confronted the
establishment, they have refused to tolerate what they consider to be unjust
treatment, and they have revolted against the system. They are concerned about

retaliation, about looking like fools, about the economic consequences and about how much support they will get from their families, their unions, their coworkers, and society if they bring legal action against their employers.

The harassed person who files an industrial claim or simply comes complaining of harassment is an outraged person. He feels that he has been done an injustice and he is angry because, although he does not yet know the outcome of his defensive and retaliatory actions, he does not believe that society will really support him but that ultimately the aggressor, the employer or consumer, will win. He is angry that he was picked as a victim. One of our subjects said in a resigned fashion, talking about himself, "Someone has to be the goat," but most patients do not feel that they should be that "someone." They see it as bad luck, and this mobilizes all of their previous anxiety about being selected by nature or fate for ill fortune. They are outraged that the aggressor is still in his position and they, the victims, are not working.

When this rage is turned inward, the result is depression. There may be a resentment of self, the victim wondering about what was wrong with him, what he had done to deserve becoming a target. His life has been disrupted, he feels he will never be able to work at his job again, and he foresees dire consequences for his relationships with his relatives and his friends.

He is a person in conflict. He is not certain whether he was right or what part he played in the harassment interaction. He is not certain whether he should have rebelled, whether he should have complained or even if he should have left his job. Perhaps it would have been better if he had gone along with the game, if he had put up with his supervisor or with his coworker. Perhaps he should not have made all this trouble. Such are the doubts that plague him.

With this composite picture of the harassed person's psychological state of fear, rage, depression, and conflict, we can outline a therapeutic program. The first goal is to give the patient an opportunity to express his feelings over an extended period of time. He should be permitted to tell his story over and over again and be encouraged to relate all the details of his plight. The victim of harassment is under pressure and must be permitted to relieve this pressure by talking. At some point, the therapist will note a change. The patient will be "talked out," and he himself will conclude that there does not seem much point in talking about it further.

At this point the therapist and patient should undertake a realistic appraisal of the patient's situation, examining alternatives, considering all his working possibilities and all his legal options. The patient should consider whether or not he wants to stay on the job at which he was harassed and whether he is prepared for the consequences of either staying or leaving.

The harassed person must be encouraged to examine his own role in the harassment interaction. At first he may be defensive and deny that he participated in any way in promoting or provoking the behavior he considered harassment. Some of our subjects could never go beyond this point. But the patient should be encouraged to see himself as part of the harassment interaction, rather than as an innocent bystander. If he can free himself of the concept of blame and become curious about the events that produced the harassment, he may come to realize that his harasser is a person, too, with his own fears and defenses, and that he must learn not to frighten that other person if he himself is to avoid attack.

Proceeding with caution, the therapist should encourage the patient to examine his past experiences. These are far less likely to be as emotionally loaded as the present experience, but the patient may discover that there are parallels to the present experience. He may recall some events from childhood, some interactions while in military service, and the like. He might remember that his parents or his siblings treated him in exactly the same way as did the alleged harasser. One black patient who felt that he was discriminated against because he was black recalled that his parents rejected him because he was darker than his siblings. Such memories provide longitudinal perspective for the experience of harassment. Although recognition that this harassment event was not a single incident and was not related only to a specific aggressor might be depressing for the patient, it also can reduce the tendency to magnify the present experience. By examining previous harassment experiences, the patient has an opportunity to recall that although at the time any one of these events occurred, he was very upset, very angry, or very depressed, he was able to deal with his feelings as time passed, and, therefore, he might be optimistic that he will be able to deal with these feelings in relation to the present incident. Such optimism is necessary because if the patient believes that nothing will change his feelings or that he cannot alter his situation, he will see no point in undertaking the psychotherapeutic effort. Further, there is always a soothing effect in the recognition that tense feelings and reactions change with time. It can be quite helpful to a depressed patient to recall his previous depressions and how they lifted.

Ultimately, one must examine the present event in the greatest detail and place it in context not only with what happened between the patient and the aggressor, but with what happened between the patient and his family and the patient and others whom he does not see as participants in the indicated situation.

Whenever possible, the therapist should work also with the patient's family as a group. The family represents a microsystem from which the patient gets most in the way of support, correction, and feedback, and the family most wants to restore him to full function. Very often, one learns that the family members know little or nothing about the work situation or the kinds of feelings the patient has about what happened at work. They might be so unsympathetic that the patient cannot discuss any aspect of what happened with them, or they might be so sympathetic that he cannot examine realistically what happened to him. In one instance, when the patient and his family met with the therapist, it became clear the although the patient had told them about his physical complaints, he had not described what he believed to be the cause of his physical complaints—namely harassment by one of his supervisors.

It usually will be difficult to bring in coworkers to participate in the process. On one occasion, a meeting with two coworkers, a supervisor, and one who worked directly with the patient resulted in a remarkable reduction in tension in the patient and a correction of his belief that he was the only one who had suffered. In the course of the discussion, the patient was able to develop a strategy for dealing with the harassing supervisor.

Psychotherapy of Work Pressure

Many of the elements of the psychotherapy of work pressure are the same as those for harassment. One must deal with the worker's concern and tension about having challenged his work system and his concern about being isolated from his fellow workers and from the community. But there are differences between the worker who complains of work pressure and the worker who complains of harassment. While the latter feels he has been victimized, the former sees himself as being both weak and courageous—weak because he could not take what his fellow workers were taking, courageous because he was the only one who could break out of the system. Often this person is a compulsive individual, and part of the work pressure comes from within; it becomes intolerable because he is unable to satisfy himself rather than because he is unable to satisfy an employer. The police sergeant whose chief did not demand the conformance to rules and regulations that the sergeant himself demanded found it intolerable to work in a setting where the written rules required so much of him and his superiors required far less; he felt he was a failure, or at least was delinquent, because he was unable to keep up with the written rules.

As has already been outlined, these workers should be permitted to ventilate their feelings. No effort should be made to instruct, argue, or explore until they have described the entire work experience in relentless detail. They should be permitted and encouraged to express feelings, fears, and hopes. The work pressure victim should be permitted to be inappropriately or even unjustly angry with his employers. He should be permitted to talk about the damage that has been done him, the suffering he has had. This phase requires great patience on the part of the listener, but the helping person, whether counselor, physician, or claims adjuster, should wait until he senses that the worker's anger and outrage have been dissipated significantly .

At that point, the helping person may undertake a careful analysis of the worker's habits and work attitudes, a study of the person and of the work environment and an attempt to understand, with the worker, how he fits or does not fit into his work environment. The function of this exercise is to inject reason into the process. The worker and the treating person have agreed that the work situation was a difficult one for the worker; now the question is one of understanding what made it so difficult and whether anything can be done to reduce the pressure. The helping person and the worker become job analysts, making recommendations for new approaches so the worker can do his job with a reduced expenditure of energy, especially psychic energy, but possibly also physical energy.

The most important aspect of this process is that the worker is a coanalyst. He is not told how to do it by someone who has not been on the scene; he is helped to analyze the body of data that only he has access to, namely the requirements of the job and his own psychological reactions to those requirements.

In the process, a study is made of how the worker communicates with those around him. For example, a secretary, outraged at her supervisor because he had accused her of not getting her work done, discovered that she had never informed him that she was overloaded. She felt that since he was the boss, he should know how much work she had done. A careful review revealed that he had no way of knowing how much work was done because the secretary worked for several different people. She had not informed him that she had to come to work forty-five minutes early and generally stayed an hour extra. Because he arrived late in the morning and left early in the afternoon, he could not have known this himself.

In this process of examining his work communications, a worker sometimes discovers that the problem is simply lack of communication skills, that he has not known how to approach his supervisors or coworkers. More often, the problems are those of personality rather than skill. The worker interprets assertiveness as equivalent to aggression. In the case of the secretary, she felt constrained not to demand more help; she felt in some way that it was not her place to do so. A careful examination of her relationships outside of work revealed the same pattern.

This examination of the person and his work environment often reveals other elements in the work situation that explain to the worker why his situation became intolerable. For example, a new owner, new work regimen, or some change in his relationships at home might have affected his reaction to work. Outrage over the coming to power of a new political administration might have made him far less accepting of work changes imposed by them than he would have been by a political administration with which he was more sympathetic.

In almost all instances, this exploration relieves some of the patient's anger, concern, and sense of impotence. If he has not left his job, one can study with him the changes he tries to make and help to devise new tactics when necessary. As problem areas are identified and explored, the worker can be helped to clarify them with his supervisors. Whenever possible, his supervisors should be included in this process. This need not be a time-consuming process. One or two joint meetings, conducted after the worker's anger has been dealt with and after some preliminary study, can be very helpful in reconciling worker and supervisor and in enlisting the supervisor as an ally in relieving the pressure.

Malingering

How are we to judge whether or not a patient is malingering, that is, "consciously" creating or exaggerating symptoms in order to gain something he wants? Study of many patients who experienced delayed recovery from seemingly minor injuries has convinced us, however, that the question about malingering cannot be answered simply for any of these patients. Both our own empirical data and the literature [81,117] indicate that malingering is a complex system and an intricate program of behavior.

Malingering is a relative, not an absolute, concept. It is not a state or a choice, but a process, an aspect of the patient's life system that is understandable only by long-term study. Such study reveals that "malingering" is not one single physical, emotional, or even social reaction. Rather, the term represents a wide range of reactions varying in intensity, duration, and frequency. Not merely a tactic nor an act nor a play for sympathy or money, malingering is instead a language, a form of communication [166], a presentation of self [53]. The malingerer is making a statement about his relationship to a whole group of activities and to the persons in his immediate and extended environment. As do all people, the malingerer lives in an immediate nuclear environment that consists of those persons with whom he spends most of his time, his family, his neighbors, a selected group of friends in his neighborhood. An extended environment includes his former work environment, those persons who are involved in deciding whether he is injured and whether he should be compensated, and a nameless, depersonalized society at large. His primary statement to society informs it that society cannot prove that he is well, that it does not have the tools for demonstrating that his illness is a sham.

Psychiatrists and other physicians have frequently recorded in their records statements like, "This man is not intelligent enough to malinger." The author has read many such statements or variations of such statements and later has sat in a hearing room while a defense attorney called a private investigator who demonstrated that indeed the patient was intelligent enough to malinger. In one such instance, following a prolonged period of questioning of the person who claimed to be disabled, in which the attorney for the insurance company asked a series of questions dealing with his ability to do specific kinds of tasks, such as lift his arms above his shoulders, bend over and touch the ground, use a hammer or a saw, climb a ladder, the attorney called in a private investigator who with the use of a telephoto lens had observed the disabled person doing all these activities and doing them over a long period of time.

There is a difference between how the intelligent malingerer writes his
script and how it is done by the less intelligent malingerer. The intelligent
malingerer learns what the defects in his initial plan are and refines his system as
he goes along. One person claiming disability was informed by a neighbor that
he had been observed by someone in a truck who seemed to have a camera. During the day that the truck had been parked outside his farm, the claimant recalled
that he had climbed up and down a ladder in order to repair the roof on the barn.
Whereas in previous reports to physicians he had told them he could not climb
ladders and could do practically nothing, after this incident, he reported that
he could climb ladders and could do certain types of work, but that there were
time limitations. He started having pain after two or three hours. He eventually
developed a statement of his illness that said he could do almost anything and
had no limitations except limitations of stamina. When he exerted himself for
any length of time, he became exhausted and later developed pain. In a way,
this is a foolproof plan, because if he is observed doing anything, he says that of
course he can do it, and if he is asked why he cannot work, he reports that he
cannot do whatever it is for very long.

The unintelligent malingerer, in contrast, cannot believe that he can be
caught. He cannot imagine that his adversaries are as intelligent as they are.
Like a young child, he tells a blatant lie and does not fully understand that he
might not be believed. The unintelligent malingerer depends on stubbornness
rather than on guile. He makes his illness statement; it is then demonstrated
to him on film that he can do all of the activities that he says he cannot do, and
he turns around and looks the lawyers and the referee in the eye and says, "I
can't do those things." For these, one might say that not only do they believe
that wishing makes it so, but they really believe that saying makes it so.

Another group of malingerers might be called compulsive malingerers, those
who use malingering as a way of interacting with others. As some people will
step aside for others when entering a door, or will have other patterns of interaction, the compulsive malingerer always will select a statement of disability.
He is conscious of the fact that he is not as sick or as disabled or as limited as
he claims to be. But being ill is his way of interacting with others. Although
there are, of course, deep and strong unconscious forces that drive him in this
direction, just as there are strong unconscious forces affecting all conscious behavior, the basic distinction for such a person is that he knows he is not as limited as he claims to be. The reason we call him compulsive is that he cannot
pass up the opportunity to make a statement of illness, even when there is no
evidence of material gain or of any of a series of secondary gains, such as protection, care, or comfort that might be obtained.

For some people, being ill represents a sanctuary. In the same way that
one might feel safe in a church or in one's own home or in a national embassy,
some people feel safer within the sanctuary of illness. It is a statement to the
world very much like the one that says, "You can't hit a man with glasses."

This one asserts, "You can't hit a man who is ill or who is disabled" and, further, "the man who is ill and disabled cannot be expected to hit back." In this sense, malingering is often a statement that protects the person against accusations of cowardice, lack of manliness, or weakness of character. In the cases we are discussing, the statement of the malingerer is, "You can't ask a man who is sick to work."

There are secondary statements addressed to society at large. The malingerer is angry with society and especially with his lot in it. He feels that he has been cheated and that his share of society's goods is unduly small. His statement says to society, "You have your devices for getting what you need; let me show you that I have mine. You have money, power, influence, position, and can make the system work the way you want it to work. I have nothing, but I understand the system and I can make the system work for me just as you can make it work for you. I can make it work by claiming to be ill, or by claiming that you injured me. You will have no way of demonstrating that I am well; that I am whole. This is the flaw in your system, and I am going to exploit it."

Underlying this statement is the malingerer's sense that the social system is unjust. Feeling deprived, he is saying, "I am going to try and get as much justice as I can for myself. This is the only way I know how to do it. I am going to take this road that is available to me." Another statement that a malingerer is making to society is that he cannot find a place for himself in the world in which he lives. He is saying that he needs to be excused from it all, but he cannot explain to others why he needs to be excused from it. He cannot make a statement of his own inability to function in the world that others can understand or will accept. Very often, he cannot make the statement in such a way that he himself can accept and understand. Consequently, he says, "I cannot explain it to you in a way that will permit you to act in a manner favorable to me. Therefore, I will tell it to you in a way that will make it possible for you to help me out of my plight." The soldier cannot say to a superior officer, "I am too afraid to go into battle." He can say, "I can't move my legs." There is a statistical advantage to this statement in the sense that all men are afraid to go into combat, but not all of them cannot move their legs. It is easier for the system to excuse the person who is paralyzed, whether from malingering or from some sort of hysterical reaction, than it is to excuse a person on the basis of fear.

Those in the immediate environment can respond to malingering in various ways. There can be acceptance and collusion, in the sense of, "Let's join together to screw society," or a tacit acceptance of the malingering because it is of mutual advantage to all the members of the immediate environment, or a rejection of the malingerer with overt statements by members of the family and work group that they believe he is malingering. Often those persons in a claimant's immediate environment are overtly supportive of his malingering.

For example, in a recent case heard before a Worker's Compensation

Appeals Board hearing, a man who demonstrated a profound tremor, especially when he tried to do something, but with some evidence of tremor even at rest, also claimed that he could not bend over, that he could not lift, and that he could not carry out fine movements. He reported all this in response to questions from his attorney. In order to support his testimony, his attorney called the applicant's wife. This woman, herself disabled, was neatly and sedately dressed, and it was known from previous testimony that she was a church-going woman who not only went to church but also served her congregation. Her husband's attorney asked her the same questions that he had asked her husband. She supported his answers fully. She, too, said he was unable to do all the things that he said he was unable to do. One of the questions that he had been asked was whether he could pick up a key in his right hand or not. He stated that in order to use a key in his right hand, he had to pick it up with his left and then insert it between the fingers of the right. She was asked specifically about this and said that often she had had to put the key into his hand. Immediately thereafter, a film was shown in which the claimant did all the things that he asserted he could not do. He climbed in and out of cars with great agility; he lifted a bundle of groceries with one arm and his dog with the other; he pulled his keys out of his pocket and inserted them into the lock of his car without any hesitation.

One can only conclude that both the man and his wife knew that he was malingering and that both had agreed that this was a good thing to do. It was a mutual enterprise, and if the outcome had been successful, they could have retired, because she had already been declared disabled, and he could have joined her. The wife's gains might be called the tertiary gains of the illness.

There are other kinds of tertiary gains for relatives of a malingerer or of anyone else who is ill. For example, in many instances the malingering male takes on the role of his wife, and his wife goes out to work. Often this arrangement is mutually satisfactory. Sometimes it is the wife as well as society against whom the malingering is taking place. Often, under circumstances of illness, whether as the result of malingering or otherwise, certain conflicts endemic in the family are set aside until such time as the sick person is once again considered recovered.

There are members of the larger environment who also will tend to support the malingerer. The society of the disabled, however informally it exists, offers ready support. The members of this society meet in physical therapy rooms, in unemployment offices, or in public parks. When they become acquainted and discover that they share disability, whether as a result of having been wounded in military service or as a result of an industrial accident, they discuss their symptoms and share information about the various support systems that are available to the disabled. Patients learn as much from other disabled people as they do from their own attorneys. Once one gets into this society of the disabled, one may be reluctant to leave it. Joining it is an affirmative act, and most people who are in it expect to remain in it for the rest of their lives. This society has never been fully studied, but represents a strong support system for its members.

There are families who do not accept the malingerer's claims of disability. Instead, they believe that he is trying to avoid responsibility and shift a greater burden of responsibility to other family members. Critical of his malingering, they resent the limitations that his illness imposes on them. Their freedom to engage in certain activities, to go certain places, is limited not only by reduced income but also by the physical disability he claims to have. When members of such families decide that one is malingering, they tend to isolate this person, to criticize him, to make fun of him, and often to separate themselves from him.

To the larger extended society, the malingerer presents a dilemma. It feels taken if it accepts him and guilty if it accuses him of malingering. The person who is taken is outraged when he first discovers it. A referee, for example, who had blasted an insurance company's lawyer because he had indicated he felt the applicant was malingering became violently angry with the applicant after films were shown demonstrating his malingering. The referee's anger was clearly the result of an unconscious recognition of the dilemma in which he found himself. If he maintained a high index of suspicion about the possibility of malingering, he could not properly care for those workers who were indeed injured. If he accepted uncritically the stories of the injured workers, then he was taken for a fool. Society in general mirrors this same conflict. The little bit of each of us that tends to malinger is projected onto the injured person. That part of us that recalls the time when we were in pain or when we were indeed disabled makes us wonder if the accusation of malingering is fair.

That virtually everyone has malingered at some time makes the complexity of the process all the more impressive. The student malingers when he has a bad enough flu syndrome or stomachache to stay home from school but is healthy enough to engage in more vigorous mental or physical activity than school would require. The spouse who is not too tired to play several sets of tennis but is too fatigued to engage in sex is frequently malingering. The professor who cannot attend a faculty meeting because of illness but can read or meet with students or colleagues in another setting is malingering, in part or entirely. Feigning illness in order to get something or to get out of something is a phenomenon that one sees in all strata of both primitive and highly technological societies. Personality type, education, and status neither insure it nor preclude it; they simply alter its manifestations.

Although most people have on occasion "played sick," we can still speak of certain extreme types for whom malingering becomes a primary coping mechanism that they are unable to stop once they have begun [139]. No typology will be exhaustive, but the most striking cases do fall into identifiable subsets.

The hypochondriac, for example, actually believes he is ill and is concerned about his symptoms. But he continues to have those symptoms after his concern diminishes, because they have been reinforced by rewards such as money, comfort, or removal from unpleasant tasks. The person who becomes addicted to medication may malinger in order to keep his supply. Childlike persons frequently play sick at critical moments. They resort to all the devices that worked in their earlier years, often acting out their symptoms in the same manner and using the same voices as they did in childhood. Feeling impotent in the face of social or interpersonal forces, the angry person sometimes continues to claim illness despite overwhelming contrary medical evidence [91]. He knows that stubbornness is the last resort of the weak and is determined to achieve his goal—and prove himself right—because unsympathetic circumstances have frustrated him [104,127].

There are also role players who slip in and out of the role of being sick, as it suits their convenience. These are hysterical personalities who, after embarking on a role, soon discover that they believe the role they are playing [154,167]. When a mysterious medical complaint reveals no organicity, and symptoms are thought to be functional, the first things to investigate are whether the patient is an hysteric, has an anxiety neurosis, or is depressed [57]. The hysteric may demand medical intervention because of a desire for attention, while those with anxiety neurosis or depression are seeking medical attention for their subjective symptoms.

Malingering is related to harassment in that in many instances it is provoked by harassment. When someone is harassed or feels he has been harassed, he seeks a way to recover for the wrong that was done him, a way to punish the wrongdoer, a way to deal with his own sense of impotence and helplessness. One such way is malingering, with symptoms that are either psychological or physical. This is especially true when the harassment takes the form of a physical attack. The physical attack might have been minor—a shove or a punch that certainly hurt but did not produce major damage—but the injured person behaves as if he had been severely wounded. Often such individuals have formed an unconscious complex, for example, a conversion reaction, related to this event. Probably as often, or even more often, a large element of malingering is present in the continued expression of pain and disability.

The nonmalingering harassed person might well claim headaches and hypertension as the result of harassment, but this person also will note that the headaches disappear as soon as he is not in the presence of his harassers, or his blood pressure may go down when he is not in the presence of his harassers. The malingerer, on the other hand, tends to have symptoms all the time.

For many patients, malingering represents a way of controlling the world. They need illness because they lack other resources. Malingering is for them a force with which to move people they normally would have little influence on. Malingering is a device of the helpless.

In any case, the malingerer disrupts his society. Those around him do not know whether to treat him as a mentally ill person, a physically ill person, or a manipulator [134]. Thus, he finds that one authoritative figure accepts his statement of illness while another rejects it. He himself becomes confused when physicians treat him as if he were actually ill. He gradually becomes an outcast, as it becomes increasingly apparent that his symptoms are voluntarily produced. As the malingerer notes the growing skepticism about his symptoms, he must go to greater lengths to convince. The more severe pain, the more exaggerated limp at particularly opportune moments provides the final proof that he has voluntary control over his symptoms. But the confusion remains. Nothing in worker's compensation or retirement systems so frustrates those dealing with applicants as the sense that they are being controlled by malingerers and knowing that they have no way of unmasking this to the satisfaction of those who will judge the case.

Physicians have the same problem as the general public in deciding who is malingering. Since a patient can have symptoms, subjective complaints, and a sense of limitation, without a concommitant set of findings indicating anatomical or physiological disruption, the physician has great difficulty in making a judgment.

A proven malingerer is one who has been observed to do those things that he claims he could not possibly do. A review of such cases makes it possible to trace the development of malingering from its first symptom until the time it is uncovered. From proven cases we can identify some of the characteristics of the malingerer: his symptoms are unanatomic; they do not follow the lines of nerve distribution; they are unphysiological, in the sense that they conform to no pattern of physiological disruption. The symptoms are shifting. The malingerer generally has to impress his audience; to do so, he exaggerates the severity of a single symptom and, even more often, its spread. His symptoms start at the toes and end at the head. They are never neatly circumscribed. The malingerer will not say, "I have a pain in this one spot, it never goes to any other place, it is constant, it is severe." The malingerer has to extend his symptoms rather than situate them.

Another factor of considerable importance is that physicians who have examined him believed that he was malingering. From very early, physicians have noted the unanatomic nature of his symptoms, using such expressions as, "maximizing symptoms," "voluntary inhibition," "obvious exaggeration," "symptoms will be altered by termination of litigation," and similar remarks. Interpretation of this type of recording utilizes the public opinion approach, that is, if a number of people think someone is doing something, it is more likely that he is in fact doing it than if few people think so.

Among malingerers we often notice a good activity pattern. For example, if a person has a certain amount of pain and restriction of motion, then we would not expect him to be able to engage in certain enterprises, certain sports, for instance, or climbing hills, or riding a motorcycle. He might not be able to drive a car long distances, or to ride a horse. But the malingerer often engages in activities that are incompatible with his symptoms or with his claimed limitations. He does too much for one who has as much pain and discomfort and disability as he claims to have. He is in too good spirits for someone who hurts as much as he claims to hurt. He eats too much and drinks too much and enjoys relationships with others too much for one who claims to be in such discomfort.

Although malingerers use medications and alcohol in the same way that nonmalingerers do, often we find that they seek or take relatively little medication in spite of their claim of being in terrible pain.

Malingerers often show an unusual pattern of development of symptoms. Initially, after some sort of injury, they start getting better in the way that would have been predicted. They reach a point where they are almost entirely well and ready to go back to work; then something happens that makes them decide that they are going to follow the other course. They discover the possibilities of disability retirement or of prolonged compensation or of Social Security disability, and the pattern of their symptoms changes. In some instances, we see patients who have already had one injury, and in a way this first injury served as their education about the potential of disability. When they have another one, they exploit that potential to the utmost, even to malingering in order to achieve their goals.

But we cannot say that there is a "pure" malingerer who has consciously plotted to play sick in order to achieve certain gain. We believe that the seemingly conscious choice of this device is based on profound and extensive unconscious mechanisms [27]. Many of our patients who seemed to be malingering had previously tried other methods of achieving their goals. Some who wanted to be free of an unpleasant job had tried to go into businesses of their own, but they had failed. Others had tried to move away but were unsuccessful in finding the type of job they sought or, if they found it, learned that the new job did not meet their expectations. The notion of using illness or disability for gain tempers the pain of the malingerer's belief that he has no other resources for achieving his goals [141].

The Impact of the Employer

California Worker's Compensation Institute reports indicate that lack of employer sympathy appeared to be the triggering element in many cases involving litigation. Apparent lack of personal concern, given as the predominant reason for regarding the employer as unsympathetic in industrial accident cases, seemed especially prominent when injuries involved subjective complaints that the employer frequently discounted or refused to believe [CWCI].

In many of the cases we studied, the supervisor or the foreman, after being told that an injury had occurred, said, "There is nothing wrong with you," or

"It was your own fault," or told the worker that he could not leave because he was needed to finish the job. The worker had approached his foreman expecting sympathy, concern, and care; instead he was told that the foreman did not care about the worker's pain or injury, but only about completing the job. This response makes a worker angry and vindictive; it indicates that if he claims to be in pain, he is no longer welcome in the society of the fit and healthy. He has the choice of giving up his symptoms or getting out. Many continue to work, even though they are hurt; others decide to get out and are then especially angry.

Disbelief and skepticism also may follow the claim of injury. "Are you sick again?" expresses the supervisor's or the coworker's disbelief and suggests the opinion they have of the worker's capability or predelection for somaticizing. The worker may be accused of malingering. "Oh, come on, you could really do it if you had to!" "You're just trying to get out on disability." Although supervisor and coworker may well be right—there often is an element of malingering or an element of the wish to terminate employment with support—the accused feels that he is being unjustly indicted, he reacts angrily, and his symptoms are consolidated.

There are many other reactions that the worker may experience as harassment. For example, an employer may reassure the worker that a job will be waiting for him, but he may start almost immediately to replace the worker, since he might not be able to function at full capacity in the foreseeable future. The employer may not accept the physician's recommendation that this worker be given a less demanding job. Even if he does find or create such a job, he may still require the worker to be fully productive immediately upon his return to work, and the worker may interpret this requirement as a lack of concern and ultimately as harassment.

Frequently, the employer may cooperate but the immediate supervisor sees the returning worker as a drag on his production schedule and presses him to leave or to produce more. The pressure often is verbalized and carries with it the threat of retaliation if the worker does not comply.

People who are sick expect sympathy from others. There is a great difference between a situation in which a person who is injured or ill is visited by his coworkers and supervisors—and is invited to continue to participate in extra work activities—and one in which he is ignored or excluded. A sick person reacts far better to those who say to him, "If you can't bowl, at least you can keep score and get the beer," than he does to those who exclude him from fellowship as soon as he leaves the work group.

Impact of the Insurance Worker

When a worker files a claim, his interaction with the adjuster will have a significant influence on the course of his claim process and even on the course of his disability. The worker often does not understand the basis on which he is to be compensated. He probably knows very little about the legal basis of the worker's compensation system. His opinions and expectations are formed largely by what he has read or seen on television about people trying to defraud insurance companies and the measures taken against them. He therefore approaches the system with his own claim in a frame of mind that is likely to be a mixture of fears of being mistreated and cheated, of being accused himself of lying and cheating, of anger at having to justify himself. He probably has had experience with other large, impersonal systems and is apprehensive about being lost in the insurance system, with no one really listening to him or interested in helping him.

The worker whose claim is based on harassment or work pressure is very likely to equate the response of the claims adjuster with that of the employer. His first contact with the adjuster, then, may determine whether the worker is going to limit his complaint of harassment to his job or is going to extend it to the compensating system itself. He may come to feel as harassed by the processing of his claim as he did in the work setting he blames for his disability. Harassment by insurance personnel that was mentioned by our subjects included the withholding of benefits of money and medical care, and of being sent to many different doctors whom the patient himself had not selected and who seemed interested only in discovering whether or not he really was injured, rather than in relieving his pain.

Patients equate investigation with harassment. One patient said, "They sent men out to harass me," referring to a private investigator who had him under surveillance with a movie camera. Patients also complain of being harassed by attorneys, both their own and those representing the insurance carrier. They may feel their own attorneys are not forceful enough in pushing their claims and in obtaining justice; these are the patients who change lawyers frequently and go looking for the "toughest" attorney in the area. Questioning at depositions by insurance company attorneys, especially the less experienced, more aggressive ones, is experienced by claimants as an effort to "brainwash" them.

The claims adjuster can minimize this aspect of the worker's relationship with the claim process by a careful determination of the facts and a thorough explanation to the worker of how his particular case relates to the system and what he can expect in the course of the claim process. If the worker understands the purposes and limitations of the compensation system, and feels the adjuster has listened to his story and been fair in evaluating it, he will be less likely to feel doubly harassed and persecuted—by the job circumstances that injured him in the first place and by the insurance system that refuses to compensate him adequately for his suffering and his loss of income. The most effective claims person is the one who deals with the claimant as a person with feelings as well as with the claim itself on its merits.

8

The Work Culture in Society

Harassment in Systems

Harassment seems to be a universal phenomenon in our industrial society. The system's underlying premise is that workers are most productive when subjected to the goad or fear of harassment. The military, prisons, police and fire departments, and sometimes schools provide ready examples of cultures in which the harassment process is inherent. The work culture is a variant of this, a system with constant pressure to produce—either on the production line or in volume of sales—where the system itself creates tension and where opportunities for additional individual harassment are thereby increased.

Systems in which rewards are distributed at the discretion of a superior place an overt premium on competition, effectively inviting the supervisor to harass his employees and the rival employees one another. The chief resident in surgery at a hospital and the senior partner in a law firm are in such positions. Although neither the hospital nor the law firm is designed as a competitive enterprise for employees, the junior members know that if they fail to please the chief or the senior partner, they probably will be passed over for promotion.

Harassment is likely to occur in a system that lacks positive mechanisms for retarding harassment. If there is no supervisor to say, "That is unacceptable behavior," or "We do not tease," would-be harassers or teasers are likely to have a significant opportunity to engage in that activity. A group such as a minority racial caucus, a labor union, or a students' grievance committee can retard harassment through direct pressure on superiors and by providing protection for the individual victim [44].

Even in the best-structured work situations, the behavior and attitudes of individuals will tend to cause harassment. It would be unrealistic to think that all employees and supervisors within an institution will always get along with each other. Some workers will be disappointed; they will decide that they were singled out for deprivation or were not given full or fair consideration. Some will require a dependent, love relationship with superiors or coworkers and will feel betrayed no matter what degree of affection is shown them. Other workers will overvalue their own contributions to an enterprise and underestimate the contribution of others and will think any reward given others is unjust. The dreamer, the fantasizer, the psychotic, the paranoid, and the delusional worker all are likely to experience subjective harassment, wherever they work. These same qualities appear in some supervisors who may perceive and also create harassment.

Social systems, including work organizations, must provide for movement and change. Retirement and promotion are formal procedures for change and for eliminating the worker. There is "kicking someone upward" or sideways, a move taken after an organization has decided that this person is no longer of value, or no longer of as much value as he was formerly, but that the organization is not going to expel him. The reasons for the decision to retain the person are complex. Morale might be negatively affected by firing someone at a given point in his career. Other workers might feel that their jobs are less secure and might come to see the organization as being ruthless rather than protective. If the organization does not want to have this image with its workers, it might well decide to keep a worker and pay him, even though it does not forsee obtaining much production from him. Often such workers are either executives or subexecutives, or they are relatives of prominent persons and firing them would bring down the wrath of their important protectors.

There are ways of encouraging workers to leave, such as withholding recognition or withholding promotion. These are messages to the worker that he is not valued by his employer. In some work situations, whole sections have been reorganized in order to get rid of one worker. One program specifically requested that a granting agency eliminate the position for one of its staff; it made this request because the members of the organization felt that they themselves could not eliminate the position with impunity.

All the above methods, and the list is not by any means complete, are designed to provide turnover in an organization when the policy and decision-making members of that organization decide that it is time to do so. They are formal mechanisms and are accepted as such.

Harassment is an informal mechanism for achieving change, and it often is not only informal, but unconscious, as well. We must hypothesize an organizational unconscious in order to explain the behavior of certain members of organizations that results in the harassment of other members. We must assume that certain workers in certain contexts function much like antibodies in the system of an allergic person. They produce irritation and a reaction. The irritation falls below the threshhold necessary to evoke formal mechanisms. In those organizations where superiors are permitted to fire people arbitrarily, there is no problem. The individual is discharged. Most often he does not know why he has been discharged, but no industrial claim is filed because of discharge; the discharge is acknowledged and accepted.

Other organizations do not permit this kind of arbitrary behavior and require supervisors to account for their actions. In this situation, the organizational unconscious comes into play. Messages are communicated at a subliminal level; certain types of behavior are reinforced, others are discouraged, and a mechanism for removing the worker and providing a change is triggered.

Although our cases seem to be divided mainly among persons harassed by their coworkers and persons harassed by their superiors, almost all harassment seems to have its origins or its support in the supervisory, managerial structure of an organizaiton. Management makes the decision to initiate or to support it, either because support is the easier course once the harassment has been initiated, or because management is uneasy about having a worker who cannot be integrated with his coworkers. When superiors decide that this is the only way to deal with a person, coworkers go alcng, either for fun or out of fear that they will be included if they do not cooperate.

Many forces work against recognition of harassment as an informal method of firing, for recognition would turn it into a formal mechanism. Conscious awareness would require justifying the mechanism, something that would be very difficult to do. Conscious awareness would produce guilt, especially when one examined exactly what he was doing. Keeping the process at the unconscious level makes it unnecessary to look at the evil inherent in it.

Since harassment behavior is a universal phenomenon, we are interested in a number of different models that make more explicit the reinforcement of harassment as an acceptable device. This includes the interaction between adolescents or children, when they smile while pushing each other around. When it seems as if the physical interaction is just about to reach the point of actual fighting, it stops and they walk away together. What is it that makes it possible for them to stop at that point? Other instances of interaction start off as enjoyable ventures but become combat. There appears to be some point in these interactions at which one person cannot ignore the behavior of another or misunderstands the behavior of another, or would be severely criticized by those around him if he continued to ignore a certain pattern of behavior and continued to see certain acts as being friendly when others had decided that in fact they were hostile and aggressive.

In work situations, too, we may seek to determine what it is that converts a simple teasing interaction into a harassment situation. In order to prevent it, we must determine the elements present so that ultimately we can build into social situations certain conditions or safety measures to convert a potentially explosive, warlike, hostile situation into one that is friendly or one in which the persons involved can resolve their differences without being destructive.

Cultural Reinforcement of Aggression

The work place is part of the larger culture and at the same time is a smaller subculture of its own. It is necessary to study both the larger culture and the subculture in order to understand the positive and negative reinforcers of aggression. Our aim is to treat not individuals but larger social entities in order to reduce this kind of interaction, which is not good for the organization or the individual.

From the positive and negative reinforcers of this kind of behavior, it is clear that there is no prohibition against aggression in our society. On the contrary, aggression is encouraged. The reinforcers are not always positive, not always negative, but where there is no specific rule, one will not expect censure for aggressive behavior. We have different limits on aggression, but while one might be arrested for jumping out into the field and attacking the umpire, the act will be considered something of a joke. One might get a reprimand from the judge, but the behavior is not really deemed bad, only impulsive and childish.

The acceptable forms of aggression change from childhood to adulthood, but not significantly. All kinds of people ask each other, under certain circumstances, "Are you going to take that?" This is a cultural assertion that one should not, that it is demeaning and one is less of a person if one "takes that." Overall, there is a notion that aggression for a reason is all right. There are certain circumstances under which it is forbidden, of course; under almost no circumstances is one to kill or injure anyone seriously, but, short of that, aggression is not only permitted and tolerated, but also encouraged.

A second permission that reinforces aggressive behavior in our culture is the reward system for winners and the relative penalty system for losers. Our society is extremely conscious of winners and losers. Where one ranks is important and must be established. One can perform grossly antisocial acts if one knows how to compensate for them. If, for example, one is a robber baron or a mobster of some kind, he can compensate for this within certain limits as long as he uses his money properly. He will be a highly respected person in political and social circules and will have influence and power. Losers, on the other hand, must not expect anything more than the crumbs of society, so there is an imperative to determine who is the winner and who is the loser.

Withdrawal is the equivalent of defeat. Once one gets involved in something, he must not quit. We hate a quitter. Once a person/worker becomes involved in an interaction, especially a competitive one, the imperative is that he continue with it until the end. If he withdraws, he has admitted that the opponent has won and is the superior. We see this in harassment situations, too. Once two people engage, or once the harassment interaction is begun, it is very difficult for either aggressor or victim to pull out. Every fight has an audience, and the behavior of the audience can be critical in determining the direction of the struggle. The audience may urge the participants on to ever greater combativeness. Or, the audience may intervene and stop the struggle, especially if it appears unequal in some way. In our harassment situations, however, we saw very little negative intervention on the part of the audience. In all but one of our cases, there was a kind of tolerance of the aggression by those around, even though many of them had been harassed themselves in the same way or by the same aggressor. There was only one instance in which a coalition was formed against the aggressor. There is a cultural imperative against becoming involved. One needs almost an organized campaign to reassure all the persons in the group that it is all right to become involved. This fear of becoming involved is one of the reasons that the group does so little to terminate a harassment situation.

It might be noted, also, that it may be somewhat comforting to see someone else suffer, for one is reassured that he himself has been spared, at least this time. This is not to say that we enjoy seeing other people suffer, but that there is some comfort and relief in knowing that one is not the target. This feeling is another of the forces making for nonintervention on the part of the group.

Related to this is the fear of standing out, of being in the spotlight. Unless the group has agreed in some way, formally and overtly, that an attack on one member will be considered an attack on all, individuals are fearful about intervening. When one goes to the police with a complaint, the police have to act; they are not acting by personal choice, but professionally. The police officer who comes to answer the complaint or to investigate it is not singled out, because he is just doing his job. But if an individual who has not been assigned a task takes it on, if he is the one who decides to right an injustice, he is at once marked. Unless he is a very strong person who can defend himself, he might well become a victim, the focus shifting from the person he was defending to himself. Unless there are institutionalized ways of dealing with harassment situations and injustices in treatment, people will remain fearful about confronting the system.

A clear double standard relating to morality and fairness exists throughout our culture. There is a set of rules of right and wrong, and society officially requires adherence to them. If a person does not declare adherence to them, he becomes suspect. At the same time, he must recognize that only a fool would consistently and in all circumstances behave in accordance with a moral standard if it functioned to his detriment. We see this standard operating in the work place, in a lack of responsiveness when confronted by injustice. When a harassed worker goes to his union representative with a complaint, the representative does not always try to protect the worker's rights. He may say, "Well, why don't you just cool it. You can take a little of that," etc. etc. The same lack of responsiveness operates informally in groups of workers who might recognize that an injustice is being done but do not necessarily feel a need to correct it or prevent its recurrence. This represents a split in our thinking. The person who is always fighting causes, who intervenes to correct injustices, is for the most part an odd character, a deviant. If he is sufficiently benign, we may smile at him, but, ultimately, we think of him as being a deviant, and no one wants to fall into that role, especially when there is no internal imperative saying that one should.

Another popular belief of almost mythic range is that unless people are driven and unless some fear is present, things are not going to happen. Both work pressure and harassment are motivated by this belief that one has to have a modicum of fear in order to engender productivity. Fear makes for conformity, for obedience to the rules; without it there will be none. Management and worker both hold the belief that, from time to time, one has to make an example of someone in order to remind everyone that there is something to fear. This element of the stressful work situation is a general cultural assumption. Therefore, the members of any work group who accept this, even though they regret or resent it, will not interfere in what they consider to be a natural situation.

There is another commonly held assumption that one gets what one deserves, that the person who has bad luck probably has done something to invite it, that the person who is hurt has been accident-prone. A variety of explanatory terms make it possible for us to attribute the calamity to the victim rather than to the aggressor, the system, or even nature in general. This cultural belief works in both harassment and work-pressure situations, and is partly responsible for the failure to help individual victims. Some persons who have a complaint will not make it, and when someone else makes the same complaint they will immediately defend the other side, presenting all the reasons why they themselves did not initiate the complaint.

Most employers, unions, and employees do not see harassment as the serious problem it actually is and do not recognize its even worse potential for creating tension that reduces productivity and accounts for conflict and strife in the work situation. Neither are they aware that harassment produces physical and mental disease that becomes social disease as it spills over to the families and communities of workers so affected. Because people take harassment for granted, they do not think in terms of prevention.

Recoveries for Psychological Disorders in Workers' Compensation[a]

The law of worker's compensation is moving toward increasing recoveries for psychic injuries. The major modernization of compensatory law is that physical trauma or injury is no longer required to recover for mental disorders stemming from work-related psychic stress. Some cases that illustrate these changes will be discussed in a later chapter.

State workers' compensation laws are statutory schemes designed to compensate workers for wages lost because of job-related injuries. Recovery in workers' compensation is based on employer liability, irrespective of fault, and

---

[a]The treatment of this subject offers a brief sidelight to the major discussion of harassment and is necessarily superficial. Selected references include: Continuing Education of the Bar, Melvin S. Witt, *California Workmen's Compensation Practice*, 1973; Warren Hanna, *California Law of Employee Injuries and Workmen's Compensation*, 2d ed., vol. 2, 1972.

stems from both the employee's status as employee and from notions of insurance. In contrast to personal injury recovery in tort, which seeks to fix blame for and indemnify for injuries, workers' compensation laws have rehabilitation as their primary purpose. Although tort and workers' compensation recovery are based on different premises, one can note a parallel development: just as in the workers' compensation situation, modern jurisdictions have also abandoned the tort requirements of physical impact as a prerequisite to recovery for mental distress.

The following discussion is based in large part on California workers' compensation statutes and case law, with the law of other jurisdictions used for comparative purposes. Because California has been in the forefront of a liberal interpretation of workers' compensation law, the cited California law may go beyond that of other jurisdictions, but it does illustrate present trends.

To recover under a workers' compensation provision, one must show that he is a "covered employee," that his injury is "compensable," and that there is a "disability" for which compensable benefits are payable. The most important requirements are an injury "arising out of the employment" and "occurring in the course of employment." Without some minimal causal connection between the work and the injury, there can be no recovery. Awards are further conditioned by the requirement, for example, that the employee not be intoxicated while injured, that he not inflict a wound on himself, not willfully and deliberately commit suicide, and not be the initial physical aggressor in an altercation resulting in injury.

"Injury" is defined as any injury or disease arising out of the employment. Such injury might be traumatic, occuring by application of physical force, or it could be nontraumatic, coming about through harmful ingestion of fumes or substances. Occupational diseases such as lead poisoning are considered injuries, for this purpose. Both the occurrence and the aggravation of such an injury can be compensated. Where preexisting conditions contribute to the injury, recovery is allowed, with an appropriate apportionment reflected in the award.

Injuries may be the result of a single incident or they may be cumulative, defined as injuries occurring as the result of repetitive mentally or physically traumatic activities extending over a period of time, the combined effect of which causes disability or need for medical treatment.

In one case in which an award was made, the claimant suffered partial paralysis from a stroke that was caused by the excessively long hours he worked as a derrick operator; he worked between ten and nineteen hours a day for an extended period of time. Another claimant also suffered a stroke that was found to have been precipitated by exposure to sixty-five consecutive days of physical and mental stress and tension during labor negotiations with unions. In another case in which the injury was also ruled cumulative, a construction worker's back disability has progressively degenerated as he continued to aggravate the problem with further work.

Workers have been awarded both temporary and permanent disability payments for psychic damage in a variety of contexts. Only a few of these circumstances are discussed here, but they suggest the range of psychological injuries that may occur and for which compensation is awarded. Again, there is a difference between workers' compensation and tort recoveries for emotional distress, but a discussion of that topic is not attempted here.

Mental and emotional injury causally connected to employment comes within the Labor Code rubric of "any injury," and can be compensated when other requisites are met. "Traumatic neurosis" is the term usually employed to describe the emotional disorder that occurs following a traumatic event.

Typically, the victim was functioning well before physical or mental trauma and claims that now he has a neurosis. This neurosis can follow typical lines of anxiety or depression or a conversion state in which one might have pain or paralysis or bizarre seizures, or it might come in the form of "I can't work," with no other concomitant symptoms, a complex that has been called "social conversion reaction" [25]. A claimant was awarded 73.25 percent permanent disability for a traumatic neurosis following a back injury, the neurosis consisting of a "disabling, resentful, defeatist attitude" plus other physical complements including headaches.

It is crucially important that there be a causal connection with the employment. California will not allow recovery unless the psychic disability was "substantially contributed to" by the employment. Here, again, as in the case of wholly physical injury where a preexisting condition is aggravated, apportionment principles apply. As noted earlier, modern jurisdictions will allow recovery for mental disturbance attributed to psychic stress without the necessity for physical trauma, provided the other requisites for recovery are met.

As long ago as 1947, recovery was allowed in such a case, where a woman who was frightened by the sight of an electrical charge, fainted and was caught by a coworker as she fell. When she again saw her coworker, she fainted, and it became impossible for her to work because of this association of the accident with the coworker. In a similar case in the same year, the claimant was frightened by lightning striking the building where she worked and developed a paralysis on her left side.

More recently, other cases have followed these precedents, allowing recovery without physical impact for work-related psychological injury. The psychic injuries in these cases were caused by pressures of the work environment itself. Baker was a fireman who developed "cardiac neurosis," a type of psychoneurotic injury of emotional origin stemming from repeated exposure to dangerous situations. He experienced unpleasant symptoms such as smoke and fume inhalation reactions; in addition, he became alarmed by the knowledge that many other firemen contracted heart disease because of such exposure on the job. He became so disturbed that he could not work. Industrial causation was shown and the California Court of Appeal annulled a decision unfavorable to Baker, clearing the way for recovery for psychic injury due to work pressure.

In 1971, a teacher claimed a cumulative psychotic disability resulting from the racial discrimination she suffered on the job. No physical trauma was required here; the "stress and strain" of the job was considered a sufficient precipitating factor.

Earlier, a Michigan Court allowed recovery for a psychotic condition resulting from work pressures for an assembly line hub assembler who felt that he could not keep up with the work. When, in an attempt to keep pace, he took components two at a time to work on, he was reprimanded by his supervisor. His fear of failure and censure became so severe that he developed a psychosis, diagnosed as paranoia or paranoid schizophrenia. He was awarded temporary disability for the duration of his psychosis. This case also illustrates the award of benefits for traumatic neurosis where the worker is diagnosed as having an underlying personality disorder, here, a predisposition to the development of schizophrenia.

Under the Longshoreman's and Harbor Worker's Compensation Act, a kind of federal workers' compensation act, a federal court allowed recovery for psychic injury without physical trauma when a Red Cross volunteer in Japan suffered a mental breakdown diagnosed as acute paranoid schizophrenia owing to abnormal job stress. His serious disagreements with other personnel and a sharply increased workload brought on the reaction, which was found to have arisen out of and in the course of employment. Workers have also been compensated for emotional shock after observing coworkers being hurt.

In a number of cases, mental and emotional disorders resulting from industrial injuries have driven workers to commit suicide. Whether compensation could be paid to surviving dependents of the decedent often turned on resolution of the causation issue. In one case where there was also an issue of whether the wound was self-inflicted, the worker had become a manic depressive because of overwork and worry. In its order annulling an Industrial Accident Commission ruling denying benefits to the widow, the Court reasoned as follows:

Where an employee receives an industrial injury and the resultant pain is such that he believes he cannot continue to stand it, where he feels that there is only one way out, where any condition results which causes him to feel that death will afford him his only relief, his act of suicide is one directly resulting from his injury, unless it appears that he could have resisted the impulse to so act.

In a similar case, one of the issues was the causal connection between a work-related injury and the suicide. Another question was about the willfulness and deliberateness of the suicide, which limits recoveries in suicides. A high school teacher had twisted his back while giving a classroom demonstration. His "industrial" injury led to a feeling of hopelessness that gradually led him to suicide. Although he was said to have had an unstable, psychopathic personality, death benefits were payable to his widow on the basis that without the industrial injury, there would have been no suicide.

Outside California, an evenly divided Michigan Supreme Court required neither a physical injury nor an occupational disease as a prerequisite to awarding death benefits to the widow of a suicide victim. This man committed suicide after becoming depressed by a state legislative committee investigation of the mental hospital where he worked, and this was sufficient to meet the causation requirement. A statutory limitation similar to California's barring compensation for voluntary, intentional, and willful suicide was avoided by reasoning analogous to "diminished capacity," that the victim's own thought processes had been too impaired by depression for his actions to be voluntary, intentional, or willful.

These developments in administrative and judicial decisions are of utmost importance in that they define a new category of illness: mental illness caused directly by work, unrelated to intermediate physical trauma or illness. It is understandable, therefore, that the worker who suffers from an emotional disturbance would consciously or unconsciously seek its causes in his work rather than in his marriage or in himself. He feels better if he can say, "They drove me crazy," rather than, "I went crazy." More and more workers who believe their jobs caused their emotional problems now file claims and often enlist the help of lawyers to fight the cases, so they can be officially declared ill because of job pressures or the harassing hostile behavior of their coworkers.

Some Recommendations for Public Policy

Broad policy measures are needed to prevent harassment in the work place. Especially in a time of economic slump, the problem becomes of great concern. Industry is pressed to reduce costs and will push its employees to produce more, faster. All workers will perceive this as pressure, but some will experience it as harassment; some will harass those who are incapable of increasing their productivity to equal the output of their coworkers. Coworkers will single out the laggards and the vulnerable. Some will attack those who produce less or produce more slowly, because they believe that this puts an additional burden on themselves; others will see this as an opportunity to identify the less productive so that if a cutback occurs, management will drop the "marked" workers first. Others, both supervisors and coworkers, will respond to the anxiety engendered by economic recession by discharging it through teasing and other forms of unpleasantness toward each other. The consuming public, feeling increasingly "ripped off" by higher prices and less service for its personal and tax dollars, will vent its anger on those with whom it comes in contact, namely the workers who deliver the products or the services—the grocery clerk, the bus driver, the school teacher, or the repairman.

Workers who fear losing their jobs because no others are available will tolerate pressure and harassment until they can no longer do so; the weak will break first. Unhappy workers will be more reluctant to use early retirement as a solution because inflation threatens to wipe out the buying power of that lesser income. Supplementary jobs would be more difficult to find. The results will be: (1) a killing of the spirit of cooperation so necessary for a society under stress; (2) a group of angry workers who will consciously or unconsciously subvert the system; (3) additional claims for compensation for mental and physical disability due to harassment; and (4) a greater demand for the services of physical and mental health facilities.

In order to minimize these undesirable developments, the Occupational Safety and Health Act of 1970 should be implemented. This is federal legislation that seeks "to assure so far as possible every working man and woman in the nation safe and healthful working conditions and to preserve our human resources. [11]. The congressional declaration of purpose states: "The Congress finds that personal injuries and illnesses arising out of work situations impose a substantial burden upon and are a hindrance to, interstate commerce in terms of lost production, wage loss, medical expenses, and disability compensation payments."

Harassment is clearly included within the rubric of occupational safety and health. Congress listed various means through which safe and healthful working conditions can be assured, including "providing for research in the field of occupational safety and health, including the psychological factors involved, and . . . developing innovative methods, techniques, and approaches for dealing with occupational safety and health problems . . ."

The Secretary of the Department of Health, Education, and Welfare is authorized to conduct such research directly or by grant or contract. A National Institute for Occupational Safety and Health is established to carry out these tasks, and is to do research on "the motivational and behavioral factors relating to the field of occupational safety and health." The legislation provides for training and education of employers and employees in "the recognition, avoidance, and prevention of unsafe or unhealthful working conditions . . . " and provides for government consultations with those groups to discuss "effective means of preventing occupational injuries and illnesses."

The Occupational Safety and Health Act authorized a study and evaluation of state workers' compensation laws as well, "to determine if such laws provide an adequate, prompt, and equitable system of compensation for injury or death arising out of or in the course of employment." The 1972 report of the National Commission on State Workmen's Compensation Laws provides a carefully documented set of recommendations for needed changes in workers' compensation laws. Many of the Commission's conclusions are in accord with the recommendations of the California Worker's Compensation Institute. These are consistent with conclusions we have drawn independently based on our observations of the workers' compensation system as it affected our patients. In general, the commission found state workers' compensation schemes inadequate and inequitable. The Commission recommended increased comprehensiveness in workers' compensation, both as to covered employees and as to covered illness or injury. Provisions for greater medical care plus vocational guidance and rehabilitation were strongly urged. The need for an effective, simplified delivery system was stressed.

Further reason for acting now to combat harassment at work is found in the growing awareness of stress at work [28,140,190,153]. Moreover, changing attitudes toward work and toward its role in our lives have become the legitimate concern of numerous groups. All levels of government—federal, state, and local— in addition to private industries large and small, are examining questions of job restructuring along with flexible work schedules. The term "job restructuring" includes, narrowly, allowing several employees to split a full-time job; broadly, the term encompasses many changes in employment that would reflect different life styles and expectations of potential employees. Thus, harassment and the host of subsidiary issues it raises are serious, pervasive public concerns that deserve full study and action.

Our approach to public policy should be from four directions: research, legislation, enforcement, and on-the-job programs to change attitudes.

Research

In any public policy matter, one must recognize the need to confront the fears of individuals and established groups. Many think government will preempt their role. Many fear that change will be costly and they therefore oppose any innova- tions. For this and other reasons, the role of the private sector, institutes, and foundations, cannot be overstressed. Private organizations can award research grants to fund pilot projects for the prevention of harassment. These projects can demonstrate that there is nothing to fear from a nonharassed work setting and that antiharassment recommendations should become public policy. Federal and state governments should lead the research, through OSHA study grants and other means such as the National Institute of Mental Health. Presidential and congressional commissions are also useful for calling attention to a problem as widespread as this and for mobilizing intellectual and experimental resources to solve the problem.

Research should consider preharassment problems such as alienation at work, the consequences of a mobile anomic society, and the need to make work more compatible with the needs of workers. The science of creating and extending social networks must be studied to find ways to increase the closeness of those who work together so that they will be happier and more productive. Evaluation research is needed to explore the thesis that when people are more productive, they not only receive more goods and services, but also derive greater emotional security from work. The benefit is universal.

Management generally has opposed worker organization, seeing it as a threat to the prosperity of the business. But when workers do organize, employers may well find that employee groups are willing and able to help meet problems of production, sales, and inflation.

National conferences, both governmental and private, on alienation at work are needed. Harassment can be properly studied only as one aspect of that broader topic. A White House conference might be held, with participants from all relevant fields who have actually studied and dealt with the problems of harassment and work pressure: workers, management, physicians, psychiatrists, clinical and social psychologists, lawyers and persons experienced in social welfare and workers' compensation administration.

The purposes of such a meeting would be to provide a forum for launching recommendations based on the above research—which would become public and private policy—and for increasing national awareness of the problem. National Advisory councils and state governor's or legislative councils dedicated to improving the work environment could also be helpful.

Legislation

Pursuant to OSHA, extensive federal regulations have been issued regarding physical aspects of occupational health and safety. The psychological aspects of work could be similarly regulated under that act. OSHA permits broad state regulation as well.

Changes in workers' compensation laws may be forthcoming as a result of the 1972 *Report of the National Commission on State Workmen's Compensation Laws* referred to above. Harassment should figure prominently as part of the current reevaluation of workers' compensation (and some retirement) systems. By providing for a legitimized yet reasonable "harassment" category within these systems, methods other than protracted and expensive litigation might be developed to handle many of the problems we have seen. A system for processing these problems would also prevent many claims of harassment. The programs put forth here would in some measure best be in legislative form; others are best implemented voluntarily in individual businesses or governmental departments.

Enforcement

Public pressure is strongly needed—pressure from public interest groups, private interest groups, private voluntary associations and unions, to name a few—to compel enforcement of existing and future legislation and to force the development of programs to prevent harassment and treat its victims. Existing enforcement offices in the employment field are overworked and ineffective: EEOC and FEPC sometimes deal marginally with cases of harassment as we define it but

have several years' accumulation of cases. Investigations actually undertaken are
usually unsatisfactory to the complainant. The same is true of enforcement of
OSHA regulations. If these groups are to take on enforcement of measures
designed to combat harassment, they will need public support.

In several metropolitan areas, people in a variety of occupations have organized
coalitions in support of occupational health and safety. Chicago's CACOSH and
San Francisco's BACOSH (Chicago and Bay Area Coalition for Occupational
Safety & Health) hold informational meetings with employees and prepare
programs to safeguard their physical and emotional health at work. Such work
will facilitate OSHA's meaningful enforcement by educating its beneficiaries. At
least one major union, the Oil, Chemical and Atomic Workers International Union
(OCAW), has implemented OSHA requirements through its negotiated contract
provisions.

Programs

Citizen participation is important in inaugurating and carrying out programs
through independent organizations or through service on governmental boards
and commissions. Community mental health boards are particularly suited to
working on harassment because they tend to be life-focused rather than symptom-
focused, as physicians are. Thus, such groups are likely to be more sensitive to
the social problem of harassment than an individual professional person might
be.

Vocational and technical schools and high school career counselors should
give serious attention to educating students about problems they may encounter
in work relationships with coworkers, management, and customers. Counseling
is offered for marriage relationships and relationships with children, but rarely
for relationships with those at work. Since work is such a significant part of life,
occupying at least forty years for most workers, and since discomfort at work is
becoming of greater concern, problems arising in the work setting should be
covered in school curricula. In addition, schools should explore with their
students the issue of how to extend work relationships into the community. The
barriers have been tremendous in the past, and, as noted elsewhere, alienation
and harassment at work are directly related to the isolation of work relationships
from home and social relationships. Schools can join with experts in looking
into the reasons why people fear extending their work ties. Classes should
provide workers (and managers) with techniques for diminishing barriers so that
they can become more of a community. Unions certainly would benefit their
members by providing such classes, and many have focused on education and
prevention.

Campaigns designed to promote the notion "be kind to your fellow worker"
should be initiated, using sound advertising and public education techniques.

Posters, buttons, meetings, and classes are all part of this effort. Such a campaign would be a useful way in which to begin a peer counseling or grievance program. Campaigns of this nature have succeeded at hospitals, for example, where "Think Patient" buttons have, at least for a brief time, impelled staff to be kinder to patients. The immediate results of such an effort cannot be very great, but it would encourage people to think in a more positive and humane way.

Work clinics should be established as part of large medical facilities. Comprising workers from the medical and rehabilitative fields, these clinics can study, diagnose, and treat persons who complain of physical symptoms or of emotional problems and who are discovered to have work problems as well. Whereas physicians of all types tend to segregate work problems and to lump them with poverty into the category of conditions about which they can do nothing, the existence of a work clinic in a medical facility provides a referral resource or even a "dumping place" where the patient who has a work problem can have it considered and treated in relationship to his medical and psychiatric symptoms.

One such clinic, organized by the author, has been in existence for two years and it has demonstrated that when work problems are considered and attended to, spurious medical symptoms are dropped, psychotherapy becomes more formal, and the outcome of medical and psychiatric treatment is easier to evaluate. Job counseling and rehabilitation can be more specific when the treating persons have a full awareness of medical and psychiatric problems and how these problems evolve as the patient seeks work or actually becomes employed.

Exiting

The patients over many years who have discussed with us the futility of their lives and of their work have led us to the conclusion that we must develop legitimate, socially respected, economically feasible exits through which people can leave jobs that discomfort them and go into new fields. They must be able to do so without losing "face" or retirement benefits and with minimal salary loss.

This program would require the cooperation of a number of social service agencies and a new view of work as well. Other writers have discussed exiting proposals. For example, the Task Force that prepared *Work in America* [164] wrote of a "self-renewal" job training program for workers who wanted to change jobs. The concept of job mobility is, of course, not new, and doubtless many facets of the subject have been extensively covered elsewhere. We offer these suggestions based on our observations of several thousand workers, with the idea that they can contribute to more comprehensive, functional planning.

After years in the same job, many workers want to get out. They are frustrated by the routine, dull nature of the tasks. No matter how challenging at the start, all jobs become repetitive. Many workers suffer discomfort.

Physically, work becomes exhausting, and the worker discovers that an assembly plant or construction job at age fifty is much harder than it was at twenty. His emotional discomfort may be even greater than his actual physical pain. He realizes that increased tenure may not mean higher status. His coworkers may regard him just as they did when he began work. His spouse and children regard other members of the community more highly than they regard him. His children do not aspire to "follow in his footsteps."

The worker becomes irritable. He becomes so concerned about his physical health that he may become hypochondriacal. He may receive some reassurance from sympathetic coworkers, but if they are unsympathetic, he becomes more fearful of physical impairments. The result is that he feels he must get out of the job that may be causing his real or imagined pain.

Whereas previously he may have been ambivalent, he no longer feels uncertain. He desperately wants to leave, though he does not consciously formulate this because to do so would run counter to his image of himself. It would mean that all his physical symptoms were in some way a ploy to get him out of difficulty. Consequently, he goes through a "social conversion reaction" saying, "I am disabled." The symptom is the disability itself. He does not say "I'm paralyzed," even though he might say that he has some muscle weakness; he does not say that the pain is overwhelming, even though he admits pain.

Many workers do not go through a full blown social conversion reaction but do grow to hate their work and would profit from the opportunity to enter a new position where they could be productively employed. An exiting program would require a significant commitment of thought, time, and money. Meaningful job counseling, training, and rehabilitation, plus psychological counseling, would be required. Federal, state, and local governments would need to cooperate as would the private employment sector. We would have to reorient our thinking about the role and modes of work in this country; notions of flexibility, mobility, compatibility and their effect on productivity would have to be fully reconsidered.

An economic feasibility study would have to be conducted before any programs were initiated, but it is our belief that both the economic and the psychic benefits would far outweigh transition costs.

Prevention aims at decreasing the frequency and intensity of undesirable conditions. This is true of disease and also of harassment. Although each preventive planner dreams of ultimately eliminating a condition, the immediate goal is to reduce the frequency and intensity of undesirable episodes. Those interested in the prevention of harassment, work pressure, and other undesirable work problems have the same goal. Although industrial accidents, harassment, and work pressure cannot be eliminated, it is hoped that through study of the causes of these problems and through education and legislation, their occurrence will be reduced.

References

1. Adams, J. S., "Wage Inequalities, Productivity and Work Quality," *Industrial Relations*, 3:9-16, 1963-1964.

2. Adorno, T. W., Frenkel-Brunswik, E., Levinson, D. J., and Sanford, R. N. *The Authoritarian Personality.* New York: Harper, 1950.

3. Allee, W. C. *Social Life of Animals.* New York: Norton, 1938.

4. Allport, G. W., "Catharsis and the Reduction of Prejudice," *Journal of Social Issues*, 1:3-10, 1945.

5. Ames, L. B., "What to Do If Your Child Is Bullied," *Family Circle*, March 1974, 34.

6. Appley, M. H. and Trumbull, R. *Psychological Stress.* New York: Appleton-Century-Crofts, 1967.

7. Ardrey, R. *African Genesis.* New York: Dell, 1971.

8. Armstrong, R. B. "Job Content and Context Factors Related to Satisfaction for Different Occupational Levels," *Journal of Applied Psychology*, 55:57-65, 1971.

9. Ash, P., "The Parties to the Grievance," *Personnel Psychology*, 23:13-37, 1970.

10. Bagatelos, P. A., "Initial Choice of Physician under Workmen's Compensation: Is California Ripe for the Panel Approach?" *University of San Francisco Law Review*, 8:149-171, Fall, 1973.

11. Bateson, G. and Mead, M. *Balinese Culture: A Photographic Analysis.* New York: New York Academy of Sciences, 1942.

12. Behan, R. C. and Hirschfield, A. H., "Disability without Disease or Accident," *Archives of Environmental Health*, 12:655-659, 1966.

13. Benedict, R. *The Chrysanthemum and the Sword.* Boston: Houghton Mifflin, 1946.

14. ____. *Patterns of Culture.* Boston: Houghton Mifflin, 1934.

15. Berkowitz, L., "Aggressive Humor as a Stimulus to Aggressive Responses," *Journal of Personality and Social Psychology*, 16:710-717, 1970.

16. ____ and Green, J. A., "The Stimulus Qualities of the Scapegoat," *Journal of Abnormal and Social Psychology*, 64:293-301, 1962.

17. Bixler, R. H., "How G. S. Became a Scapegoater," *Journal of Abnormal and Social Psychology*, 43:230-232, 1948.

18. Bradney, P., "The Joking Relationship in Industry," *Human Relations*, 10:179-187, 1957.

19. Bragg, R. L., "A Study of Certain Psychological Aspects of Vocational (Occupational) Disability," *American Journal of Psychiatry*, 119: 570-571, 1962.

20. Braverman, M. and Hacker, F. J., "Psychotraumatic Reactions," *Industrial Medicine and Surgery*, 35:957-966, 1966.

21. Brenman, M., "On Teasing and Being Teased: And the Problem of 'Moral Masochism,'" *Psychoanalytic Studies of the Child*, 7:264-285, 1952.

22. Brill, N. Q. and Glass, J., "Workmen's Compensation for Psychiatric Disorders," *Journal of the American Medical Association*, 193:345-348, August 2, 1965.

23. Brodsky, C. M., "Compensation Illness as a Retirement Channel," *Journal of the American Geriatrics Society*, 19:51-60, 1971.

24. _____, "Personality disorders," in *The New Catholic Encyclopedia*. New York: McGraw-Hill, 1966, 768-776.

25. _____, "Social Psychiatric Consequences of Job Incompetence," *Comprehensive Psychiatry*, 12:526-536, 1971.

26. _____, "The Systemic Incompatibility of Medical Practice and Psychotherapy," *Diseases of the Nervous System*, 31:597-603, 1970.

27. Bromberg, W., "The Clinical Picture of Traumatic Neurosis," *Journal of Forensic Sciences*, 1:80-85, 1956.

28. Buck, B. E. *Working under Pressure*. New York: Russak Crane, 1972.

29. Buss, A. H. *The Psychology of Aggression*. New York: Wiley, 1961.

30. Byrne, D., "The Relationship between Humor and the Expression of Hostility," *Journal of Abnormal and Social Psychology*, 53:84-89, 1956.

31. Chambers, W. N., "Emotional Factors Complicating Industrial Injuries," *Journal of Occupational Medicine*, 5:568-574, 1963.

32. Coffee, D. and McLean, A. A., "Mental Health in Industry: Whose Responsibility?" *Journal of Occupational Medicine*, 9:213-214, 1967.

33. Coser, R. L., "Laughter among Colleagues: A Study of Social Functions of Humor among Staff of a Mental Hospital," *Psychiatry*, 23:81-95, 1960.

34. _____, "Some Social Functions of Laughter: A Study of Humor in a Hospital Setting," *Human Relations*, 12:171-182, 1959.

35. Creedman, N. and Creedman, M., "Angst, the Curse of the Working Class," *Human Behavior*, 1:9-14, 1972.

36. Daniels, A. K. and Daniels, R. R., "The Social Function of the Career Fool," *Psychiatry*, 27:219-229, 1964.

37. Davis, A. and Dollard, J. *Children of Bondage*. Washington, D. C.: American Council on Education, 1940.

38. DeCharms, R. and Wilkins, E. J., "Some Effects of Verbal Expression of Hostility," *Journal of Abnormal and Social Psychology*, 66:462-470, 1963.

39. Deci, E. L., "Work, Who Does Not Like It and Why," *Psychology Today*, 6:57-58, 1972.

40. *Diagnostic and Statistical Manual of Mental Disorders*, 2d ed., vol. 2. Washington, D. C.: American Psychiatric Association, 1968.

41. Dworkin, E. S. and Efran, J. S., "The Angered: Their Susceptibility to Varieties of Humor," *Journal of Personality and Social Psychology*, 6:233-236, 1967.

42. Erikson, E. H., "Childhood and Tradition in Two American Indian Tribes," *The Psychoanalytic Study of the Child*, 1:319-350, 1945.

43. Etkin, W. (ed.) *Social Behavior and Organization among Vertebrates*. Chicago: University of Chicago Press, 1964.

44. Feldman, R. A., "Group Integration and Intense Interpersonal Disliking," *Human Relations*, 22:405-413, 1969.

45. Fenn, D. H. and Yankelovich, D., "Responding to the Employee Voice," *Harvard Business Review*, 50:83-91, 1972.

46. Foster, M. W., "Neurosis and Trauma," *Clinical Orthopaedics*, 32:54-59, 1964.

47. French, J. R. P., "Person Role Fit," *Occupational Mental Health*, 3:15-20, 1973.

48. Freud, S., "Humor," *International Journal of Psycho-Analysis*, 9:1-6, 1928.

49. Fry, W. F. *Sweet Madness: A Study of Humor*. Palo Alto, Calif.: Pacific Books, 1963.

50. Glaser, D. *The Effectiveness of a Prison and Parole System*. New York: Bobbs-Merrill, 1969.

51. Goffman, E. *Asylums*. New York: Doubleday, 1961.

52. _____, "On Face-Work: An Analysis of Ritual Elements in Social Interaction," *Psychiatry*, 18:213-231, 1955.

53. _____. *Presentation of Self in Everyday Life*. New York: Doubleday, Anchor Books, 1959.

54. _____. *Stigma: Notes on the Management of Spoiled Identity*. Englewood Cliffs, N.J.: Prentice-Hall, 1963.

55. Golightly, C. and Scheffler, I., "Playing the Dozens: A Note," *Journal of Abnormal and Social Psychology*, 43:104-105, 1948.

56. Goodrich, A. T., Henry, J., and Goodrich, D. W., "Laughter in Psychiatric Staff Conferences: A Sociopsychiatric Analysis," *American Journal of Orthopsychiatry*, 24:175-184, 1954.

57. Goodwin, D. W., "Psychiatry and the Mysterious Medical Complaint," *Journal of the American Medical Association*, 209:1884-1888, September 22, 1969.

58. Grieff, B. S., "To What Degree Is Work Performance Related to Occupational Stress?" *Occupational Mental Health*, 2:11, 1973.

59. Griggs, J. F., "Differentiation of Neurosis from Organic Disease," *Postgraduate Medicine*, 29:301-308, 1961.

60. Gross, E. *Work and Society.* New York: Thomas Y. Crowell, 1958.

61. Gusinde, M. Die Feuerland Indioner. Wien: Modling, 1931-1939.

62. Haire, M., Ghiselli, E. E., and Porter, L. W., "Psychological Research on Pay: An Overview," *Industrial Relations*, 3:3-8, 1963-1964.

63. Hall, E. T. *The Silent Language.* New York: Doubleday, 1959.

64. Hanna, W. *California Law of Employee Injuries and Workmen's Compensation.* 3rd. ed., vols. 1, 2, 1972.

65. Herford, M. E. M. "The Effect of Psychosomatic Disorders in Industry," in J. O. Wisdom and H. H. Wolff (eds.), *The Role of Psychosomatic Disorder in Adult Life, Proceedings of the Society for Psychosomatic Research at the Royal College of Physicians, London, 1961.* 1965.

66. Hermann, J. A., De Montes, A. I., Dominguez, B., Montes, F., and Hopkins, B. L., "Effects of Bonuses for Punctuality on the Tardiness of Industrial Workers," *Journal of Applied Behavior Analysis*, 6:563-570, 1973.

67. Hertzler, J. O. *Laughter: A Socio-Scientific Analysis.* New York: Exposition Press, 1970.

68. Herzberg, F. "The Motivation to Work," in E. A. Fleishman (ed.), *Studies in Personnel and Industrial Psychology.* Homewood, Ill.: Dorsey, 1967, 282-287.

69. _____, "One More Time: How Do You Motivate Employees?" *Harvard Business Review*, 46:53-62, 1968.

70. Hetherington, E. M. and Wray, N. P., "Aggression, Need for Social Approval, and Humor Preferences," *Journal of Abnormal and Social Psychology*, 68:685-689, 1964.

71. Hinrichs, J. R., "Psychology of Men at Work," *Annual Review of Psychology*, 21:519-554, 1970.

72. Hirschfeld, A. H. and Behan, R. C., "The Accident Process, II. Toward a More Rational Treatment of Industrial Injuries," *Journal of the American Medical Association*, 186:300, 1963.

73. _____, and _____, "Disability," *International Psychiatry Clinic*, 6:239-248, 1969.

74. _____, and _____, "The Seminar Method for the Treatment of Disability, III. Factors in the Doctor-Patient Relationship," *Journal of Occupational Medicine*, 9:48-52, 1967.

75. Hodge, J. R., "The Passive-Dependent versus the Passive-Aggressive Personality," *United States Armed Forces Medical Journal*, 6:84-90, 1955.

76. Jacobson, E., "The Child's Laughter," *The Psychoanalytic Study of the Child*, 2:39-61, 1946.

77. Jurgensen, C. E., "What Job Applicants Say They Want," in E. A. Fleishman (ed.), *Studies in Personnel and Industrial Psychology*. Homewood, Ill.: Dorsey, 1967.

78. Kahn, R. L., "Conflict, Ambiguity, and Overload: Three Elements in Job Stress," *Occupational Mental Health*, 3:2-9, 1973.

79. Kahy, R. L., Wolfe, D. M., Quinn, R. P., and Snoek, J. D. *Organizational Stress: Studies in Role Conflict and Ambiguity*. New York: Wiley, 1964.

80. Kaufmann, H. *Aggression and Altruism*. New York: Holt, 1970.

81. Keiser, L. *The Traumatic Neurosis*. Philadelphia: Lippincott, 1968.

82. Kiev, A., "Crisis Intervention in Industry," *Journal of Occupational Medicine*, 12:158-163, 1970.

83. Klapp, O. E., "Heroes, Villains and Fools, as Agents of Social Control," *American Sociological Review*, 19:56-62, 1954.

84. Klein, S. M. *Workers Under Stress: The Impact of Work Pressure on Group Cohesion*. Lexington, Ky.: University of Kentucky Press, 1971.

85. Kornhauser, A. *Mental Health of the Industrial Worker*. New York: Wiley, 1965.

86. Kreps, J. M., "Modern Man and his Instinct of Workmanship," *American Journal of Psychiatry*, 130:179-183, 1973.

87. Kubie, L. S., "The Destructive Potential of Humor in Psychotherapy," *American Journal of Psychiatry*, 127:37-42, 1971.

88. Landy, D. and Mettee, D., "Evaluation of an Aggressor as a Function of Exposure to Cartoon Humor," *Journal of Personality and Social Psychiatry*, 12:66-71, 1969.

89. Langner, R. and Michael, S. T. *Life Stress and Mental Health. The Midtown Manhattan Study*. New York: Free Press, 1963.

90. Larson, D. L. and Spreitzer, E. A., "Education, Occupation, and Age as Correlates of Work Orientation," *Psychological Reports*, 33:879-884, 1973.

91. Layden, M., "Psychiatric Aspects of Malingering," *Southern Medical Journal*, 60:1237-1239, 1967.

92. Leary, T. *Interpersonal Diagnosis of Personality*. New York: Ronald Press, 1959.

93. Leedy, J. (ed.) *Compensation in Psychiatric Disability and Rehabilitation*. Springfield, Ill.: Charles C Thomas, 1972.

94. Lemert, E. M., "Paranoia and the Dynamics of Exclusion," *Sociometry*, 25:2-20, 1962.

95. Levin, S.,"Toward a Classification of External Factors Capable of Inducing Psychological Stress," *International Journal of Psycho-Analysis*, 47:546-551, 1966.

96. Levine, J. and Redlich, F. C., "Failure to Understand Humor," *Psychoanalytic Quarterly*, 24:560-572, 1955.

97. Levinson, D. J., "Role, Personality, and Social Structure in the Organization Setting," *Journal of Abnormal and Social Psychology*, 58:170-180, 1959.

98. Levinson, H. "Easing the Pain of Personal Loss," *Harvard Business Review*, 50:80-88, 1972.

99. _____, "Emotional Toxicity of the Work Environment," *Archives of Environmental Health*, 19:239-243, 1969.

100. _____, "A Psychoanalytic View of Occupational Stress," *Occupational Mental Health*, 3:2-13, 1973.

101. Lieblich, A., "Reaction to the Frustration of the Other," *Human Relations*, 23:335-344, 1970.

102. Lipowski, Z. J., "Psychosocial Aspects of Disease," *Annals of Internal Medicine*, 71:1197-1206, 1969.

103. Lomas, P. "Family Interaction and the Sick Role," in J. O. Wisdom and H. H. Wolff (eds.), *The Role of Psychosomatic Disorder in Adult Life. Proceedings of the Society for Psychosomatic Research at the Royal College of Physicians, London, November, 1961.* 1965.

104. McDanald, E. C., "Susceptibility of the Neurotic to Trauma," *Diseases of the Nervous System*, 16:218-221, 1955.

105. McGrady, P. M., "The Worksick Virus," *True*, January 1974, 23, 70-71.

106. McLean, A., "Occupational 'Stress,' a Misnomer," *Occupational Mental Health*, 2:12-15, 1973.

107. McMurry, R. N., "Conflicts in Human Values," *Harvard Business Review*, 41:130-145, 1963.

108. Margolis, B. K. and Kroes, W. H., "Occupational Stress and Strain," *Occupational Mental Health*, 2:4-6, 1973.

109. Martineau, W. H. "A Model of the Social Functions of Humor," in J. H. Goldstein and P. E. McGhee (eds.), *The Psychology of Humor.* New York: Academic Press, 1972, pp. 114-125.

110. Mead, M. "Sex and Temperament in Three Primitive Societies, in M. Mead, *From the South Seas.* New York: Morrow, 1939.

111. Megargee, E. I. and Hokanson, J. E. (eds.) *The Dynamics of Aggression.* New York: Harper & Row, 1970.

112. Meineker, R. L., "Psychology of Work," *Journal of Occupational Medicine*, 14:212-215, 1972.

113. Menninger, W. C. "The Meaning of Work in Western Society," in H. Borow (ed.), *Man in A World of Work.* Boston: Houghton Mifflin, 1964.

114. Mulcahy, M. "Accident Neurosis," *Journal of the Irish Medical Association,* 58:197-201, 1966.

115. Murray, H. A., "The Psychology of Humor: 2. Mirth Responses to Disparagement Jokes as a Manifestation of an Aggressive Disposition," *Journal of Abnormal and Social Psychology*, 29:66-81, 1934.

116. Murstein, B. I., "The Effect of Amount of Possession of the Trait of Hostility on Accuracy of Perception of Hostility in Others," *Journal of Abnormal and Social Psychology*, 62:216-220, 1961.

117. Nahum, L. H., "Pathologic Malingering," *Connecticut Medicine*, 28:858-862, 1964.

118. Nealey, S. M., "Pay and Benefit Preference," *Industrial Relations*, 3:17-28, 1963-1964.

119. Neff, W. S. *Work and Human Behavior.* New York: Atherton, 1968.

120. Newcomb, T. M., "Autistic Hostility and Social Reality," *Human Relations,* 1:69-86, 1947.

121. O'Brien, D. W. *An Analysis of Special California Workman's Insurance Programs.* 2d. ed., Winter Brook Publishing, 1972.

122. O'Connell, W. E., "The Adaptive Functions of Wit and Humor," *Journal of Abnormal and Social Psychology*, 61:263-270, 1960.

123. O'Leary, D., "The Ontario System: Non-Adversary Workmen's Compensation," *Trial*, 9:33-35, 38, November-December 1973.

124. Overley, T. M., "Discovering the Functional Illness in Interview," *Journal of the American Medical Association*, 186:776-777, November 23, 1963.

125. Owens, W. H., Jr., "The Less They Have, the More They Want: Reexamination of Concern with Status," *Psychological Reports*, 33:828-830, 1973.

126. Parkinson, C. N. *Parkinson's Law.* Boston: Houghton Mifflin, 1957.

127. Pokorney, A. D. and Moore, F. J., "Neuroses and Compensation: Chronic Psychiatric Disorders Following Injury or Stress in Compensable Situations," *Archives of Industrial Hygiene and Occupational Medicine*, 8:547-563, 1953.

128. Radcliffe-Brown, A. R. *Structure and Function in Primitive Society.* New York: Free Press, 1968.

129. Radin, S. S., "Job Phobia: School Phobia Revisited," *Comprehensive Psychiatry*, 13:251-257, 1972.

130. Rank, B. and MacNaughton, D., "A Clinical Contribution to Early Ego Development," *Psychoanalytic Study of the Child*, 5:53-65, 1950.

131. Reich, A., "The Structure of the Grotesque-Comic Sublimation," *Menninger Clinic Bulletin*, 13:160-171, 1949.

132. Roethlisberger, F. J. "The Foreman: Master and Victim of Double Talk, in S. D. Hoslet (ed.), *Human Factors in Management*. New York: Harper, 1951, 39-59.

133. Rogg, S. G. and D'Alonzo, C. A. *Emotions and the Job*. Springfield, Ill.: Charles C Thomas, 1965.

134. Ross, W. D. *Practical Psychiatry for Industrial Physicians*. Springfield, Ill.: Charles C Thomas, 1956.

135. Ruesch, J. and Brodsky, C. M., "The Concept of Social Disability," *Archives of General Psychiatry*, 19:394-403, 1968.

136. *San Fransisco Chronicle*, July 17, 1974, 3.

137. Schaller, G. B. *The Mountain Gorilla*. Chicago: University of Chicago Press, 1963.

138. Schlessinger, N. and Blau, D., "A Psychiatric Study of a Retraining Command," *United States Armed Forces Medical Journal*, 8:397-405, 1957.

139. Schneck, J. M., "Pseudo-Malingering," *Diseases of the Nervous System*, 23:396-398, 1962.

140. Selye, H. *Stress and Distress*. Philadelphia: Lippincott, 1974.

141. Shaw, R. S., "Pathologic Malingering: The Painful Disabled Extremity," *New England Journal of Medicine*, 271:22-26, 1964.

142. Shuval, J., Antonovsky, A., and Davies, A. M., "Illness: A Mechanism for Coping with Failure," *Social Science and Medicine*, 7:259-265, 1973.

143. Singer, D. L., "Aggression Arousal, Hostile Humor, Catharsis," *Journal of Personality and Social Psychology*, Monograph Supplement, 8(1): part 2, 1-14, 1968.

144. _____, Gollob, H. F., and Levine, J., "Mobilization of Inhibitions and the Enjoyment of Aggressive Humor," *Journal of Personality*, 35:562-569, 1967.

145. Singer, R. C. and Shaw, C. C., "The Passive-Aggressive Personality," *United States Armed Forces Medical Journal*, 8:62-69, 1957.

146. Sommer, R. *Personal Space: The Behavioral Basis of Design*. Englewood Cliffs, N. J.: Prentice-Hall, 1969.

147. Sperling, S. J., "On the Psychodynamics of Teasing," *American Psychoanalytic Association Journal*, 1:458-483, 1953.

148. Stellman, J. M. and Daum, S. M. *Work Is Dangerous to Your Health*. New York: Vintage Books, 1973.

149. Stephenson, R. M., "Conflict and Control Functions of Humor," *American Journal of Sociology*, 56:569-574, 1950-1951.

150. Street, L., "Game Forms in the Factory Group," *Berkeley Journal of Sociology*, 4:44-55, 1958.

151. Sykes, G. M. *Society of Captives: A Study of a Maximum Security Prison.* Princeton, N. J.: Princeton University Press, 1958.

152. Taylor, F. K., "A Logical Analysis of the Medico-Psychological Concept of Disease," *Psychological Medicine*, 1:356-364, 1971.

153. Terkel, S. *Working.* New York: Pantheon, 1974.

154. Thompson, G. N., "Posttraumatic Psychoneurosis: A Statistical Survey," *American Journal of Psychiatry*, 121:1043, 1965.

155. *Time*, "The Law: Hell in the Factory," June 7, 1971, 39.

156. Toch, H. *Violent Men.* Chicago: Aldine, 1969.

157. Trahair, R. C. S., "The Workers' Judgment of Pay and Additional Benefits: An Empirical Study," *Human Relations*, 23:201-223, 1970.

158. Uyterhoeven, H. E. R., "General Managers in the Middle," *Harvard Business Review*, 50:75-85, 1972.

159. *Wall Street Journal*, "Athletes Break Bones, Workers Get Hernias: Me, I Get Spit at." October 25, 1973, 1.

160. Webber, R. A., "Perceptions of Interactions between Superiors and Subordinates," *Human Relations*, 23:235-248, 1970.

161. Weinberg, S. K., "Aspects of the Prison's Social Structure," *American Journal of Sociology*, 47:717-726, 1941-1942.

162. Wilensky, H. L., "The Moonlighter: A Product of Relative Deprivation," *Industrial Relations*, 3:105-124, 1963-1964.

163. Witt, M. S. (ed.) *Continuing Education of the Bar. California Workmen's Compensation Practice.* California CEB, 1973.

164. *Work in America.* Report of A Special Task Force to the Secretary of Health, Education, and Welfare. Prepared under the auspices of the W. E. Upjohn Institute for Employment Research. Cambridge, Mass.: Massachusetts Institute of Technology Press, 1973.

165. Wrenn, C. G. "Human Values and Work in American Life," in H. Borow (ed.), *Man in A World At Work.* Boston: Houghton Mifflin, 1964, 24-44.

166. Ziegler, F. J. and Imboden, J. B., "Contemporary Conversion Reactions," *Archives of General Psychiatry*, 6:279-287, 1962.

167. _____, Imboden, J. B., and Meyer, E., "Contemporary Conversion Reactions: A Clinical Study," *American Journal of Psychiatry*, 116:901-910, 1960.

Index

About the Author

Carroll M. Brodsky is a professor of psychiatry at the University of California School of Medicine and is director of the Ambulatory Psychiatric Service. He founded the Work Clinic at the University of California and it has received national recognition. Dr. Brodsky received the Ph.D. in anthropology from Catholic University in Washington, D.C. and the M.D. from the University of California School of Medicine in San Francisco.